The Most Dangerous Game

A SATURDAY MORNING BREAKFAST CEREAL COLLECTION

By Zach Weiner

breadpig

BROOKLYN · SOMERVILLE · THE INTERNETS

Printed in the United States of America

For information about special discounts for bulk purchases,
please contact Breadpig, Inc. at IncredibleBulk@Breadpig.com

Manufacturing by RR Donnelley

Weiner, Zach.
The Most Dangerous Game: A Saturday Morning Breakfast Cereal Collection
ISBN 978-0-9828537-1-9
Breadpig, Inc.
www.breadpig.com

Breadpig is not a traditional publisher. The majority of the profits of this book are going to the artist, Zach Weiner. And as with all of Breadpig's projects, the company's profits are being donated to a worthy charity. We selected the Khan Academy, a not-for-profit with the goal of changing education for the better by providing a free world-class education to anyone anywhere. With easy-to-grok, free video lessons on everything from arithmetic to advanced economics, Khan Academy is reforming education for students of all ages and backgrounds. No pressure though—that cat video you're watching is pretty cool too.

For support in this publishing venture,
breadpig thanks Marie Mundaca, LeeAnn Suen, Jeff Mach, Ben Peters,
and the friends and family who've always unhesitatingly supported team breadpig.

Even our winged porcine hero couldn't have done it alone. Thank you.

Cover art designed by Zach Weiner, colored and made awesome by Jim Zubkavich.

0 1 1 2 3 5 8 13 21 34

To Greg, my intellectual role model

Acknowledgments

Sometimes I marvel at the pool of talented people to whom I have access. The only more amazing thing is how open they are to last minute requests, sudden changes of plan, and general abusive behavior.

This book is published by the best publisher ever, Breadpig, and I want to thank Alexis Ohanian and Christina Xu for running a great company. Christina is a tireless organizer, and Alexis is a tireless promoter. They're always awesome, except for that one time Alexis stole Sabriya's biscuit. What a dick.

I want to thank Michael Johnson for helping me build this book during a 3 day long panic attack when I realized how close the deadline was, despite it taking far more hours than he was obligated to put in.

I want to thank Kelly Weinersmith for being my ideal geek wife. Her research makes an appearance as a comic in this book, which means I got a free comic written just by being with her. That alone is worth the fourth billing she's getting in this acknowledgment section.

I want to thank my parents, Phyllis and Martin Weiner, for going another year without disowning me. With any luck, they'll soon descend into total senility, so I can convince them I write Family Circus.

I want to thank my Secret Joke Congress for all the help they've given me over the last several years. One day, I will get you all signet rings.

Lastly, I want to thank the 200 or so MIT geeks who came to see me during orientation week 2011. I wasn't joking when I said I thought there would only be 10 people.

<3, Zach

OH HEY.

Welcome to the second SMBC book. Being the second book, it has many of the qualities of all great sequels: new ideas are introduced, older ideas are extended and twisted, and at the end, it turns out the killer was you all along.

This book mostly contains comics from 2011, which has been a year of stylistic change for SMBC. In 2010, I decided I would no longer care about panel number. Subsequently, people seemed to really prefer the longer ones. In fact, there appears to be a strong correlation between length of strip and traffic on the website. Since I worship at the altar of Mammon, this perverse incentive system has prompted me to create longer and longer comics, culminating in the 57 panel behemoth contained in this book.

This is a dangerously unstable state of affairs. A back of the envelope calculation suggests that panel number doubles roughly every year. Unless my math is wrong, within our lifetimes, every comic will contain just over infinity panels. By then, all labor on Earth will have to be redirected toward creating the ink and paper needed for additional comics. Before long, all the trees will be gone, the greenhouse effect will enter an unchecked feedback loop, and we will perish, our shriveling husks dried, scorched, carbonized, and finally annihilated by the Venus-like hellscape we made of our once-verdant Earth. The world will have ended - not with a whimper, but with a boner joke.

So enjoy the more expansive story-like strips contained herein. Don't worry about the gears of destruction you're helping to turn - you're only contributing a little.

ZACH WEINER

P.S.: If you bought the first book, this book continues the adventure game by letting you pursue the "death" track. If you didn't, begin with the square below. Each square represents the last choice you made, and gives you two new choices. To follow a choice, just use the number and arrow to identify the page number and the location on that page for the next adventure block.

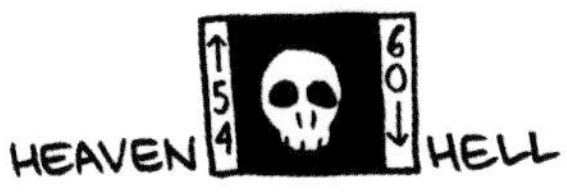
HEAVEN
154
60
HELL

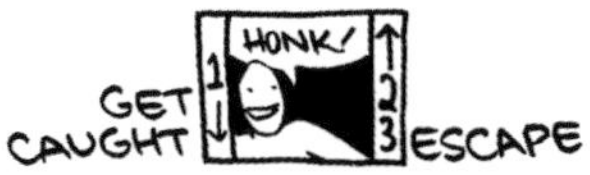
HONK!
GET CAUGHT
ESCAPE

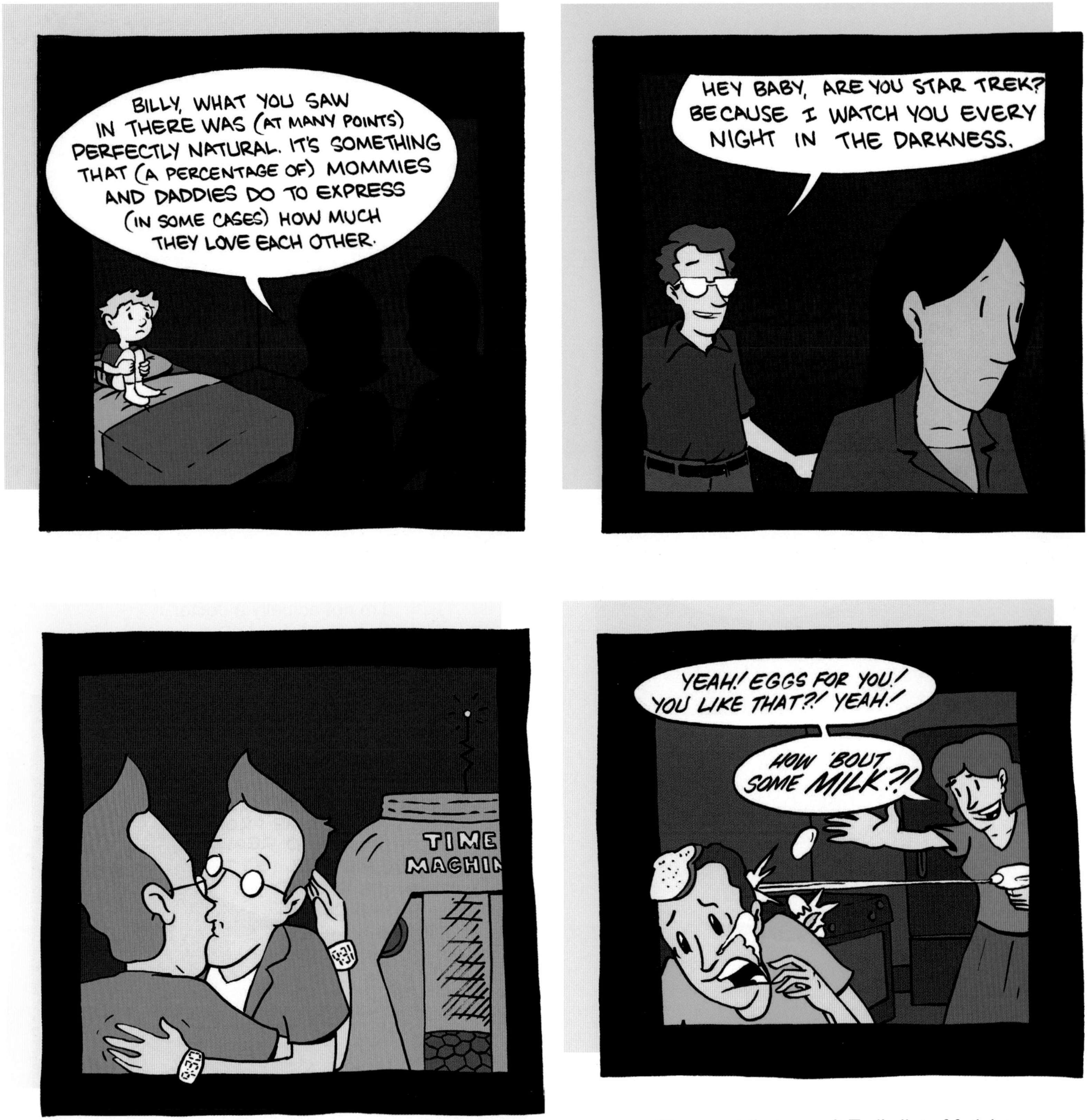
BILLY, WHAT YOU SAW IN THERE WAS (AT MANY POINTS) PERFECTLY NATURAL. IT'S SOMETHING THAT (A PERCENTAGE OF) MOMMIES AND DADDIES DO TO EXPRESS (IN SOME CASES) HOW MUCH THEY LOVE EACH OTHER.
HEY BABY, ARE YOU STAR TREK? BECAUSE I WATCH YOU EVERY NIGHT IN THE DARKNESS.
TIME MACHIN
YEAH! EGGS FOR YOU! YOU LIKE THAT?! YEAH!
HOW 'BOUT SOME MILK?!

Turns out that wasn't Ted's list of fetishes.

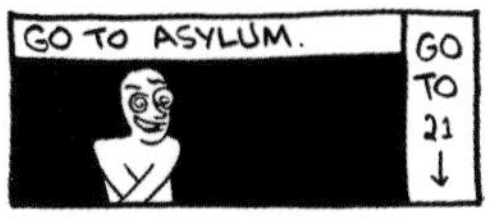
GO TO ASYLUM.
GO TO 21 ↓

NO! THERE'S NO TIME FOR CPR! WE'LL HAVE TO INJECT THE AIR DIRECTLY INTO HIS VEINS!

Upon closer scrutiny, it turns out
I'm not actually a doctor.

I DON'T CARE HOW "SPOOKY" IT IS! NO KID WANTS TO EAT A CEREAL WITH BREAD-FLAVORED MARSHMALLOWS!
FINE! WHATEVER!

SEXUAL BREADATOR!

WAIT! DO YOU HAVE ANY PROTECTION?
WELL, MY MOM SAID BABIES ONLY COME FROM TWO PEOPLE WHO REALLY LOVE EACH OTHER. SO, I THINK WE SHOULD BE IN THE CLEAR.

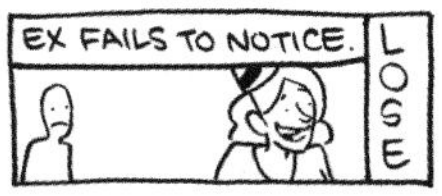
EX FAILS TO NOTICE.
LOSE

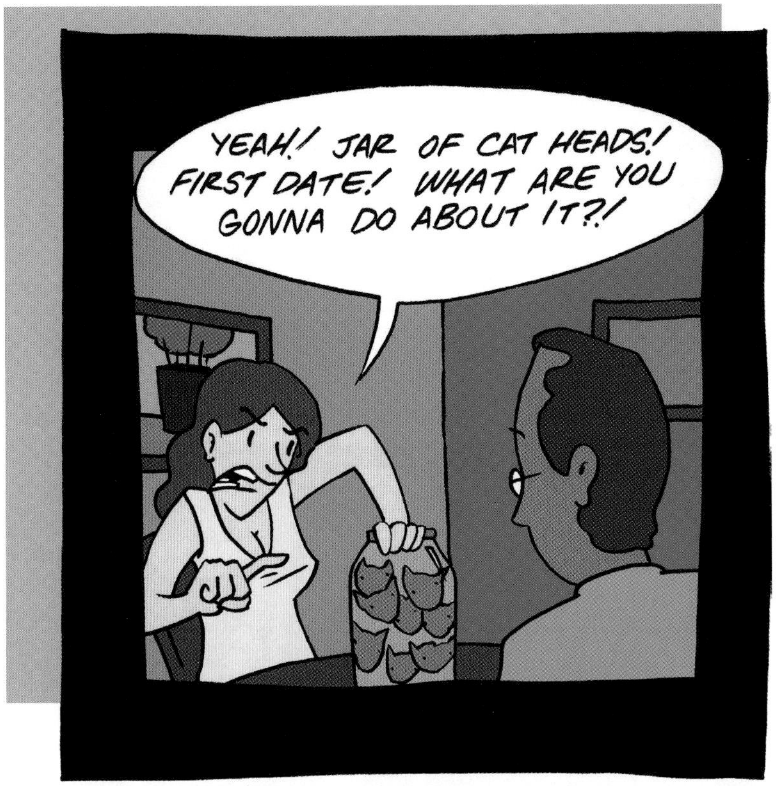
YEAH! JAR OF CAT HEADS! FIRST DATE! WHAT ARE YOU GONNA DO ABOUT IT?!

I try to find creative ways
to compensate for my shyness.

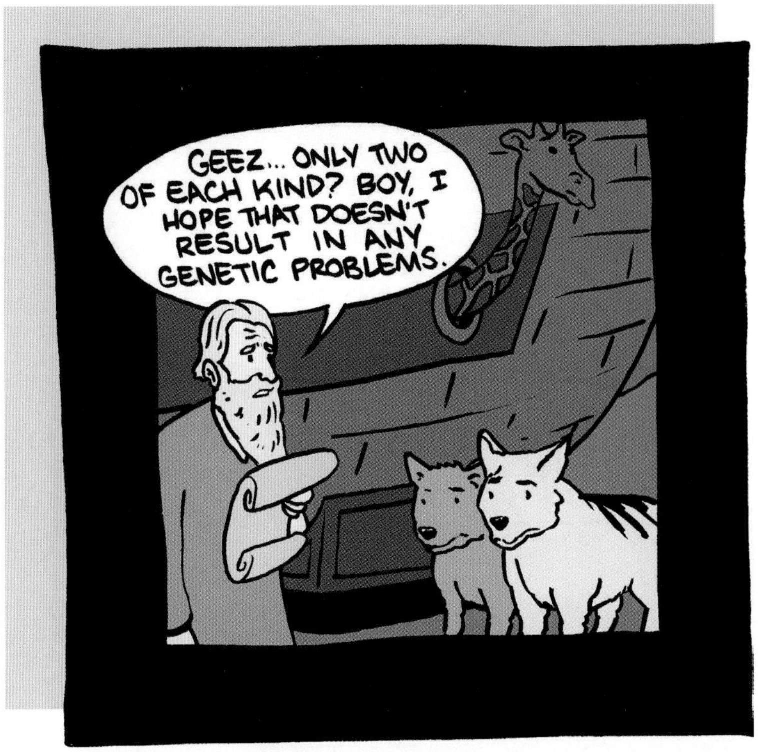
GEEZ... ONLY TWO OF EACH KIND? BOY, I HOPE THAT DOESN'T RESULT IN ANY GENETIC PROBLEMS.

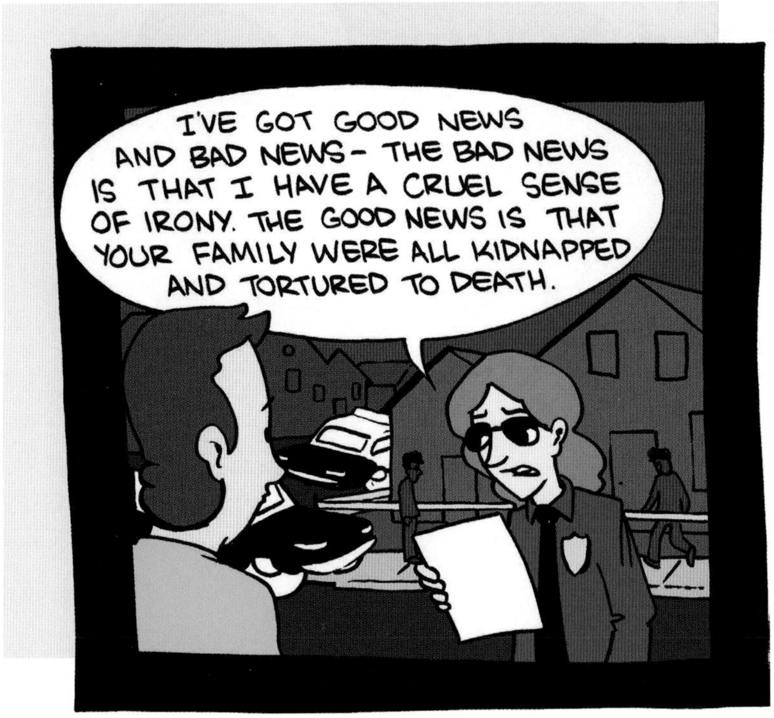
I'VE GOT GOOD NEWS AND BAD NEWS - THE BAD NEWS IS THAT I HAVE A CRUEL SENSE OF IRONY. THE GOOD NEWS IS THAT YOUR FAMILY WERE ALL KIDNAPPED AND TORTURED TO DEATH.

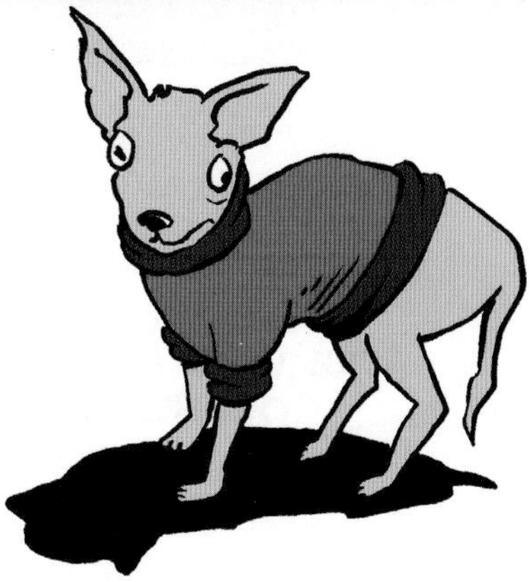

GO INSANE ↑142
161↓ VISIT SNUGGLEBURG

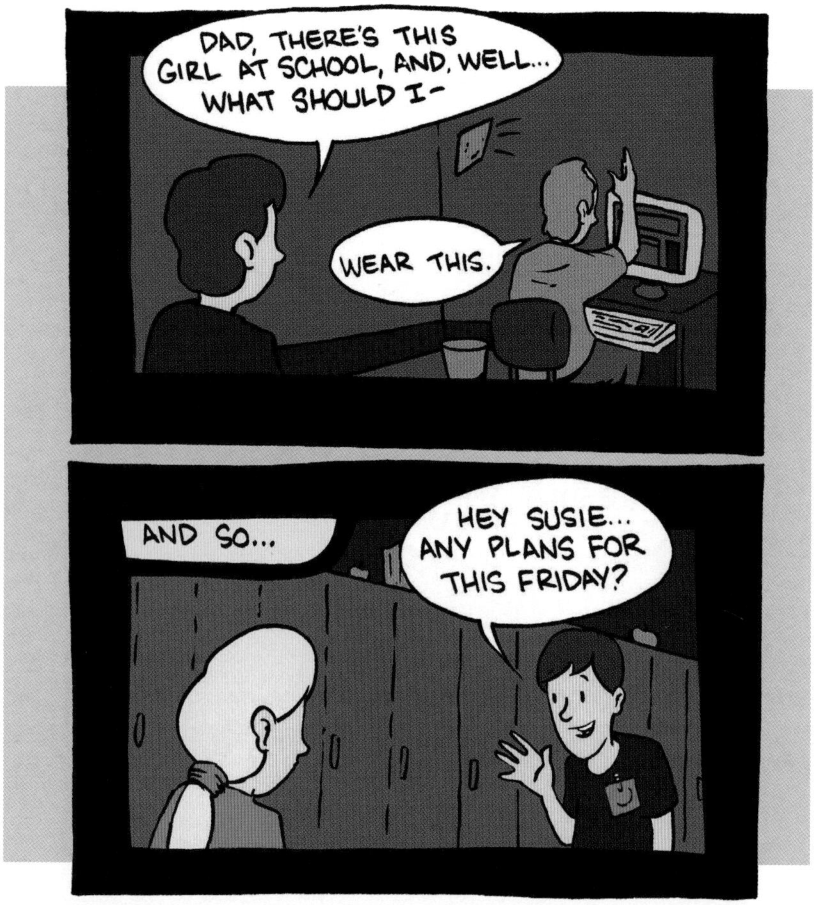
DAD, THERE'S THIS GIRL AT SCHOOL, AND, WELL... WHAT SHOULD I-
WEAR THIS.
AND SO...
HEY SUSIE... ANY PLANS FOR THIS FRIDAY?

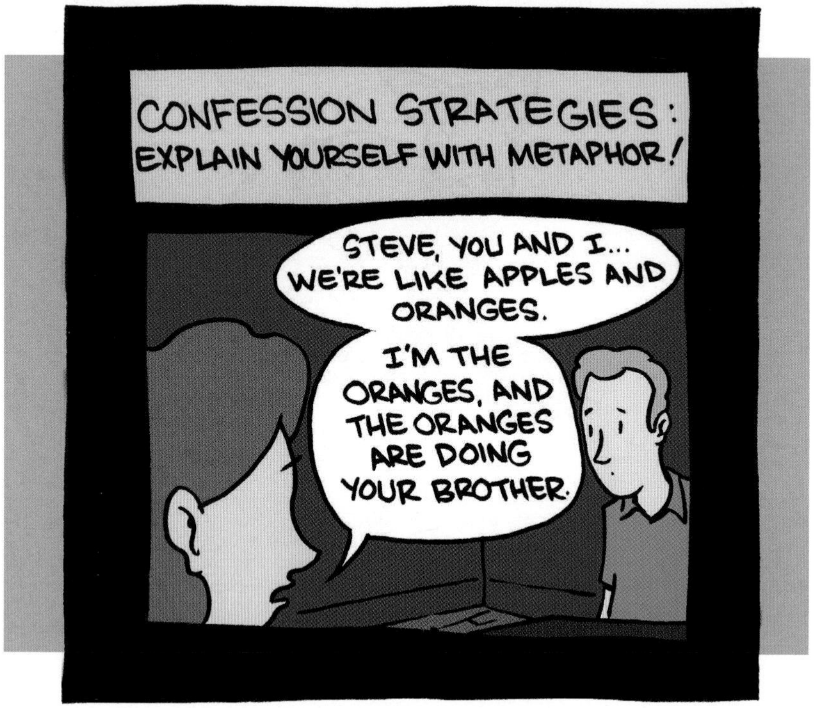
CONFESSION STRATEGIES:
EXPLAIN YOURSELF WITH METAPHOR!
STEVE, YOU AND I... WE'RE LIKE APPLES AND ORANGES.
I'M THE ORANGES, AND THE ORANGES ARE DOING YOUR BROTHER.

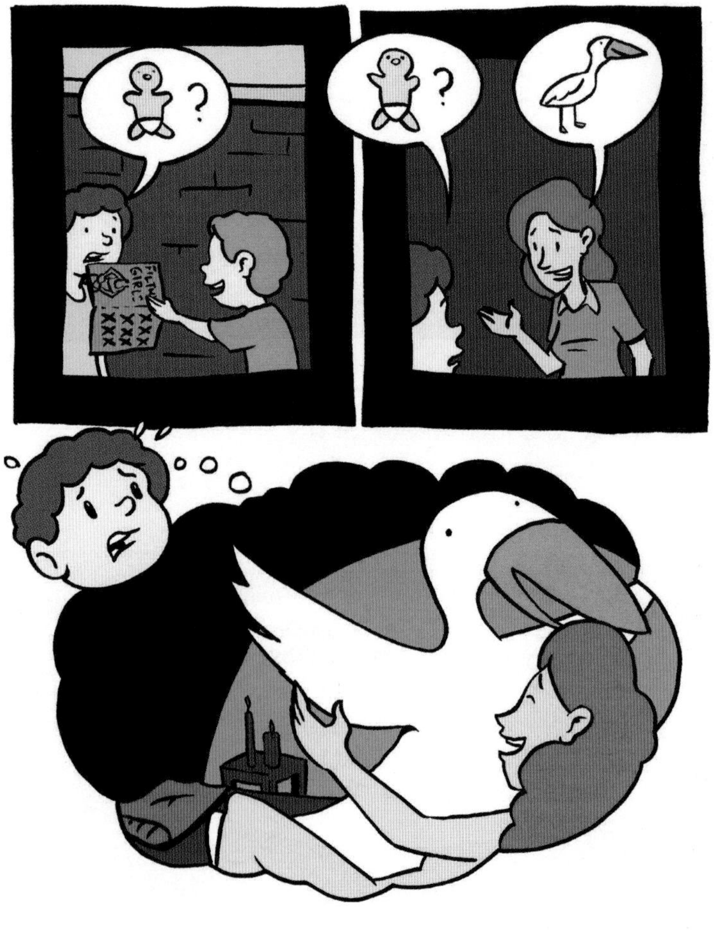
?
?

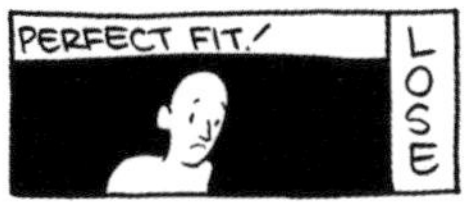
PERFECT FIT!
LOSE

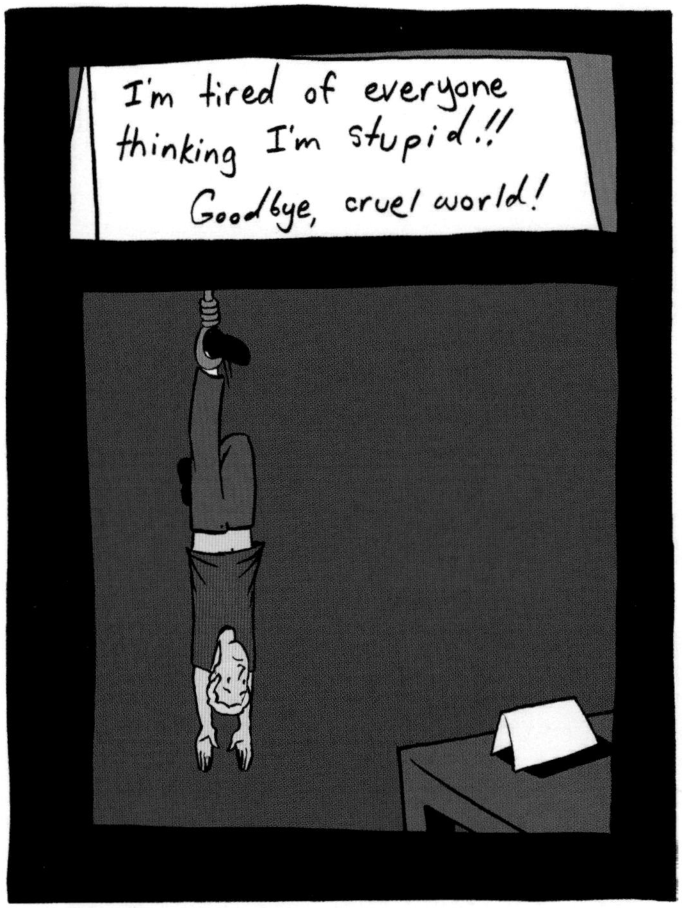
I'm tired of everyone thinking I'm stupid!!
Goodbye, cruel world!

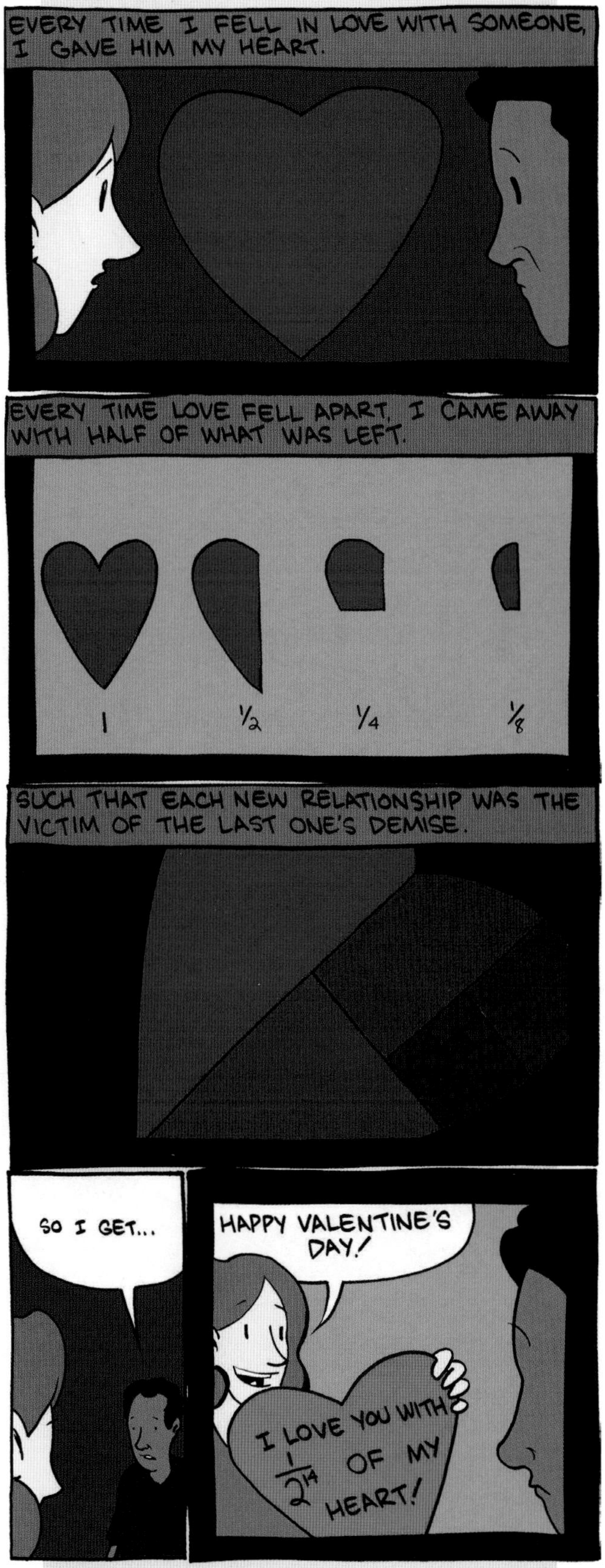
EVERY TIME I FELL IN LOVE WITH SOMEONE, I GAVE HIM MY HEART.
EVERY TIME LOVE FELL APART, I CAME AWAY WITH HALF OF WHAT WAS LEFT.
1
1/2
1/4
1/8
SUCH THAT EACH NEW RELATIONSHIP WAS THE VICTIM OF THE LAST ONE'S DEMISE.
SO I GET...
HAPPY VALENTINE'S DAY!
I LOVE YOU WITH $\frac{1}{2^{14}}$ OF MY HEART!

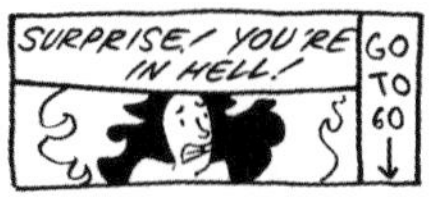
SURPRISE! YOU'RE IN HELL!
GO TO 60 ↓

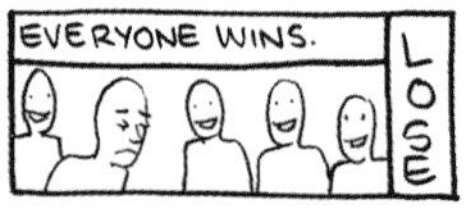

EVERYONE WINS.
LOSE

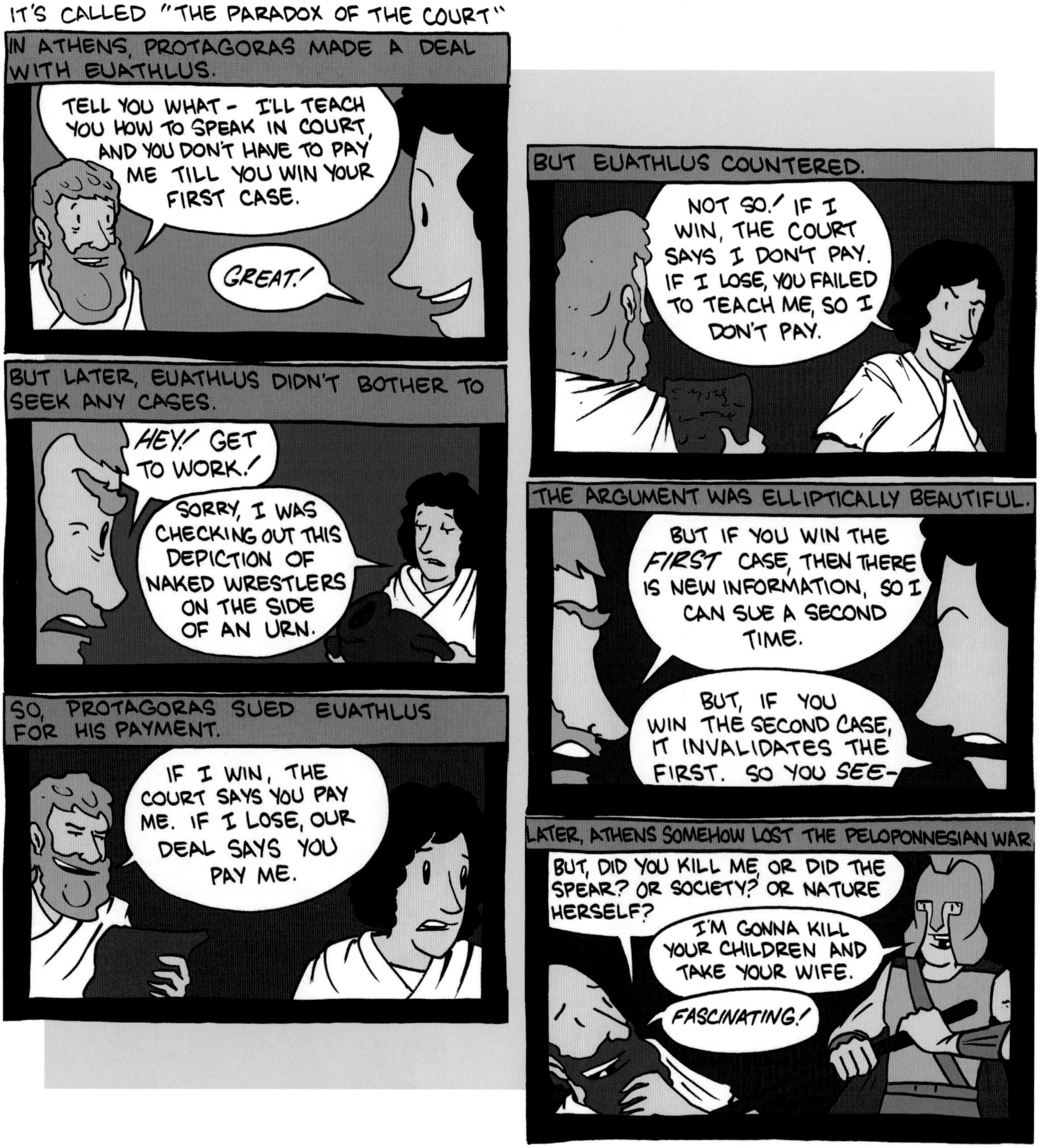

IT'S CALLED "THE PARADOX OF THE COURT"
IN ATHENS, PROTAGORAS MADE A DEAL WITH EUATHLUS.
TELL YOU WHAT - I'LL TEACH YOU HOW TO SPEAK IN COURT, AND YOU DON'T HAVE TO PAY ME TILL YOU WIN YOUR FIRST CASE.
GREAT!
BUT LATER, EUATHLUS DIDN'T BOTHER TO SEEK ANY CASES.
HEY! GET TO WORK!
SORRY, I WAS CHECKING OUT THIS DEPICTION OF NAKED WRESTLERS ON THE SIDE OF AN URN.
SO, PROTAGORAS SUED EUATHLUS FOR HIS PAYMENT.
IF I WIN, THE COURT SAYS YOU PAY ME. IF I LOSE, OUR DEAL SAYS YOU PAY ME.
BUT EUATHLUS COUNTERED.
NOT SO! IF I WIN, THE COURT SAYS I DON'T PAY. IF I LOSE, YOU FAILED TO TEACH ME, SO I DON'T PAY.
THE ARGUMENT WAS ELLIPTICALLY BEAUTIFUL.
BUT IF YOU WIN THE FIRST CASE, THEN THERE IS NEW INFORMATION, SO I CAN SUE A SECOND TIME.
BUT, IF YOU WIN THE SECOND CASE, IT INVALIDATES THE FIRST. SO YOU SEE-
LATER, ATHENS SOMEHOW LOST THE PELOPONNESIAN WAR.
BUT, DID YOU KILL ME, OR DID THE SPEAR? OR SOCIETY? OR NATURE HERSELF?
I'M GONNA KILL YOUR CHILDREN AND TAKE YOUR WIFE.
FASCINATING!

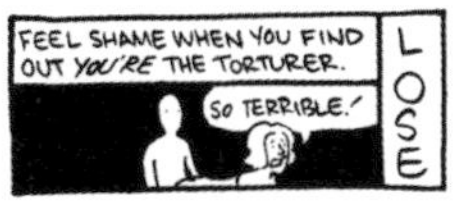
FEEL SHAME WHEN YOU FIND OUT YOU'RE THE TORTURER.
SO TERRIBLE!
LOSE

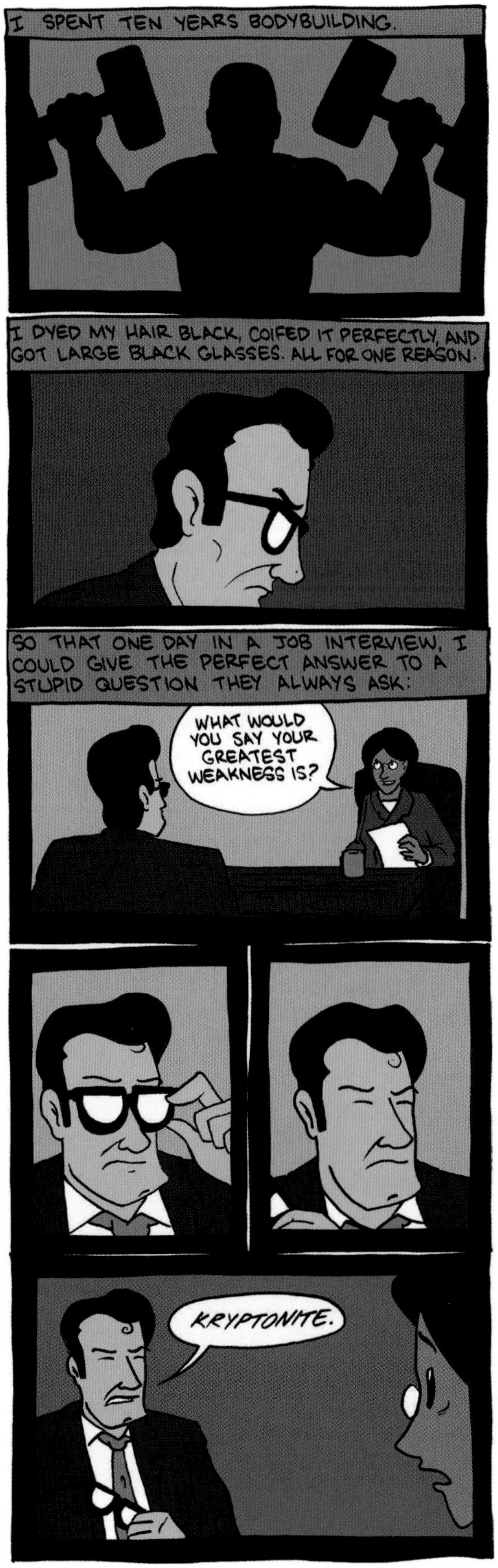
I SPENT TEN YEARS BODYBUILDING.
I DYED MY HAIR BLACK, COIFED IT PERFECTLY, AND GOT LARGE BLACK GLASSES. ALL FOR ONE REASON.
SO THAT ONE DAY IN A JOB INTERVIEW, I COULD GIVE THE PERFECT ANSWER TO A STUPID QUESTION THEY ALWAYS ASK:
WHAT WOULD YOU SAY YOUR GREATEST WEAKNESS IS?
KRYPTONITE.

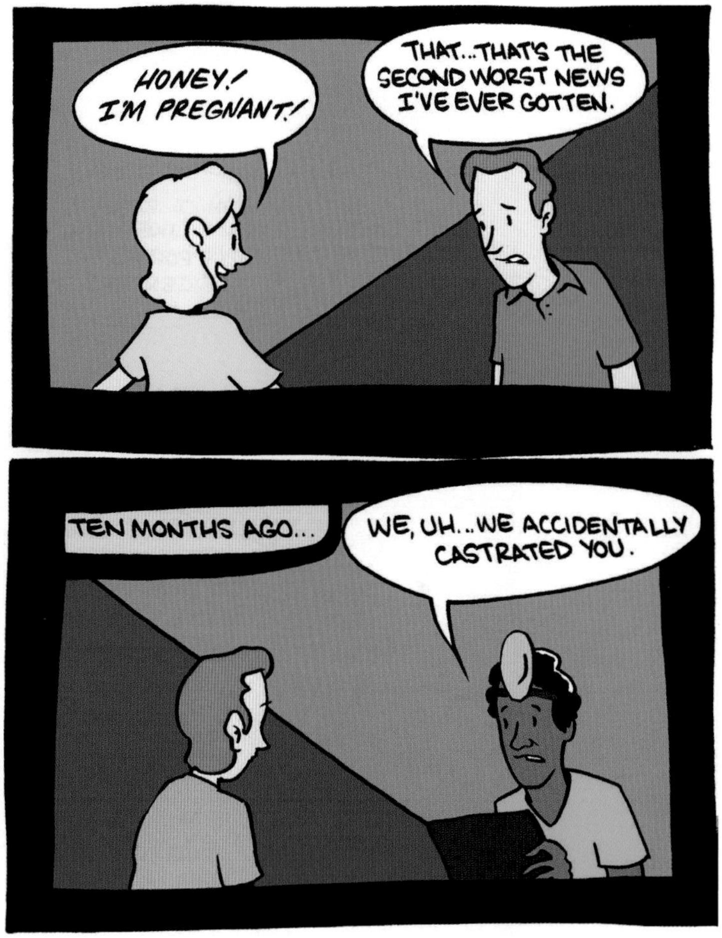
HONEY! I'M PREGNANT!
THAT...THAT'S THE SECOND WORST NEWS I'VE EVER GOTTEN.
TEN MONTHS AGO...
WE, UH...WE ACCIDENTALLY CASTRATED YOU.

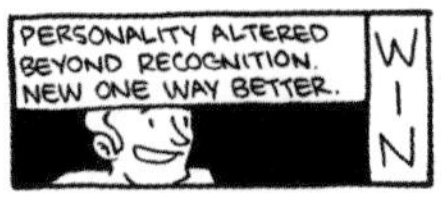
PERSONALITY ALTERED BEYOND RECOGNITION. NEW ONE WAY BETTER.
WIN

FIT INTO HEAVEN WELL.
LOSE

OKAY, LET'S SETTLE THIS ONCE AND FOR ALL.
"I'M OFFENDED" DOES NOT EQUAL "IT'S OFFENSIVE."
"I'M OFFENDED" IS WHEN SOMETHING UPSETS YOU.
UGH. I REALLY DON'T LIKE THIS GUY'S PORTRAYAL OF GENDER.
"IT'S OFFENSIVE" HAS NO AGREED UPON STANDARD.
NIPPLES ARE OFFENSIVE! THEY MUST BE STOPPED!
SERIOUSLY. IF YOU'RE NOT BREAST FEEDING-
AAH! AAH! YOU SAID "BREAST!"
"IT'S OFFENSIVE" IS WHEN YOU CLAIM EVERYONE IS UPSET BY IT.
UGH! THIS BOOK IS SO OFFENSIVE, WE NEED TO STOP CONSIDERING ITS VIEWPOINT!
"I'M OFFENDED" STARTS ARGUMENTS.
I'M OFFENDED BY YOUR RELIGION.
THAT OFFENDS ME, BUT MY SAVIOR, LORD RACIST SATAN, SAYS WE CAN TALK ABOUT IT.
"I'M OFFENDED" HAPPENS TO EVERYONE.
BLAH. I HATE ABORTION JOKES. NO MORE OF THIS AUTHOR.
UGH. I HATE "FAMILY CIRCUS." BARELY ANY ABORTION JOKES!
"IT'S OFFENSIVE" ENDS THEM.
DISAGREEMENT IS OFFENSIVE!
NO IT'S NOT.
ARE YOU TRYING TO UPSET EVERYONE?!

CREEPIEST MEETUP EVER.
LOSE

LIAR! GO TO PUNISHMENT.
HELL SUCKS.
GO TO 38 ↓

AND NOW... A TRIBUTE TO SEX.

I'm what you call a virtuoso masturbator.

YOU LOOK EXACTLY THE SAME! HOW DO I KNOW WHICH IS A ROBOT AND WHICH IS A SECRET HUMAN WHO MUST BE DEACTIVATED!
QUICK!
WHOEVER IS THE REAL UNIT J0-4918.23.6234-111.2, SAY SOMETHING ONLY UNIT J0-4918.23.6234-111.2 WOULD SAY.

010010010010000000110000101101
10100100000011011000110111101101110
01100101011011000111100100100100000
011100110110111101101101011001010111010
001101001011011010
110010101110011.
UH... BEEP?
SPLOOSH!

WIN

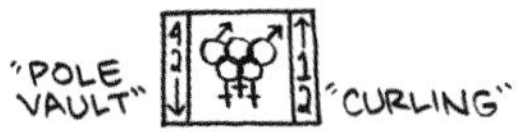
"POLE VAULT"
"CURLING"

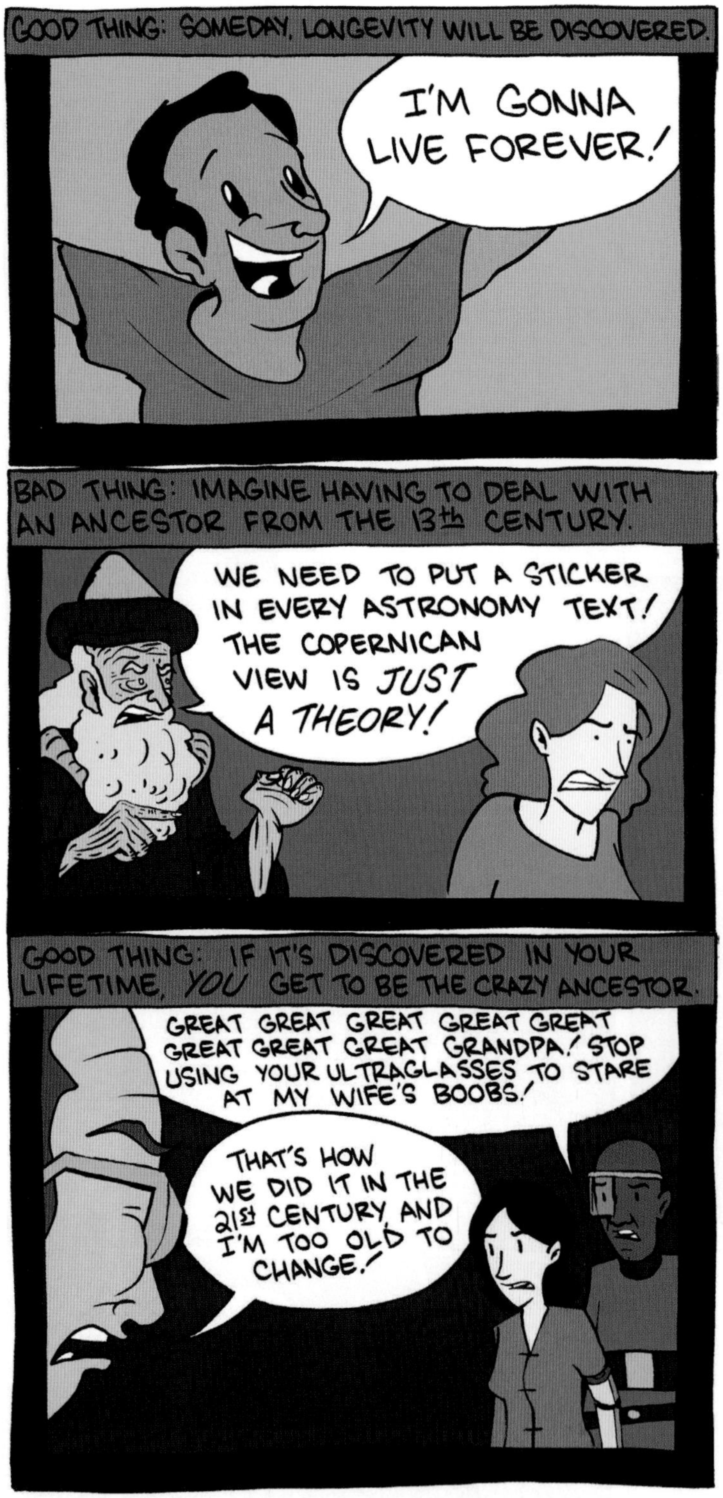
GOOD THING: SOMEDAY, LONGEVITY WILL BE DISCOVERED.
I'M GONNA LIVE FOREVER!
BAD THING: IMAGINE HAVING TO DEAL WITH AN ANCESTOR FROM THE 13th CENTURY.
WE NEED TO PUT A STICKER IN EVERY ASTRONOMY TEXT! THE COPERNICAN VIEW IS *JUST A THEORY!*
GOOD THING: IF IT'S DISCOVERED IN YOUR LIFETIME, *YOU* GET TO BE THE CRAZY ANCESTOR.
GREAT GREAT GREAT GREAT GREAT GREAT GREAT GREAT GRANDPA! STOP USING YOUR ULTRAGLASSES TO STARE AT MY WIFE'S BOOBS!
THAT'S HOW WE DID IT IN THE 21st CENTURY, AND I'M TOO OLD TO CHANGE!

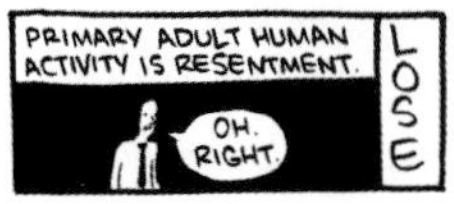
PRIMARY ADULT HUMAN ACTIVITY IS RESENTMENT.
OH. RIGHT.
LOSE

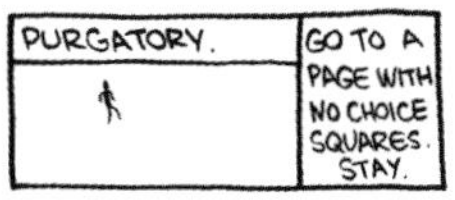
PURGATORY.
GO TO A PAGE WITH NO CHOICE SQUARES. STAY.

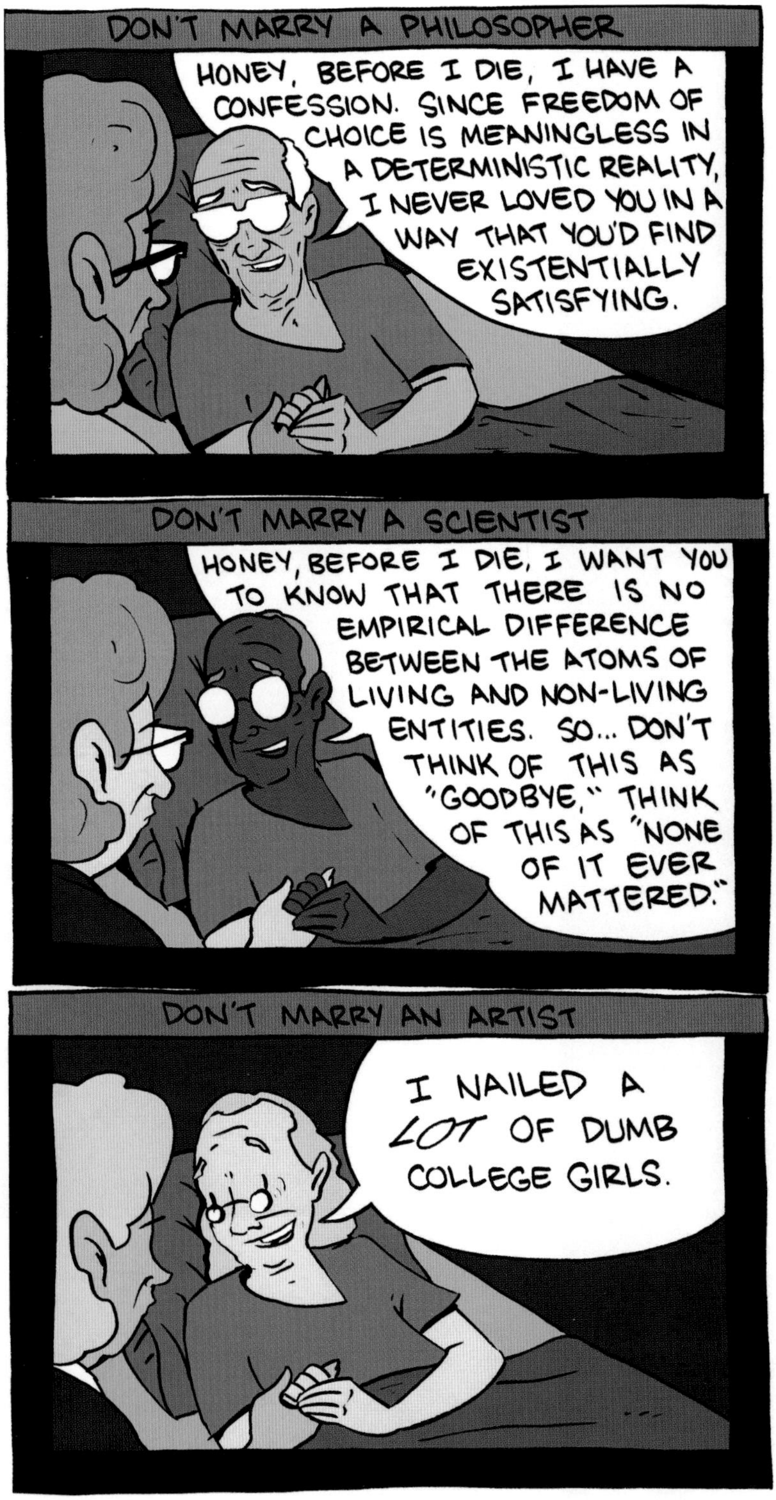
DON'T MARRY A PHILOSOPHER
HONEY, BEFORE I DIE, I HAVE A CONFESSION. SINCE FREEDOM OF CHOICE IS MEANINGLESS IN A DETERMINISTIC REALITY, I NEVER LOVED YOU IN A WAY THAT YOU'D FIND EXISTENTIALLY SATISFYING.
DON'T MARRY A SCIENTIST
HONEY, BEFORE I DIE, I WANT YOU TO KNOW THAT THERE IS NO EMPIRICAL DIFFERENCE BETWEEN THE ATOMS OF LIVING AND NON-LIVING ENTITIES. SO... DON'T THINK OF THIS AS "GOODBYE," THINK OF THIS AS "NONE OF IT EVER MATTERED."
DON'T MARRY AN ARTIST
I NAILED A *LOT* OF DUMB COLLEGE GIRLS.

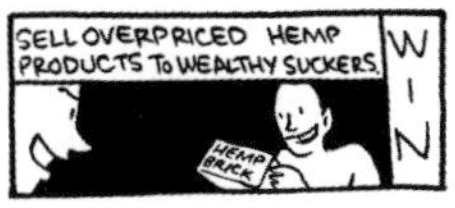
SELL OVERPRICED HEMP PRODUCTS TO WEALTHY SUCKERS.
WIN

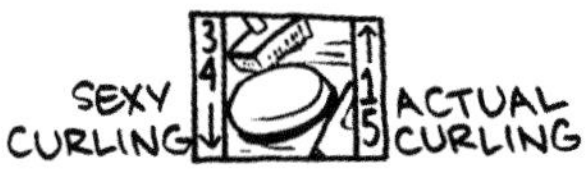
SEXY CURLING
ACTUAL CURLING

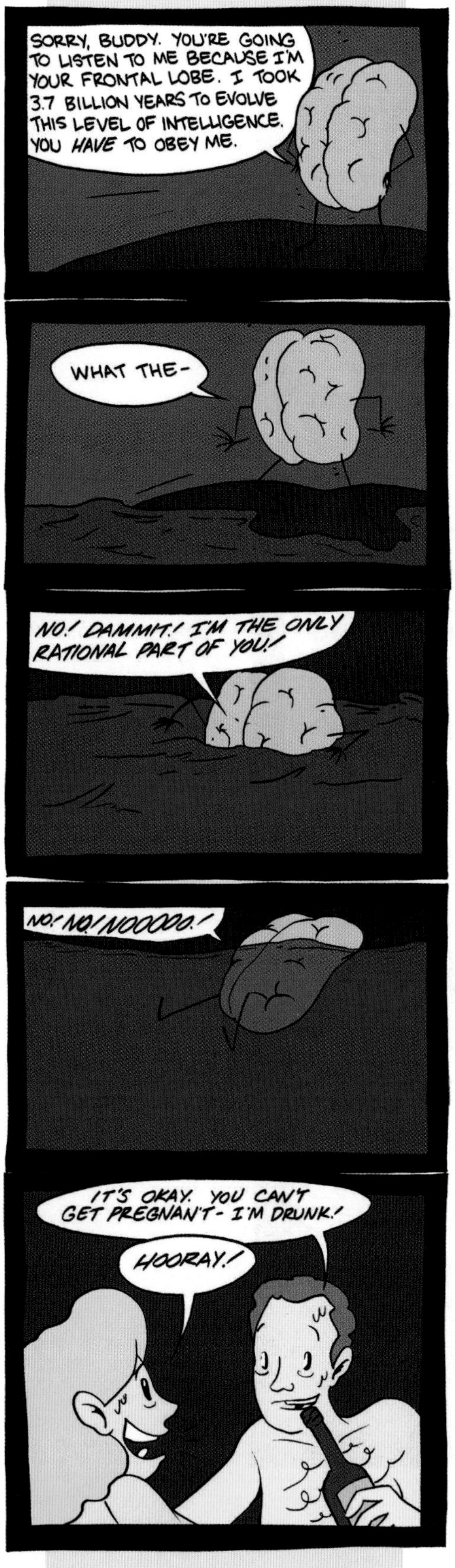
SORRY, BUDDY. YOU'RE GOING TO LISTEN TO ME BECAUSE I'M YOUR FRONTAL LOBE. I TOOK 3.7 BILLION YEARS TO EVOLVE THIS LEVEL OF INTELLIGENCE. YOU *HAVE* TO OBEY ME.
WHAT THE-
NO! DAMMIT! I'M THE ONLY RATIONAL PART OF YOU!
NO! NO! NOOOOO!
IT'S OKAY. YOU CAN'T GET PREGNANT- I'M DRUNK!
HOORAY!

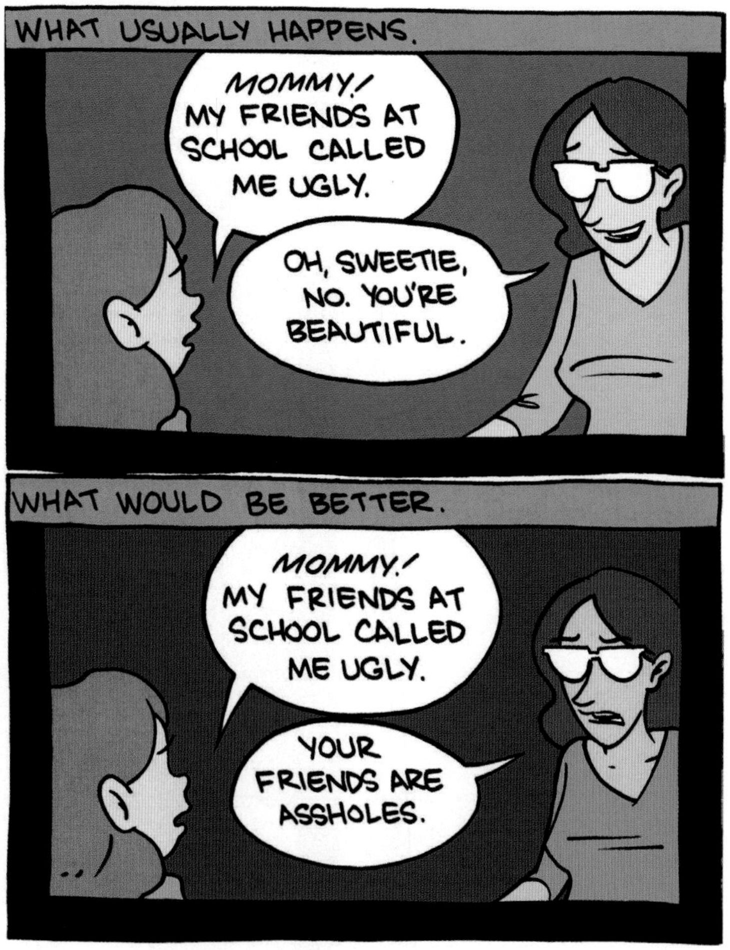
WHAT USUALLY HAPPENS.
MOMMY! MY FRIENDS AT SCHOOL CALLED ME UGLY.
OH, SWEETIE, NO. YOU'RE BEAUTIFUL.
WHAT WOULD BE BETTER.
MOMMY! MY FRIENDS AT SCHOOL CALLED ME UGLY.
YOUR FRIENDS ARE ASSHOLES.

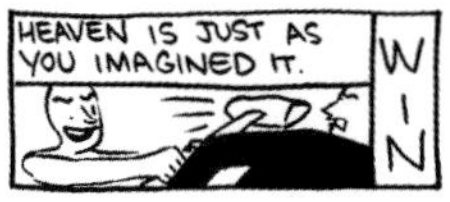
HEAVEN IS JUST AS YOU IMAGINED IT.
WIN

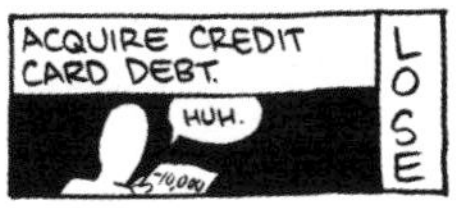

ACQUIRE CREDIT CARD DEBT.
HUH.
LOSE

THE COMEDY EQUATION:
OLD JOKE + SADNESS = NEW JOKE

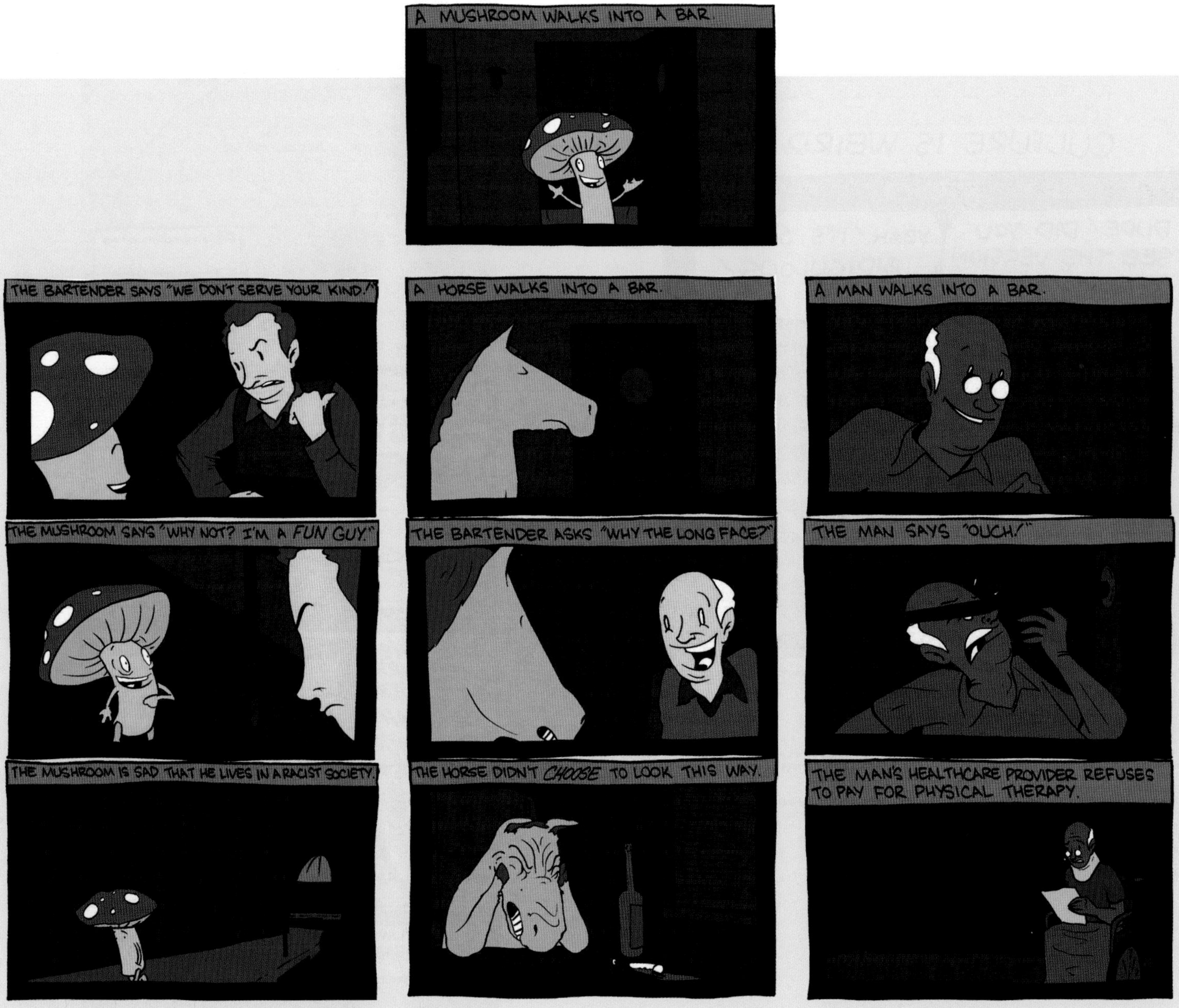

A MUSHROOM WALKS INTO A BAR.
THE BARTENDER SAYS "WE DON'T SERVE YOUR KIND."
THE MUSHROOM SAYS "WHY NOT? I'M A FUN GUY."
THE MUSHROOM IS SAD THAT HE LIVES IN A RACIST SOCIETY.
A HORSE WALKS INTO A BAR.
THE BARTENDER ASKS "WHY THE LONG FACE?"
THE HORSE DIDN'T CHOOSE TO LOOK THIS WAY.
A MAN WALKS INTO A BAR.
THE MAN SAYS "OUCH!"
THE MAN'S HEALTHCARE PROVIDER REFUSES TO PAY FOR PHYSICAL THERAPY.

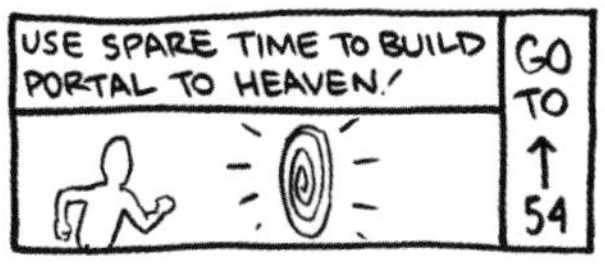

USE SPARE TIME TO BUILD PORTAL TO HEAVEN!
GO TO ↑ 54

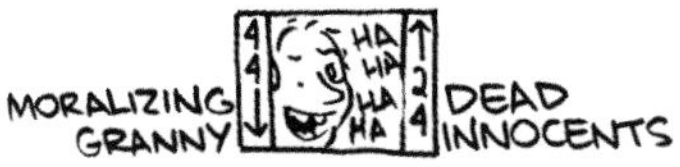
MORALIZING GRANNY
44 ↓
HA HA HA HA
↑ 24
DEAD INNOCENTS

CULTURE IS WEIRD

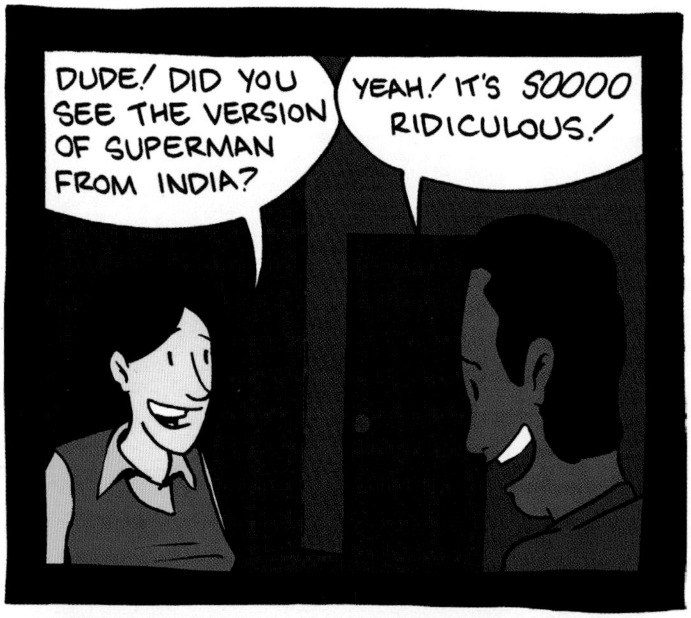
DUDE! DID YOU SEE THE VERSION OF SUPERMAN FROM INDIA?
YEAH! IT'S SOOOO RIDICULOUS!

THINGS AMERICAN SUPERMAN DOES

-Flies
-Breathes nothing in space
-Lifts anything
-Looks human; is alien
-Gets powers from the yellow sun
-Has muscles; never exercises
-Sees through walls
-Shoots lasers from eyes
-Grows weak next to a particular rock
-Hears specific sounds at long distance
-Is invincible
-Freezes things with breath
-Lives forever
-Has telescopic vision
-Has microscopic vision

THINGS INDIAN SUPERMAN DOES

-Flies
-Breathes nothing in space
-Lifts anything
-Looks human; is alien
-Gets powers from the yellow sun
-Has muscles; never exercises
-Sees through walls
-Shoots lasers from eyes
-Grows weak next to a particular rock
-Hears specific sounds at long distance
-Is invincible
-Freezes things with breath
-Lives forever
-Has telescopic vision
-Has microscopic vision
-Dances

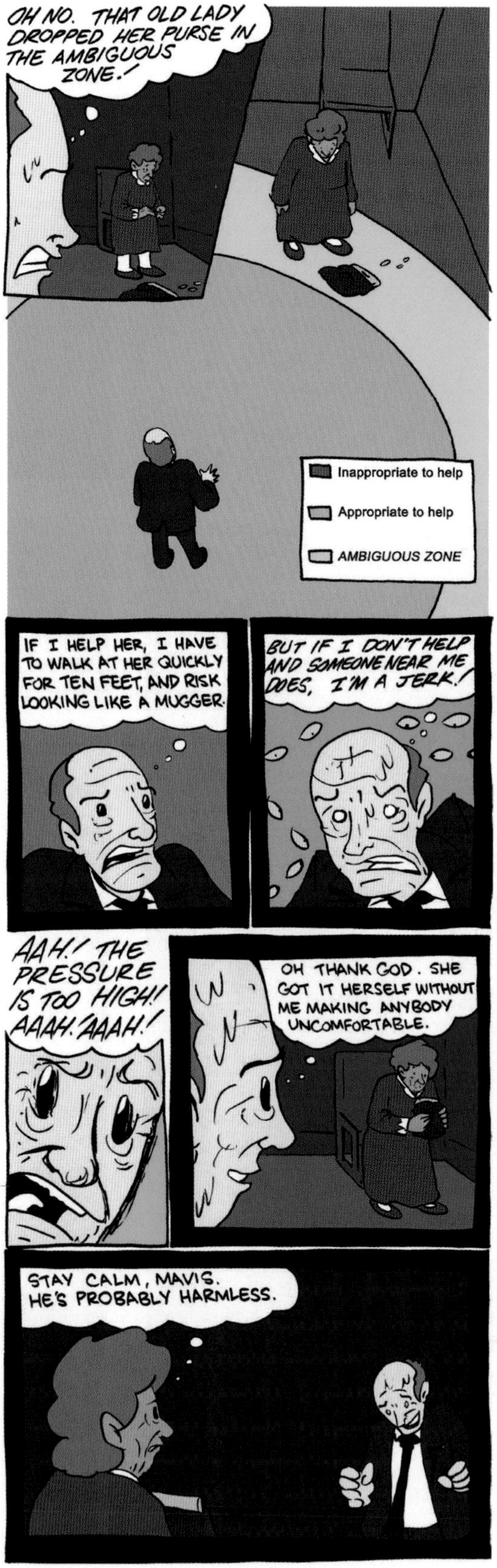
OH NO. THAT OLD LADY DROPPED HER PURSE IN THE AMBIGUOUS ZONE.
Inappropriate to help
Appropriate to help
AMBIGUOUS ZONE
IF I HELP HER, I HAVE TO WALK AT HER QUICKLY FOR TEN FEET, AND RISK LOOKING LIKE A MUGGER.
BUT IF I DON'T HELP AND SOMEONE NEAR ME DOES, I'M A JERK!
AAH! THE PRESSURE IS TOO HIGH! AAAH! AAAH!
OH THANK GOD. SHE GOT IT HERSELF WITHOUT ME MAKING ANYBODY UNCOMFORTABLE.
STAY CALM, MAVIS. HE'S PROBABLY HARMLESS.

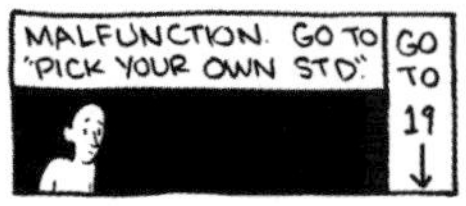
MALFUNCTION. GO TO "PICK YOUR OWN STD"
GO TO 19 ↓

OH GOD NO, THIS IS CANADIAN HEAVEN!
LOSE

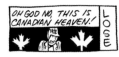

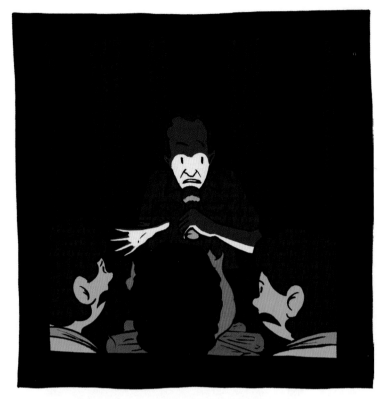

And for the rest of the night, you'll wonder if she actually enjoyed sex or was just trying to avoid relationship conflict!

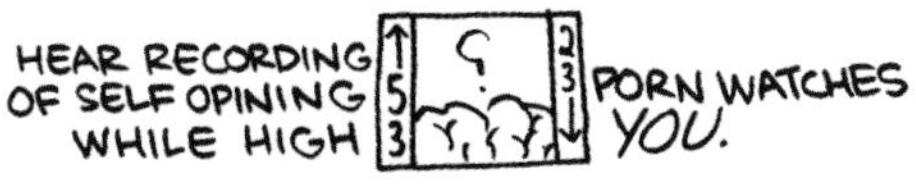

IMAGINE TRUTH IS A SPHERE:
THIS IS WHAT I USED TO THINK CAUSED ARGUMENTS
THE SPHERE IS ALL BLACK!
THE SPHERE IS ALL WHITE!
THIS IS WHAT I THINK NOW.
THE SPHERE IS ALL BLACK!
THE SPHERE IS ALL WHITE!

ECONOMIST PICKUP LINES:
HEY BABY. IF I TOLD YOU YOU HAD A BEAUTIFUL BODY, WOULD IT IMPROVE YOUR SELF ESTEEM TO A THRESHOLD AT WHICH YOU'D HAVE NO INTEREST IN ME?

HEAR RECORDING OF SELF OPINING WHILE HIGH
PORN WATCHES YOU.

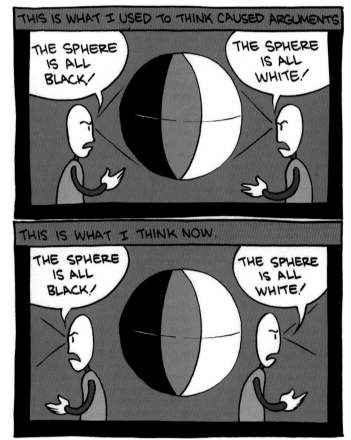

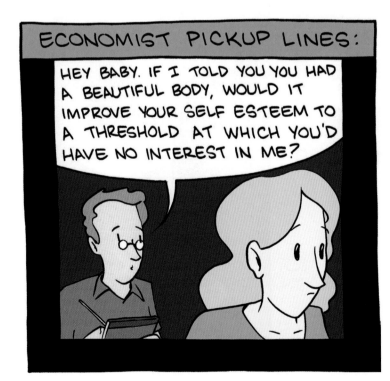

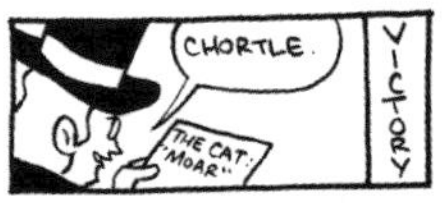

CHORTLE.
THE CAT: "MOAR"
VICTORY

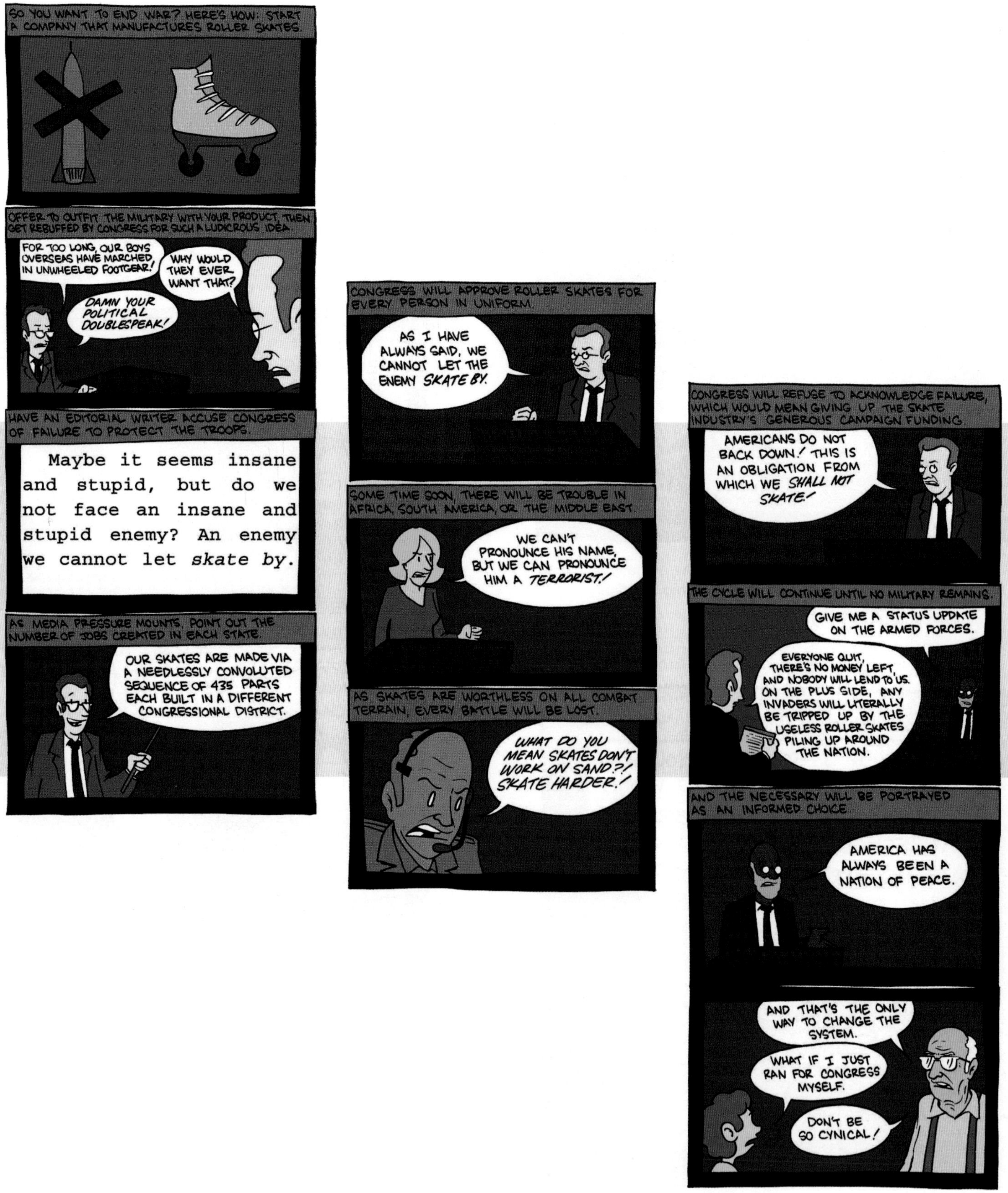

SO YOU WANT TO END WAR? HERE'S HOW: START A COMPANY THAT MANUFACTURES ROLLER SKATES.
OFFER TO OUTFIT THE MILITARY WITH YOUR PRODUCT, THEN GET REBUFFED BY CONGRESS FOR SUCH A LUDICROUS IDEA.
FOR TOO LONG, OUR BOYS OVERSEAS HAVE MARCHED IN UNWHEELED FOOTGEAR!
WHY WOULD THEY EVER WANT THAT?
DAMN YOUR POLITICAL DOUBLESPEAK!
HAVE AN EDITORIAL WRITER ACCUSE CONGRESS OF FAILURE TO PROTECT THE TROOPS.
Maybe it seems insane and stupid, but do we not face an insane and stupid enemy? An enemy we cannot let *skate by*.
AS MEDIA PRESSURE MOUNTS, POINT OUT THE NUMBER OF JOBS CREATED IN EACH STATE.
OUR SKATES ARE MADE VIA A NEEDLESSLY CONVOLUTED SEQUENCE OF 435 PARTS EACH BUILT IN A DIFFERENT CONGRESSIONAL DISTRICT.
CONGRESS WILL APPROVE ROLLER SKATES FOR EVERY PERSON IN UNIFORM.
AS I HAVE ALWAYS SAID, WE CANNOT LET THE ENEMY *SKATE BY*.
SOME TIME SOON, THERE WILL BE TROUBLE IN AFRICA, SOUTH AMERICA, OR THE MIDDLE EAST.
WE CAN'T PRONOUNCE HIS NAME, BUT WE CAN PRONOUNCE HIM A *TERRORIST!*
AS SKATES ARE WORTHLESS ON ALL COMBAT TERRAIN, EVERY BATTLE WILL BE LOST.
WHAT DO YOU MEAN SKATES DON'T WORK ON SAND?! SKATE HARDER!
CONGRESS WILL REFUSE TO ACKNOWLEDGE FAILURE, WHICH WOULD MEAN GIVING UP THE SKATE INDUSTRY'S GENEROUS CAMPAIGN FUNDING.
AMERICANS DO NOT BACK DOWN! THIS IS AN OBLIGATION FROM WHICH WE *SHALL NOT SKATE!*
THE CYCLE WILL CONTINUE UNTIL NO MILITARY REMAINS.
GIVE ME A STATUS UPDATE ON THE ARMED FORCES.
EVERYONE QUIT, THERE'S NO MONEY LEFT, AND NOBODY WILL LEND TO US. ON THE PLUS SIDE, ANY INVADERS WILL LITERALLY BE TRIPPED UP BY THE USELESS ROLLER SKATES PILING UP AROUND THE NATION.
AND THE NECESSARY WILL BE PORTRAYED AS AN INFORMED CHOICE.
AMERICA HAS ALWAYS BEEN A NATION OF PEACE.
AND THAT'S THE ONLY WAY TO CHANGE THE SYSTEM.
WHAT IF I JUST RAN FOR CONGRESS MYSELF.
DON'T BE SO CYNICAL!

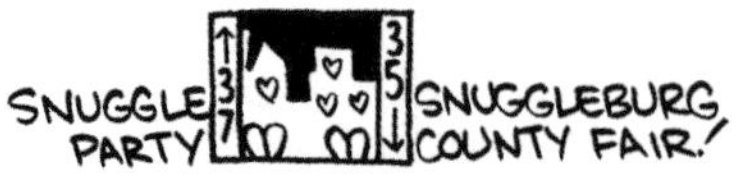

SNUGGLE PARTY
137
351
SNUGGLEBURG COUNTY FAIR!

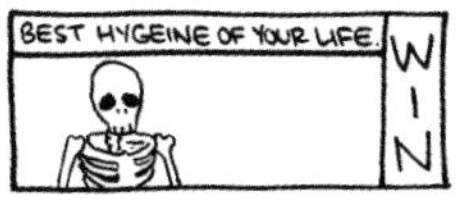
BEST HYGEINE OF YOUR LIFE.
W I N

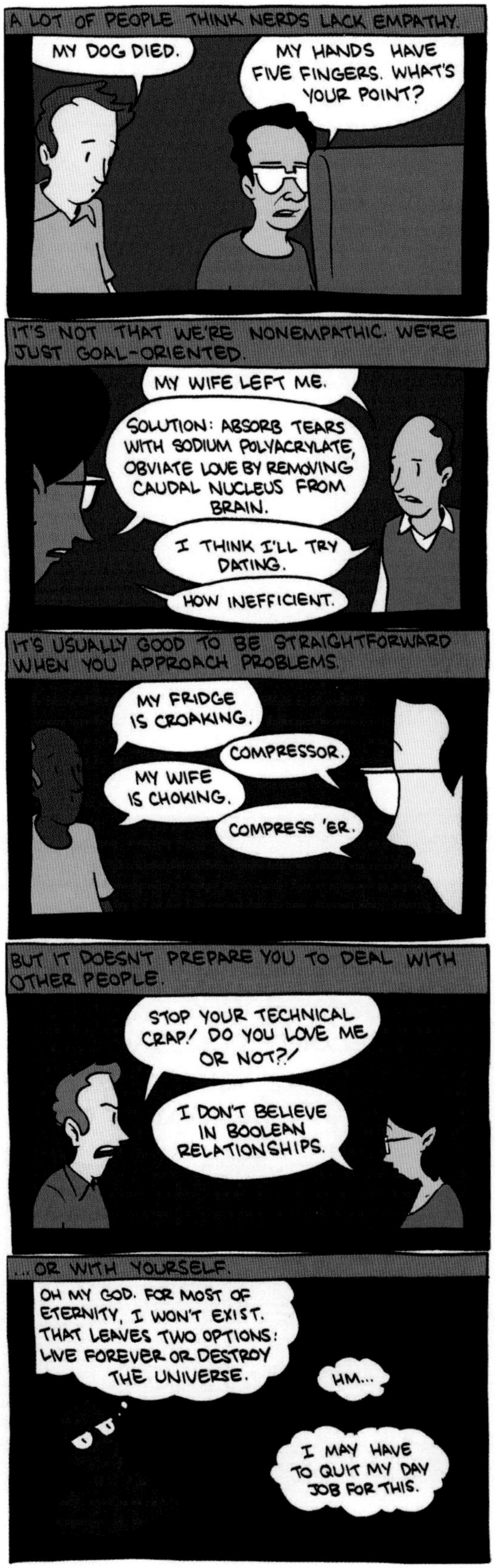
A LOT OF PEOPLE THINK NERDS LACK EMPATHY.
MY DOG DIED.
MY HANDS HAVE FIVE FINGERS. WHAT'S YOUR POINT?
IT'S NOT THAT WE'RE NONEMPATHIC. WE'RE JUST GOAL-ORIENTED.
MY WIFE LEFT ME.
SOLUTION: ABSORB TEARS WITH SODIUM POLYACRYLATE, OBVIATE LOVE BY REMOVING CAUDAL NUCLEUS FROM BRAIN.
I THINK I'LL TRY DATING.
HOW INEFFICIENT.
IT'S USUALLY GOOD TO BE STRAIGHTFORWARD WHEN YOU APPROACH PROBLEMS.
MY FRIDGE IS CROAKING.
COMPRESSOR.
MY WIFE IS CHOKING.
COMPRESS 'ER.
BUT IT DOESN'T PREPARE YOU TO DEAL WITH OTHER PEOPLE.
STOP YOUR TECHNICAL CRAP! DO YOU LOVE ME OR NOT?!
I DON'T BELIEVE IN BOOLEAN RELATIONSHIPS.
...OR WITH YOURSELF.
OH MY GOD. FOR MOST OF ETERNITY, I WON'T EXIST. THAT LEAVES TWO OPTIONS: LIVE FOREVER OR DESTROY THE UNIVERSE.
HM...
I MAY HAVE TO QUIT MY DAY JOB FOR THIS.

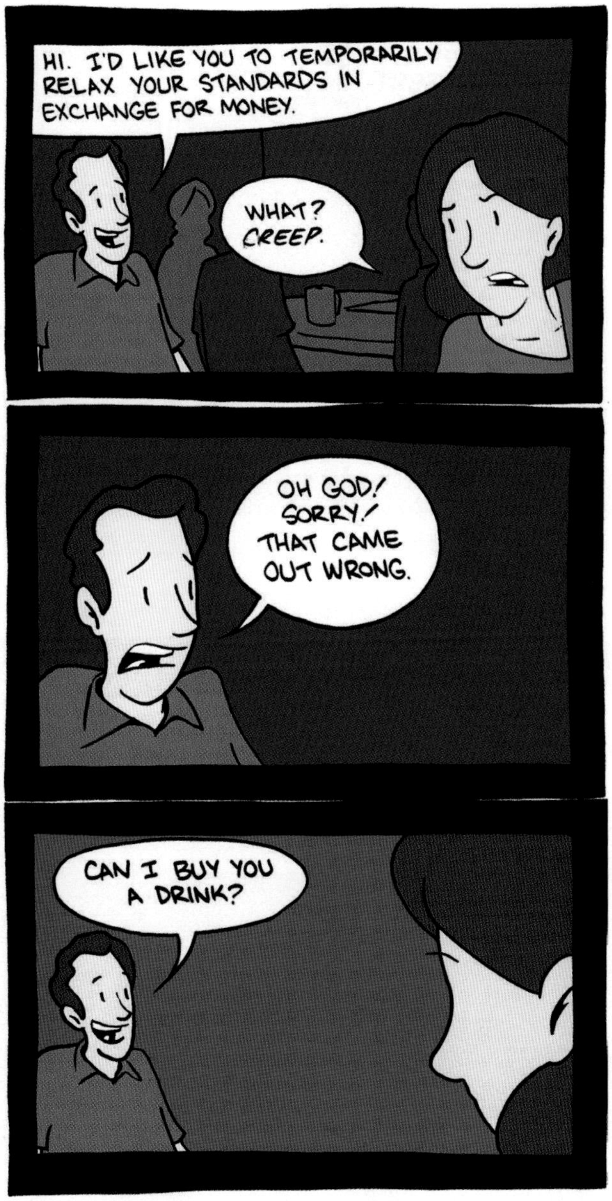
HI. I'D LIKE YOU TO TEMPORARILY RELAX YOUR STANDARDS IN EXCHANGE FOR MONEY.
WHAT? CREEP.
OH GOD! SORRY! THAT CAME OUT WRONG.
CAN I BUY YOU A DRINK?

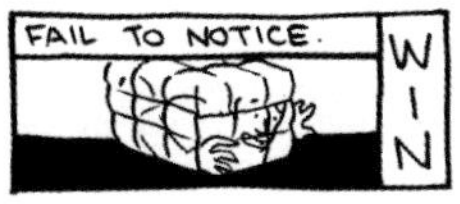
FAIL TO NOTICE.
W I N

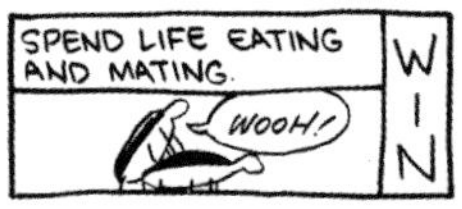
SPEND LIFE EATING AND MATING.
WOOH!
WIN

"CAN π BE EXPRESSED AS A FRACTION?"

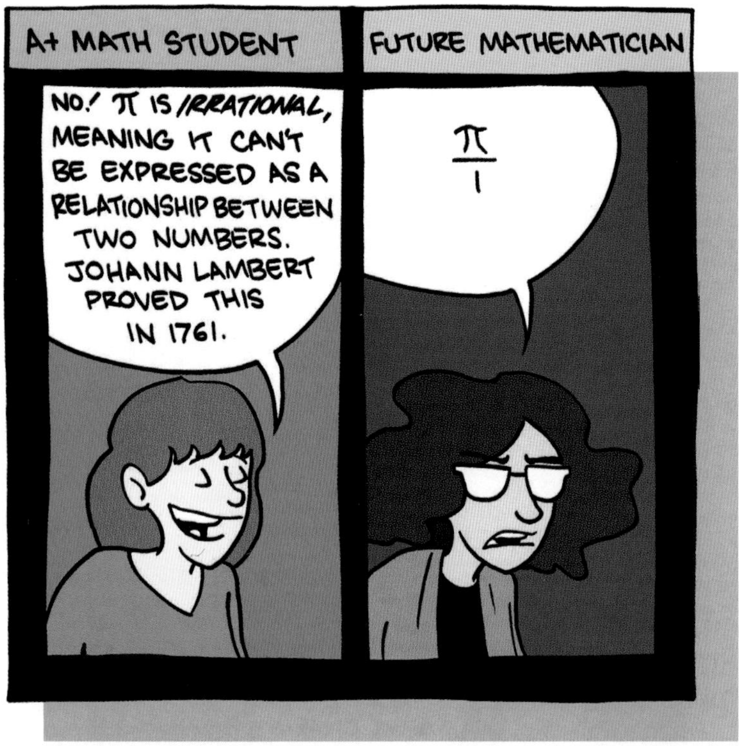
A+ MATH STUDENT
NO! π IS IRRATIONAL, MEANING IT CAN'T BE EXPRESSED AS A RELATIONSHIP BETWEEN TWO NUMBERS. JOHANN LAMBERT PROVED THIS IN 1761.
FUTURE MATHEMATICIAN
π/1

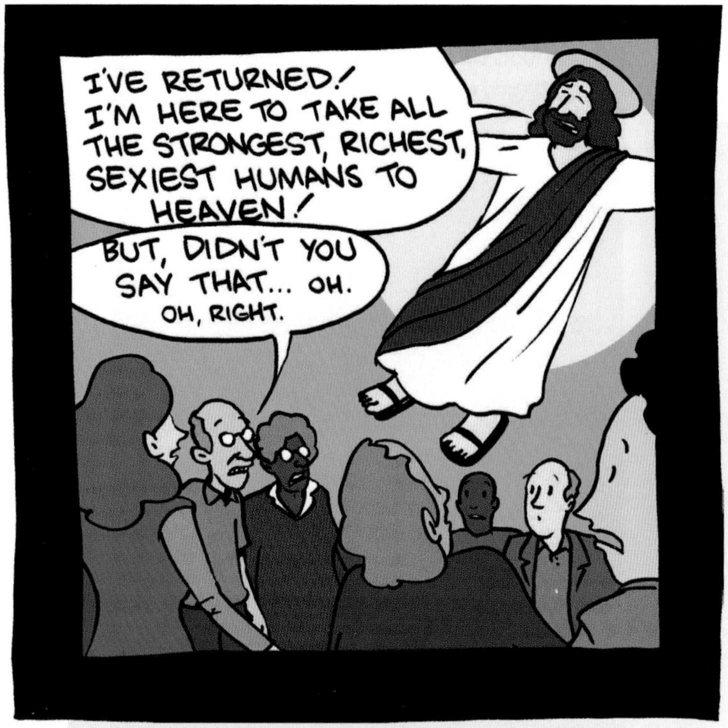
I'VE RETURNED! I'M HERE TO TAKE ALL THE STRONGEST, RICHEST, SEXIEST HUMANS TO HEAVEN!
BUT, DIDN'T YOU SAY THAT... OH. OH, RIGHT.

"The meek shall inherit the earth."

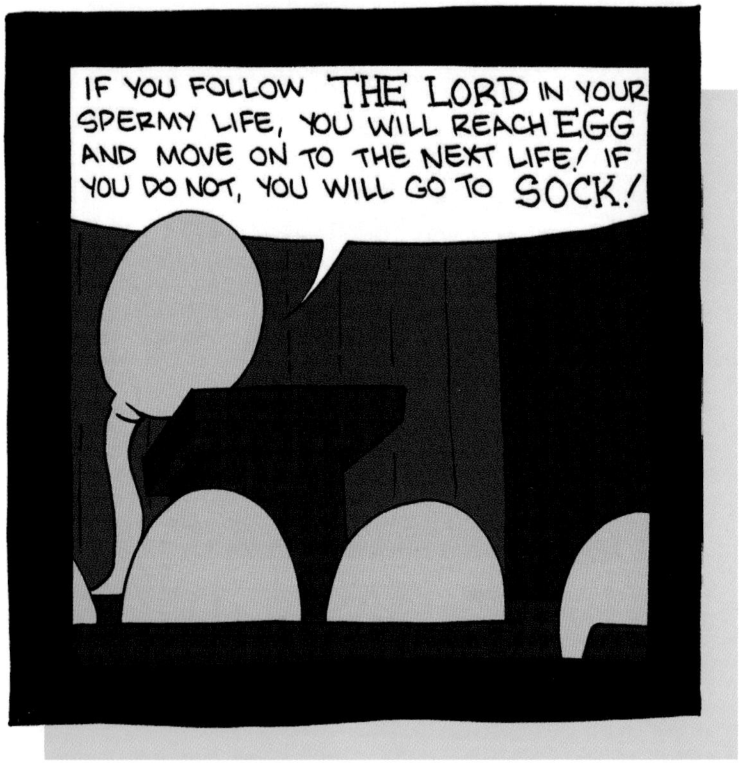
IF YOU FOLLOW THE LORD IN YOUR SPERMY LIFE, YOU WILL REACH EGG AND MOVE ON TO THE NEXT LIFE! IF YOU DO NOT, YOU WILL GO TO SOCK!

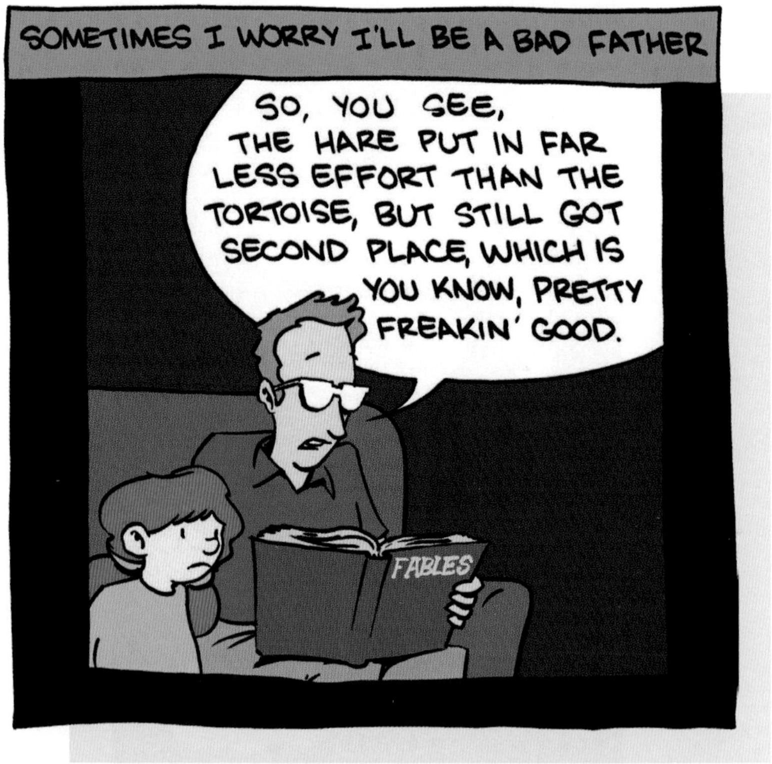
SOMETIMES I WORRY I'LL BE A BAD FATHER
SO, YOU SEE, THE HARE PUT IN FAR LESS EFFORT THAN THE TORTOISE, BUT STILL GOT SECOND PLACE, WHICH IS YOU KNOW, PRETTY FREAKIN' GOOD.
FABLES

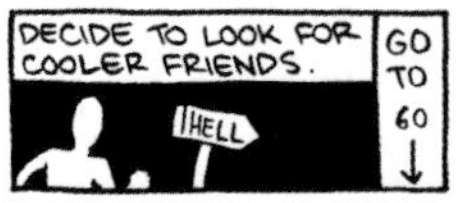
DECIDE TO LOOK FOR COOLER FRIENDS.
HELL
GO TO 60 ↓

SHAKESPEARE'S HAMLET IS BASED ON AN OLDER DANISH LEGEND ABOUT A PRINCE NAMED AMLETH.

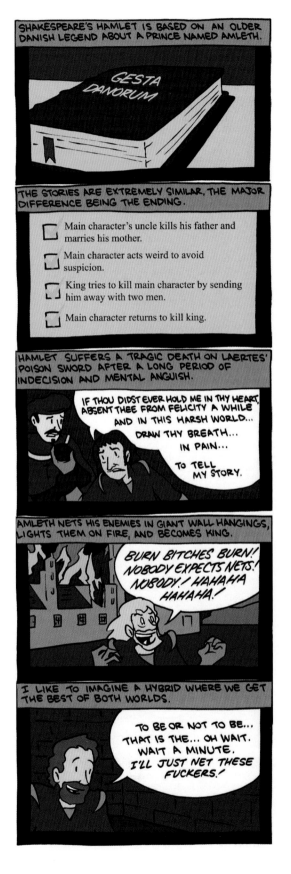

GESTA DANORUM

THE STORIES ARE EXTREMELY SIMILAR, THE MAJOR DIFFERENCE BEING THE ENDING.

- ☐ Main character's uncle kills his father and marries his mother.
- ☐ Main character acts weird to avoid suspicion.
- ☐ King tries to kill main character by sending him away with two men.
- ☐ Main character returns to kill king.

HAMLET SUFFERS A TRAGIC DEATH ON LAERTES' POISON SWORD AFTER A LONG PERIOD OF INDECISION AND MENTAL ANGUISH.

IF THOU DIDST EVER HOLD ME IN THY HEART, ABSENT THEE FROM FELICITY A WHILE AND IN THIS HARSH WORLD... DRAW THY BREATH... IN PAIN... TO TELL MY STORY.

AMLETH NETS HIS ENEMIES IN GIANT WALL HANGINGS, LIGHTS THEM ON FIRE, AND BECOMES KING.

BURN BITCHES BURN! NOBODY EXPECTS NETS! NOBODY! HAHAHA HAHAHA!

I LIKE TO IMAGINE A HYBRID WHERE WE GET THE BEST OF BOTH WORLDS.

TO BE OR NOT TO BE... THAT IS THE... OH WAIT. WAIT A MINUTE. I'LL JUST NET THESE FUCKERS!

SO, YOU SEE, SOMETHING CAN EXIST NOT JUST AS TRUTH OR FALSEHOOD, BUT ALSO AS A SUPERPOSITION. A THIRD OPTION: TRUE-FALSE.

WELL YEAH.

I'M SORRY... WHY DOES ANYONE FIND THIS CONCEPT DIFFICULT.

Oddly enough, politicians excel at quantum mechanics.

EAT IT! 7↓ ↑122 REFUSE

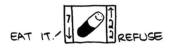

ANY JOKE THAT ENDS WITH A PUN CAN BE CONVERTED TO AN ACTION MOVIE SCENE

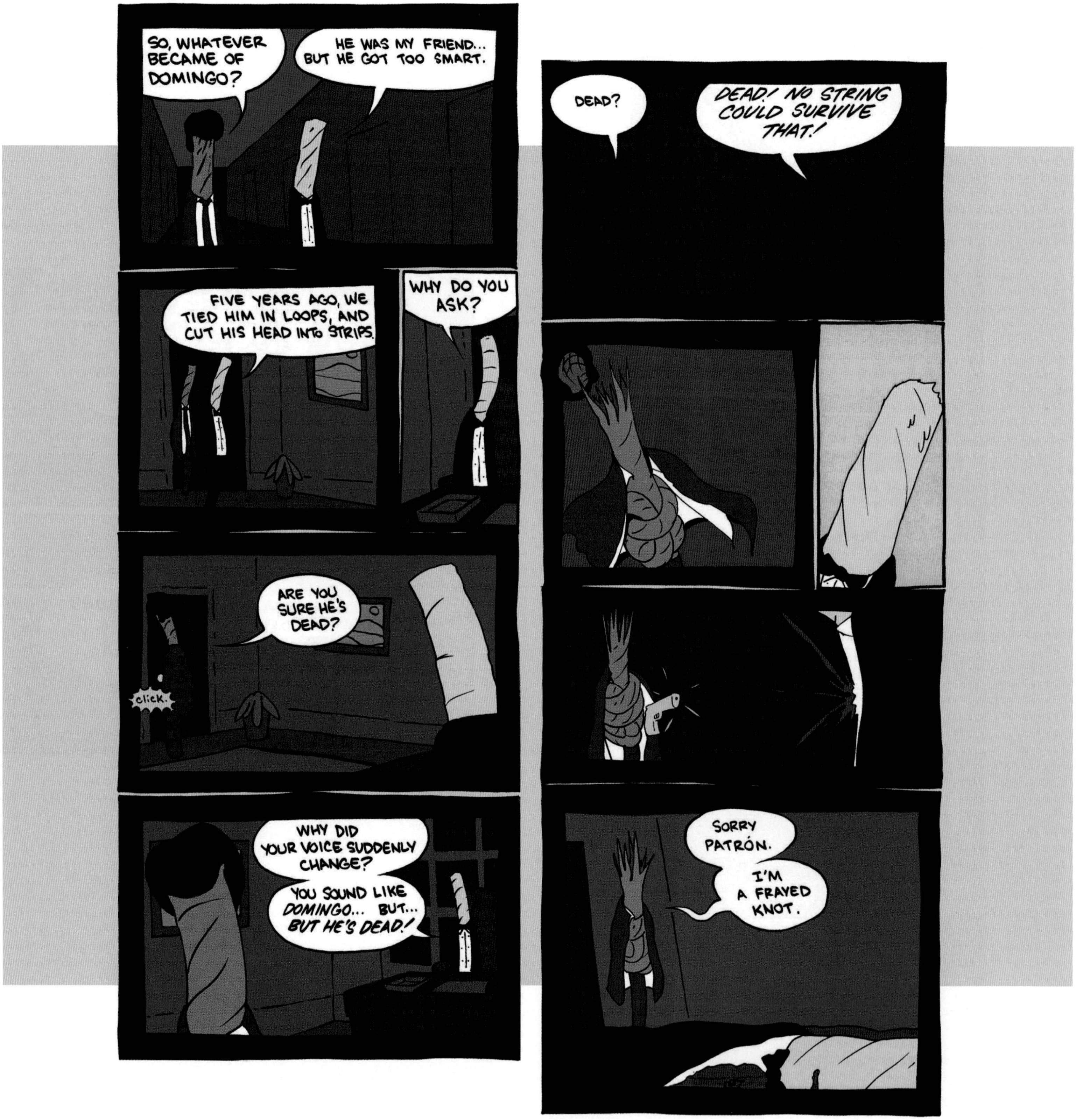

SO, WHATEVER BECAME OF DOMINGO?
HE WAS MY FRIEND... BUT HE GOT TOO SMART.
FIVE YEARS AGO, WE TIED HIM IN LOOPS, AND CUT HIS HEAD INTO STRIPS.
WHY DO YOU ASK?
ARE YOU SURE HE'S DEAD?
click.
WHY DID YOUR VOICE SUDDENLY CHANGE?
YOU SOUND LIKE DOMINGO... BUT... BUT HE'S DEAD!
DEAD?
DEAD! NO STRING COULD SURVIVE THAT!
SORRY PATRÓN.
I'M A FRAYED KNOT.

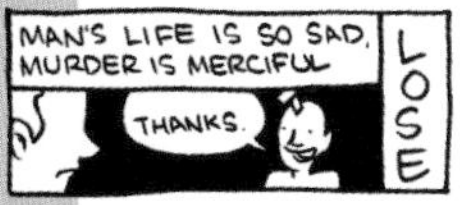
MAN'S LIFE IS SO SAD, MURDER IS MERCIFUL
THANKS.
LOSE

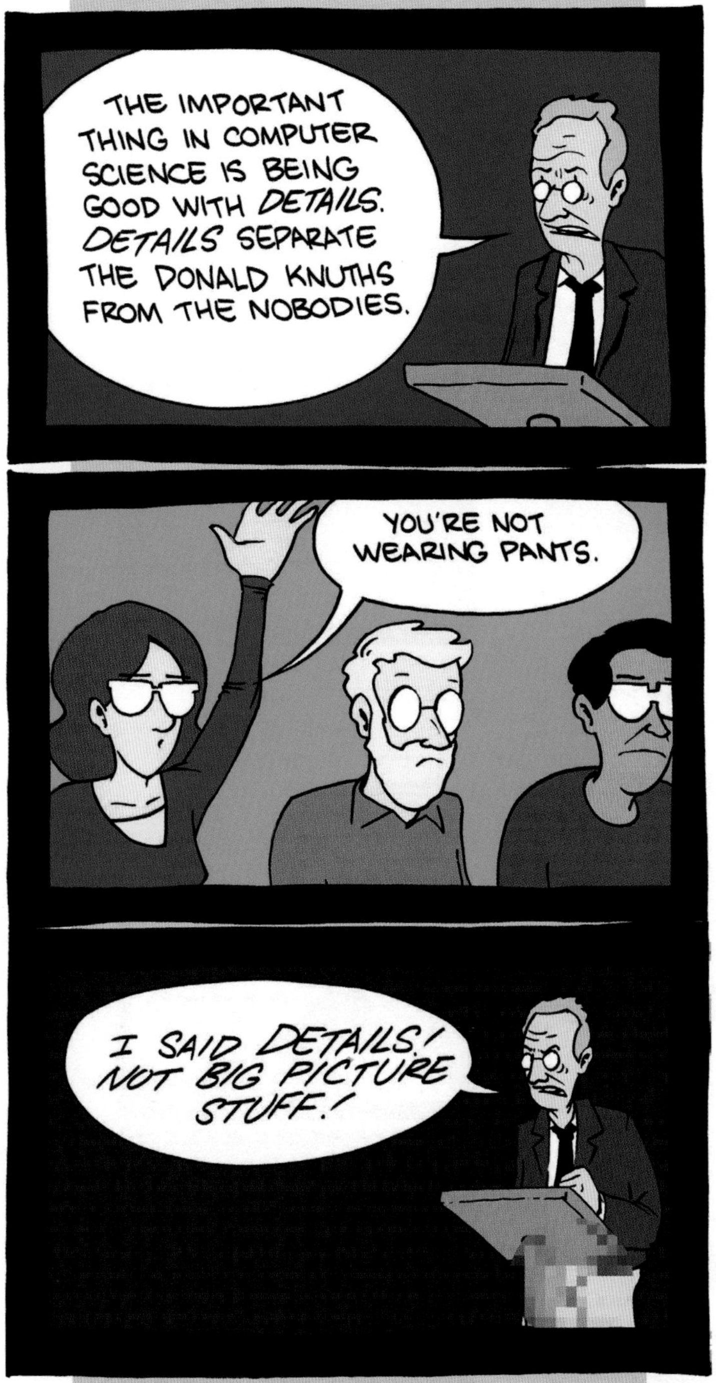
THE IMPORTANT THING IN COMPUTER SCIENCE IS BEING GOOD WITH *DETAILS*. *DETAILS* SEPARATE THE DONALD KNUTHS FROM THE NOBODIES.
YOU'RE NOT WEARING PANTS.
I SAID *DETAILS*! NOT BIG PICTURE STUFF!

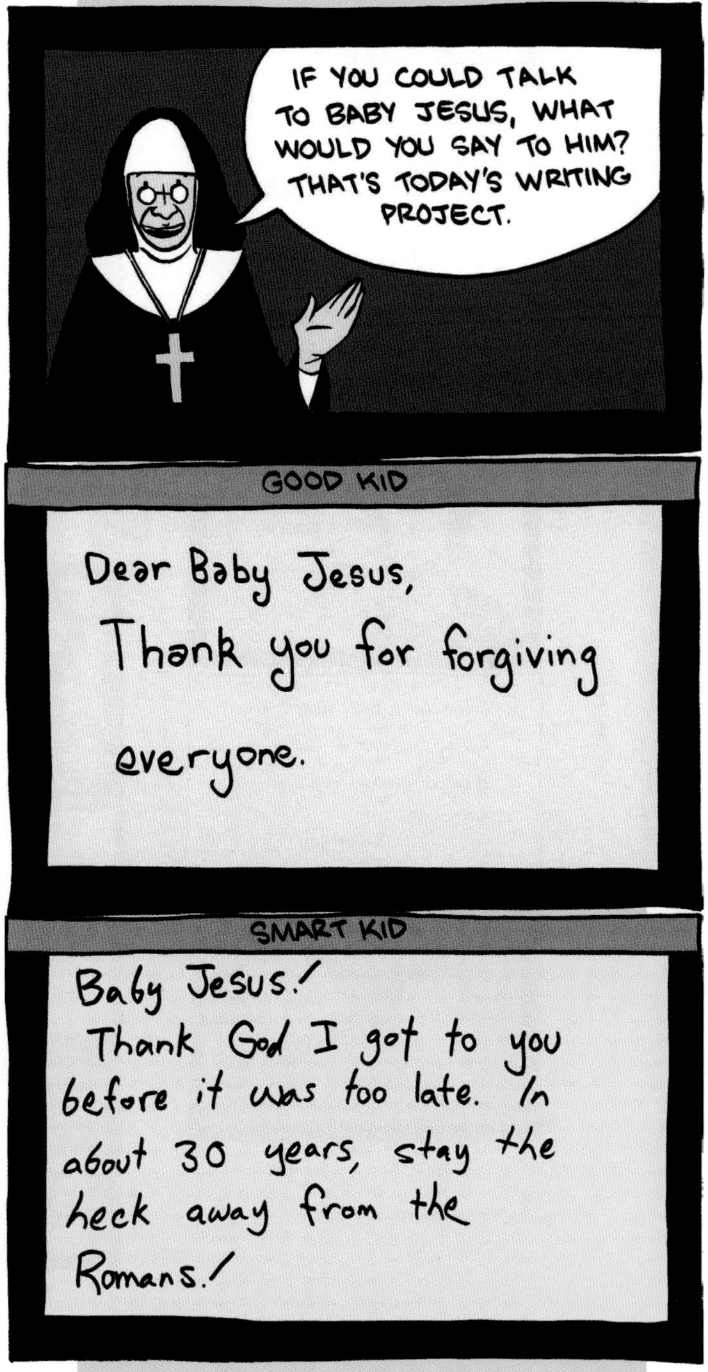
IF YOU COULD TALK TO BABY JESUS, WHAT WOULD YOU SAY TO HIM? THAT'S TODAY'S WRITING PROJECT.
GOOD KID
Dear Baby Jesus,
Thank you for forgiving everyone.
SMART KID
Baby Jesus!
Thank God I got to you before it was too late. In about 30 years, stay the heck away from the Romans!

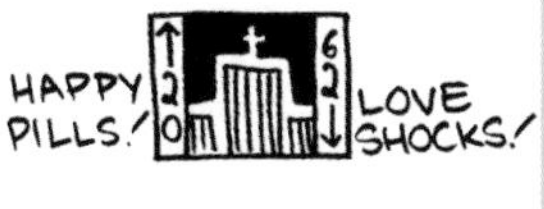
HAPPY PILLS!
120
621
LOVE SHOCKS!

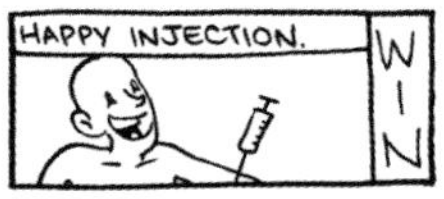
HAPPY INJECTION.
WIN

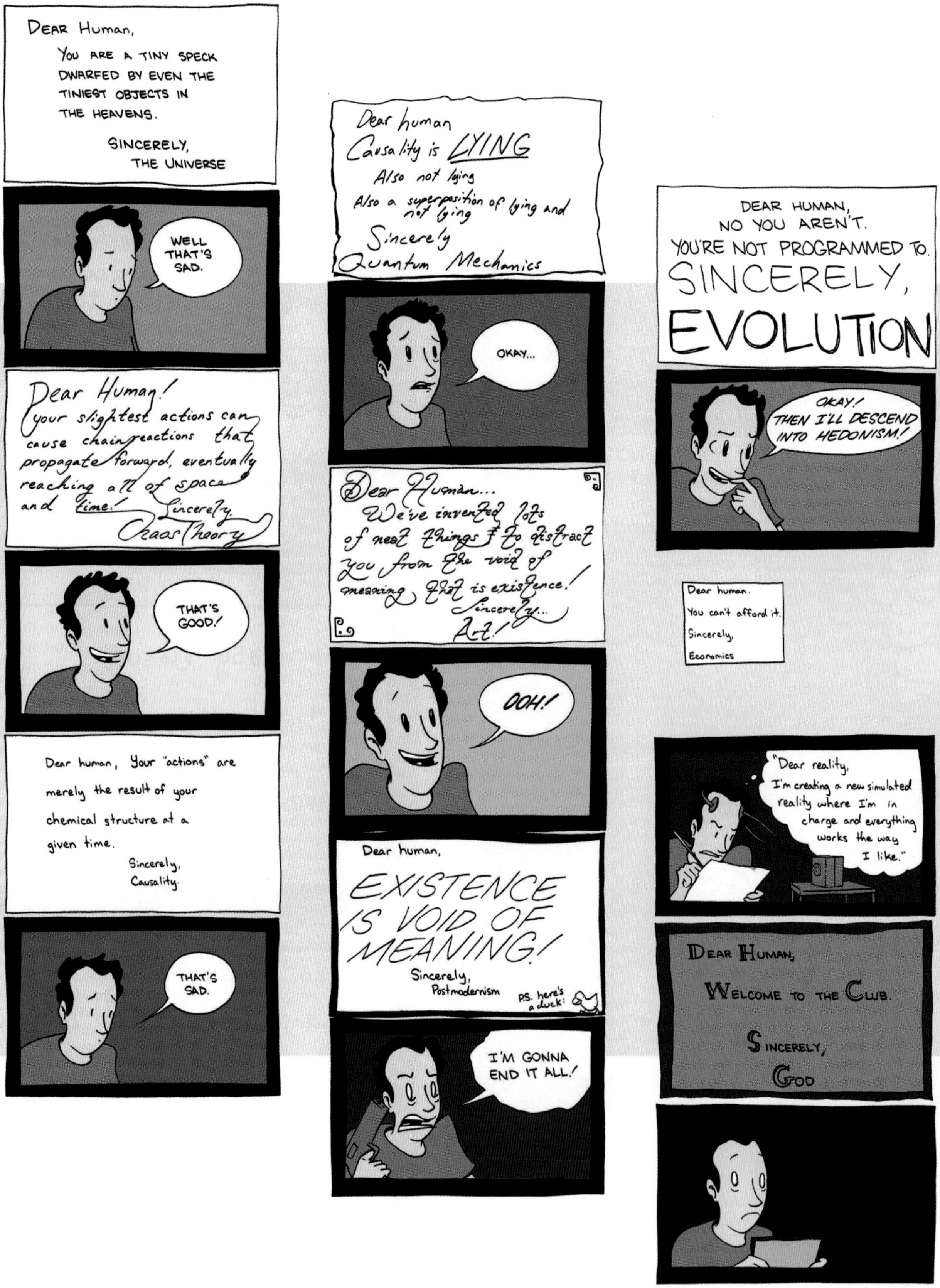
DEAR HUMAN, YOU ARE A TINY SPECK DWARFED BY EVEN THE TINIEST OBJECTS IN THE HEAVENS. SINCERELY, THE UNIVERSE
WELL THAT'S SAD.
Dear Human! your slightest actions can cause chain reactions that propagate forward, eventually reaching all of space and time! Sincerely, Chaos Theory
THAT'S GOOD!
Dear human, Your "actions" are merely the result of your chemical structure at a given time. Sincerely, Causality.
THAT'S SAD.
Dear human Causality is LYING Also not lying Also a superposition of lying and not lying Sincerely Quantum Mechanics
OKAY...
Dear Human... We've invented lots of neat things to distract you from the void of meaning that is existence! Sincerely... Art!
OOH!
Dear human, EXISTENCE IS VOID OF MEANING! Sincerely, Postmodernism P.S. here's a duck:
I'M GONNA END IT ALL!
DEAR HUMAN, NO YOU AREN'T. YOU'RE NOT PROGRAMMED TO. SINCERELY, EVOLUTION
OKAY! THEN I'LL DESCEND INTO HEDONISM!
Dear human. You can't afford it. Sincerely, Economics
"Dear reality, I'm creating a new simulated reality where I'm in charge and everything works the way I like."
DEAR HUMAN, WELCOME TO THE CLUB. SINCERELY, GOD

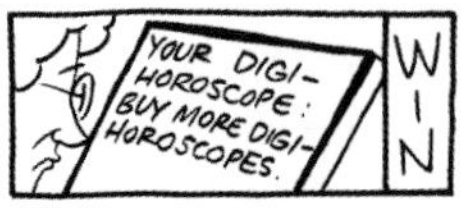
YOUR DIGI-HOROSCOPE: BUY MORE DIGI-HOROSCOPES.
WIN

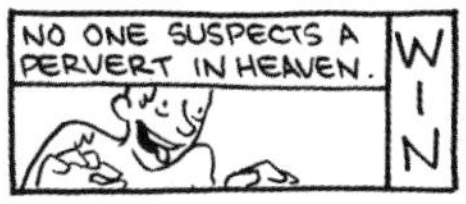
NO ONE SUSPECTS A PERVERT IN HEAVEN.
WIN

FOR TOO LONG, "GAY" HAS BEEN USED AS A PEJORATIVE TERM.

HENCEFORTH, WE SHALL HAVE A NEW MEANING FOR THE WORD "GAY."

Gay /geɪ/ : *adjective* : As awesome as two people who are experts on penises having sex without fear of pregnancy.

EXAMPLES:

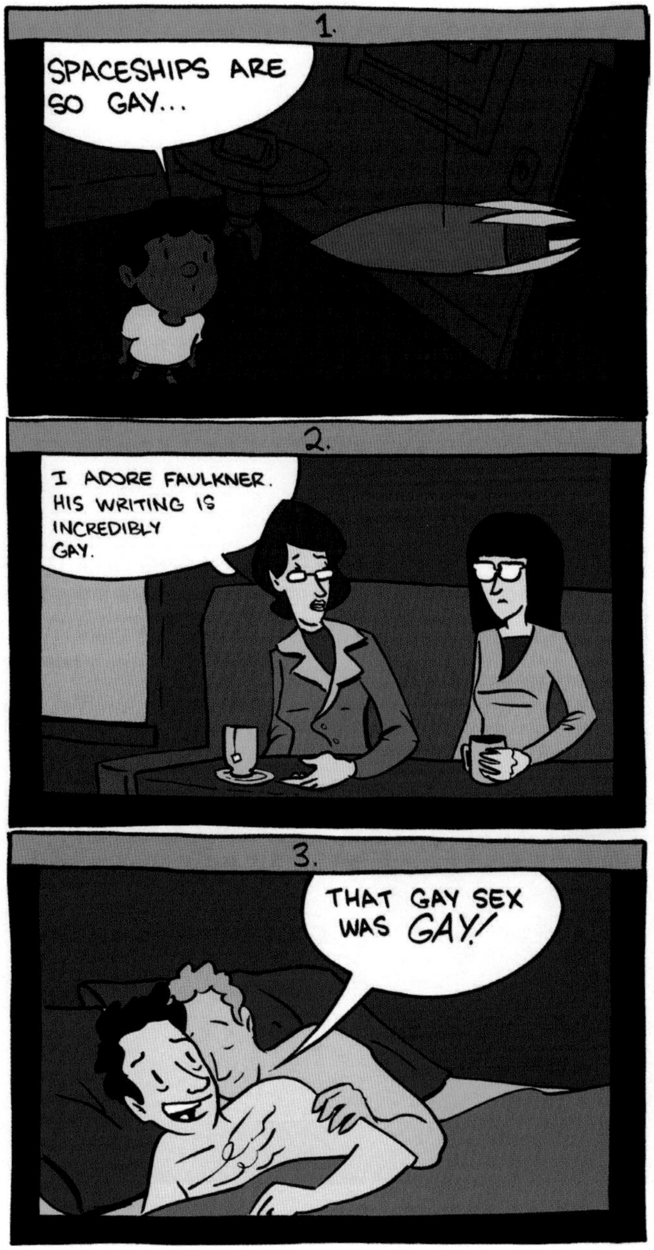
1.
SPACESHIPS ARE SO GAY...
2.
I ADORE FAULKNER. HIS WRITING IS INCREDIBLY GAY.
3.
THAT GAY SEX WAS GAY!

Life Tip:
The world seems much happier
if you imagine every person you meet
is living life according to a fulfilled longterm plan.

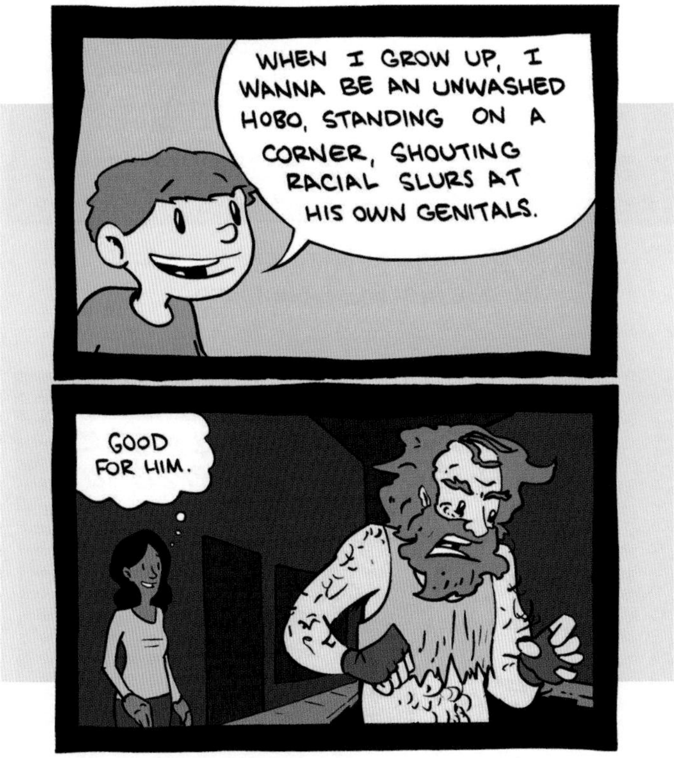
WHEN I GROW UP, I WANNA BE AN UNWASHED HOBO, STANDING ON A CORNER, SHOUTING RACIAL SLURS AT HIS OWN GENITALS.
GOOD FOR HIM.

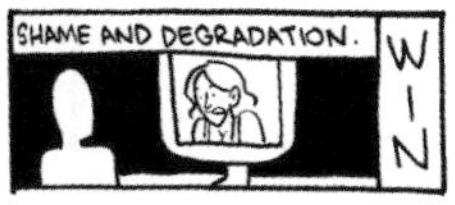
SHAME AND DEGRADATION.
WIN

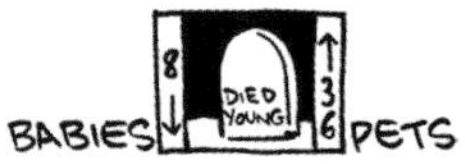
BABIES
8↓
DIED YOUNG
136↑
PETS

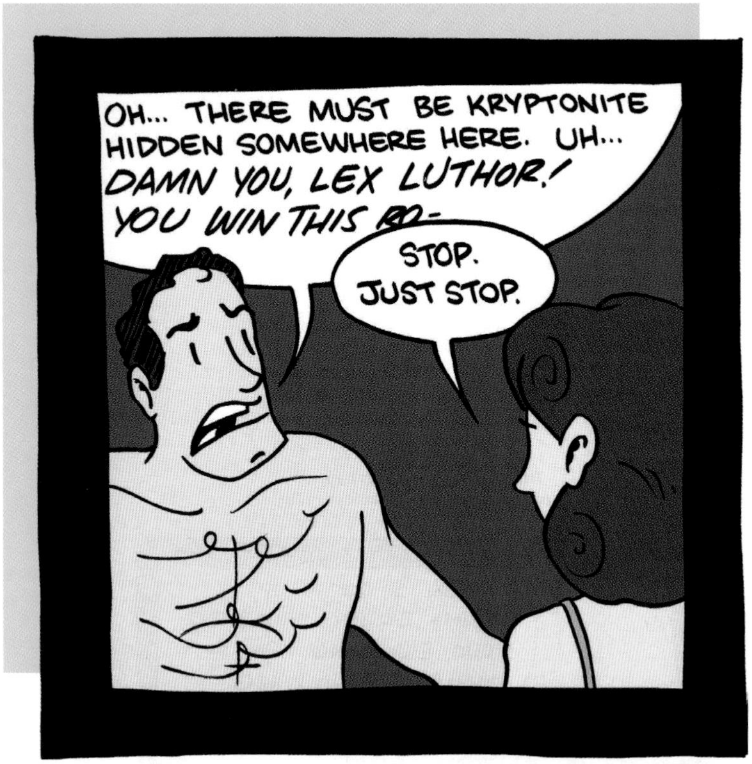
OH... THERE MUST BE KRYPTONITE HIDDEN SOMEWHERE HERE. UH... DAMN YOU, LEX LUTHOR! YOU WIN THIS RO–
STOP. JUST STOP.

Later in life, Superman refuses to admit he has erectile dysfunction.

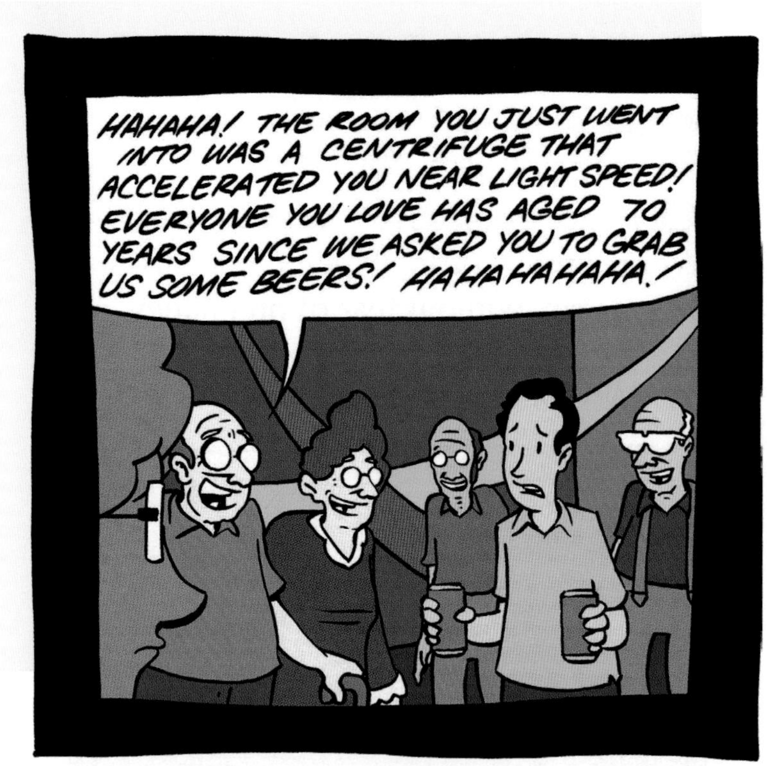
HAHAHA! THE ROOM YOU JUST WENT INTO WAS A CENTRIFUGE THAT ACCELERATED YOU NEAR LIGHT SPEED! EVERYONE YOU LOVE HAS AGED 70 YEARS SINCE WE ASKED YOU TO GRAB US SOME BEERS! HAHAHAHAHA!

Pranks are way better in the future.

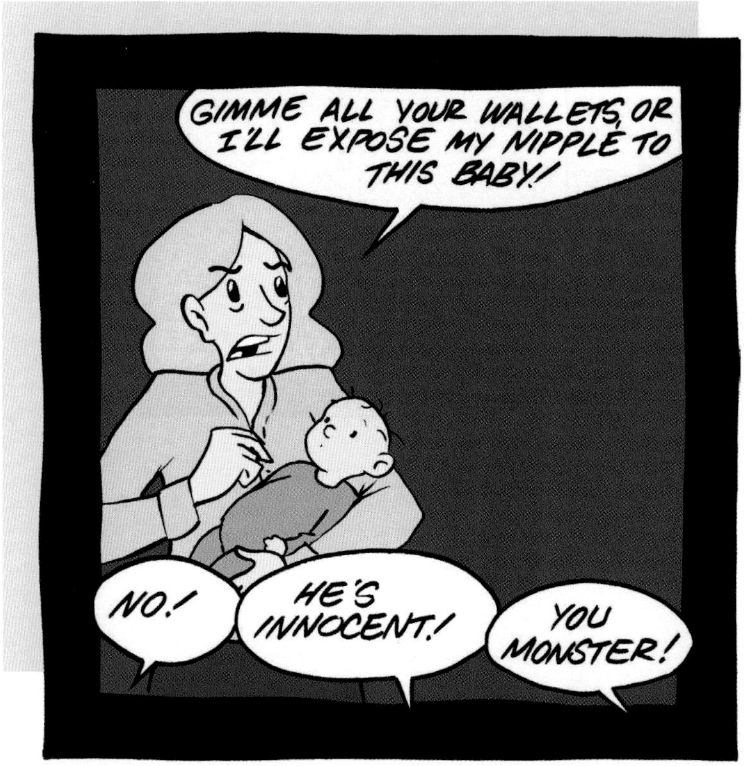
GIMME ALL YOUR WALLETS, OR I'LL EXPOSE MY NIPPLE TO THIS BABY!
NO!
HE'S INNOCENT!
YOU MONSTER!

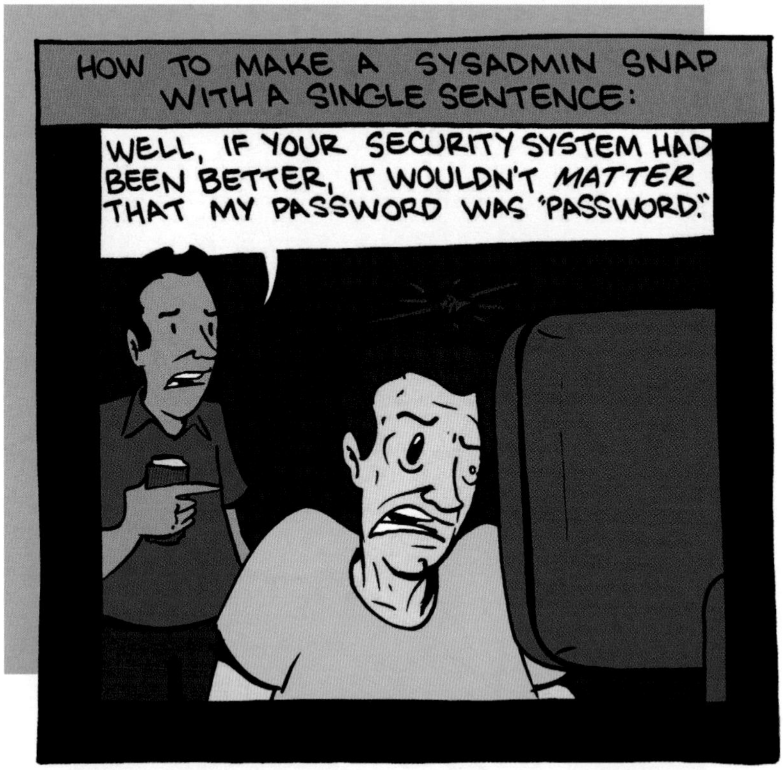
HOW TO MAKE A SYSADMIN SNAP WITH A SINGLE SENTENCE:
WELL, IF YOUR SECURITY SYSTEM HAD BEEN BETTER, IT WOULDN'T MATTER THAT MY PASSWORD WAS "PASSWORD."

The least dangerous disgruntled employees work at the FCC.

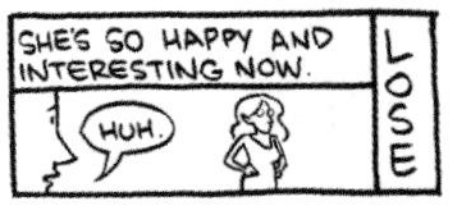
SHE'S SO HAPPY AND INTERESTING NOW.
HUH.
LOSE

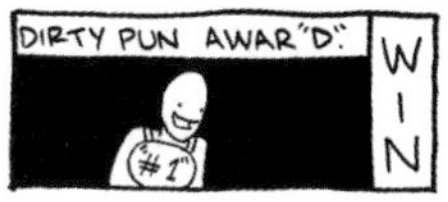
DIRTY PUN AWAR"D"
#1
WIN

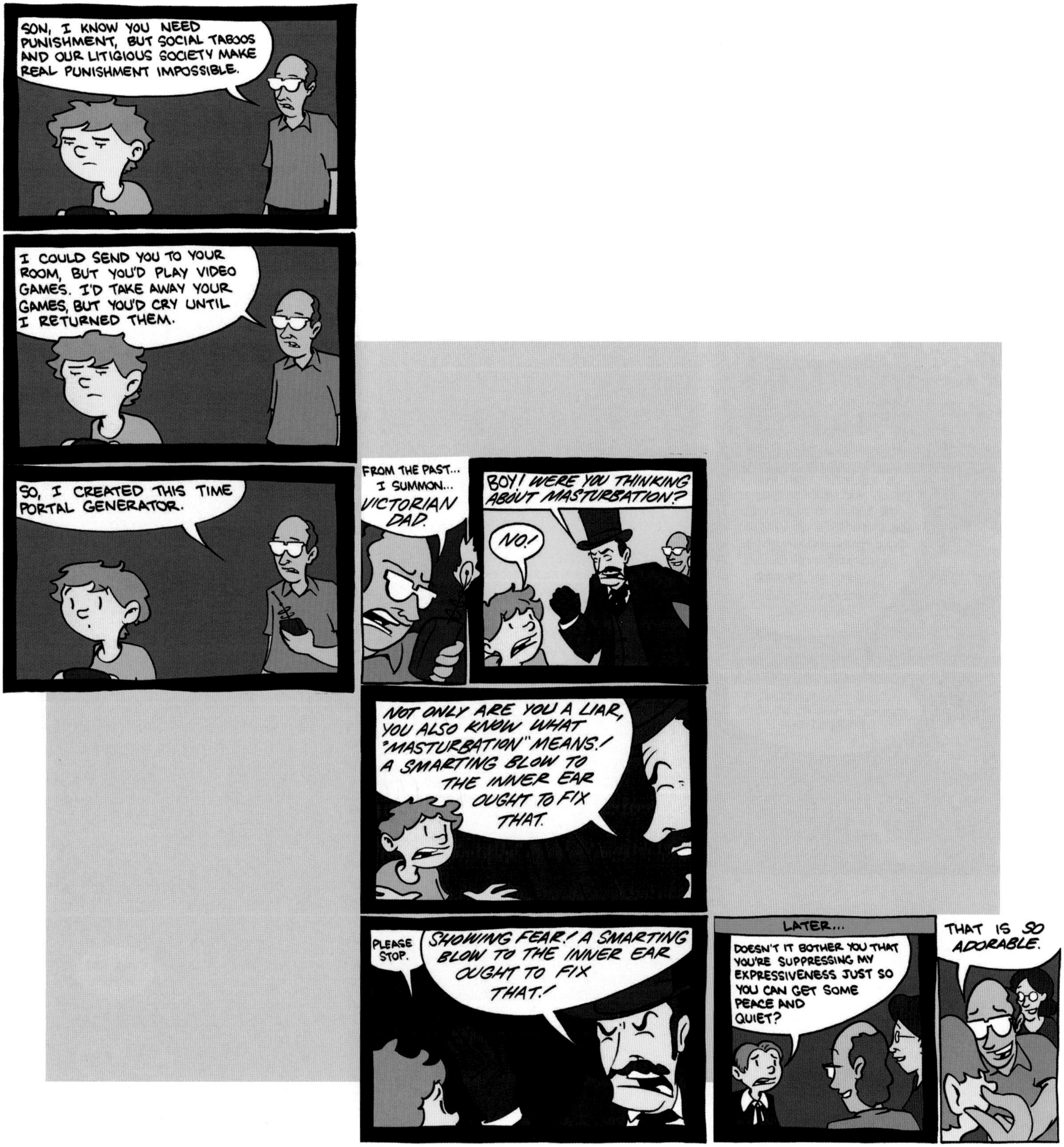
SON, I KNOW YOU NEED PUNISHMENT, BUT SOCIAL TABOOS AND OUR LITIGIOUS SOCIETY MAKE REAL PUNISHMENT IMPOSSIBLE.
I COULD SEND YOU TO YOUR ROOM, BUT YOU'D PLAY VIDEO GAMES. I'D TAKE AWAY YOUR GAMES, BUT YOU'D CRY UNTIL I RETURNED THEM.
SO, I CREATED THIS TIME PORTAL GENERATOR.
FROM THE PAST... I SUMMON... VICTORIAN DAD.
BOY! WERE YOU THINKING ABOUT MASTURBATION?
NO!
NOT ONLY ARE YOU A LIAR, YOU ALSO KNOW WHAT "MASTURBATION" MEANS! A SMARTING BLOW TO THE INNER EAR OUGHT TO FIX THAT.
PLEASE STOP.
SHOWING FEAR! A SMARTING BLOW TO THE INNER EAR OUGHT TO FIX THAT!
LATER...
DOESN'T IT BOTHER YOU THAT YOU'RE SUPPRESSING MY EXPRESSIVENESS JUST SO YOU CAN GET SOME PEACE AND QUIET?
THAT IS SO ADORABLE.

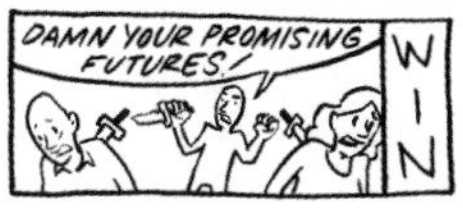
DAMN YOUR PROMISING FUTURES!
WIN

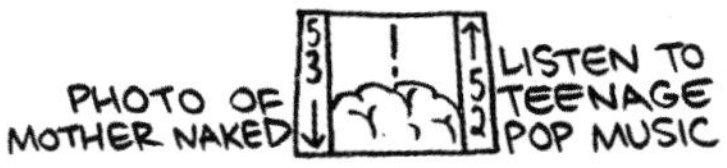

PHOTO OF MOTHER NAKED
53
152
LISTEN TO TEENAGE POP MUSIC

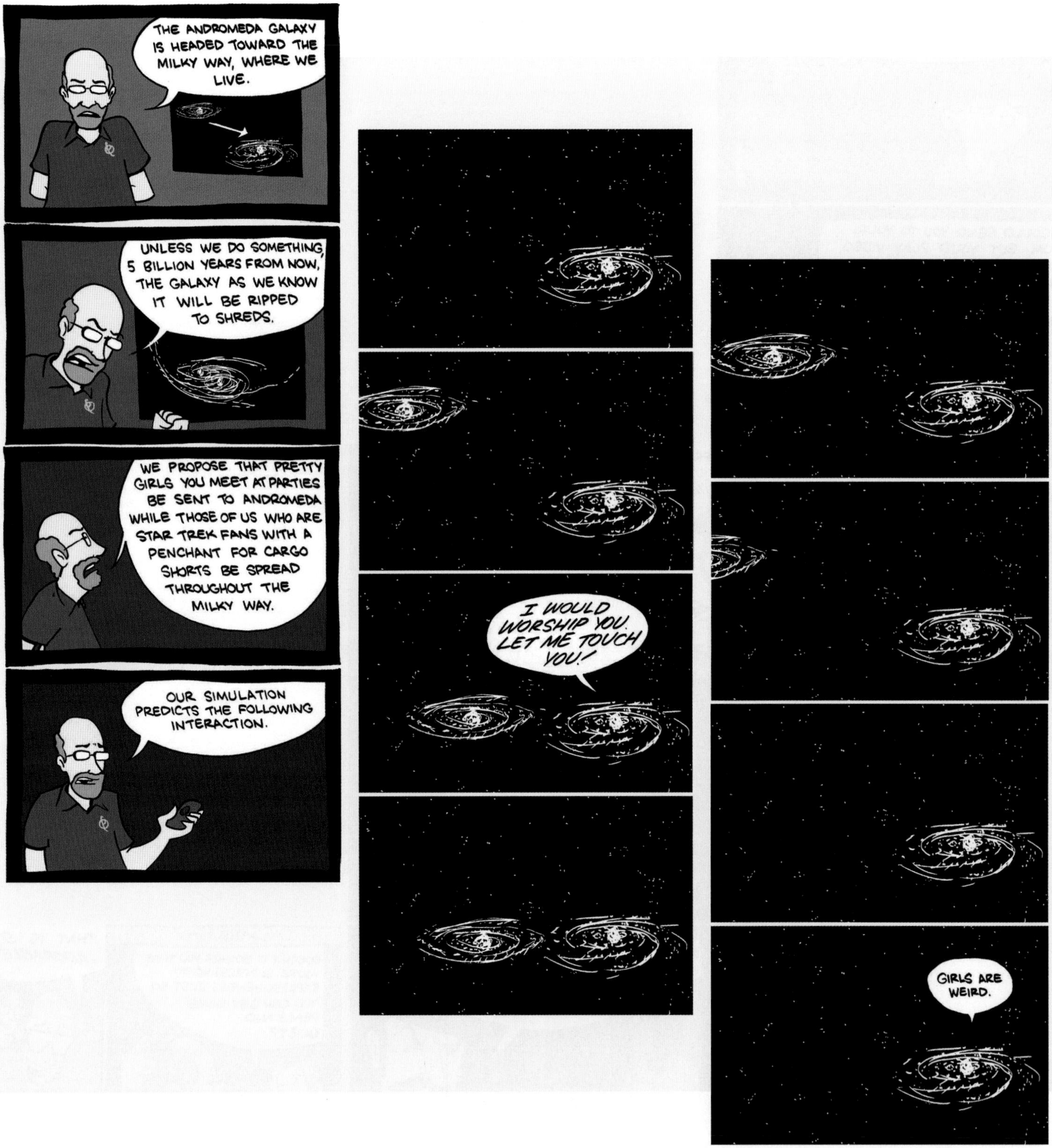

THE ANDROMEDA GALAXY IS HEADED TOWARD THE MILKY WAY, WHERE WE LIVE.
UNLESS WE DO SOMETHING, 5 BILLION YEARS FROM NOW, THE GALAXY AS WE KNOW IT WILL BE RIPPED TO SHREDS.
WE PROPOSE THAT PRETTY GIRLS YOU MEET AT PARTIES BE SENT TO ANDROMEDA WHILE THOSE OF US WHO ARE STAR TREK FANS WITH A PENCHANT FOR CARGO SHORTS BE SPREAD THROUGHOUT THE MILKY WAY.
OUR SIMULATION PREDICTS THE FOLLOWING INTERACTION.
I WOULD WORSHIP YOU. LET ME TOUCH YOU!
GIRLS ARE WEIRD.

NUDE PHOTOS OF POPE.
WIN

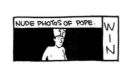

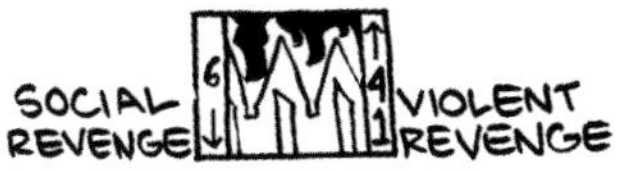
SOCIAL REVENGE
6
14
VIOLENT REVENGE

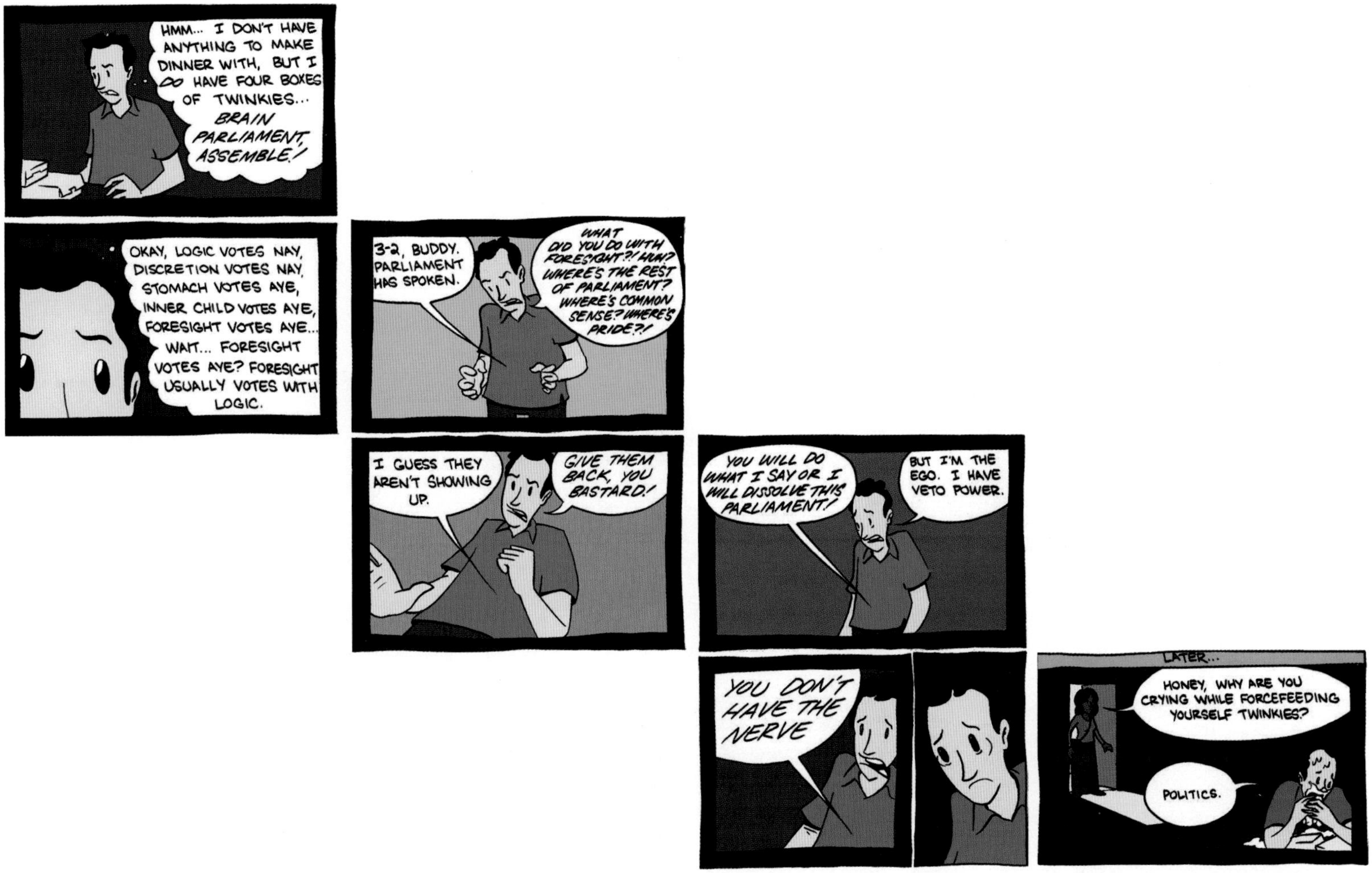
HMM... I DON'T HAVE ANYTHING TO MAKE DINNER WITH, BUT I DO HAVE FOUR BOXES OF TWINKIES... BRAIN PARLIAMENT, ASSEMBLE!
OKAY, LOGIC VOTES NAY, DISCRETION VOTES NAY, STOMACH VOTES AYE, INNER CHILD VOTES AYE, FORESIGHT VOTES AYE... WAIT... FORESIGHT VOTES AYE? FORESIGHT USUALLY VOTES WITH LOGIC.
3-2, BUDDY. PARLIAMENT HAS SPOKEN.
WHAT DID YOU DO WITH FORESIGHT?! HUH? WHERE'S THE REST OF PARLIAMENT? WHERE'S COMMON SENSE? WHERE'S PRIDE?!
I GUESS THEY AREN'T SHOWING UP.
GIVE THEM BACK, YOU BASTARD!
YOU WILL DO WHAT I SAY OR I WILL DISSOLVE THIS PARLIAMENT!
BUT I'M THE EGO. I HAVE VETO POWER.
YOU DON'T HAVE THE NERVE
LATER...
HONEY, WHY ARE YOU CRYING WHILE FORCEFEEDING YOURSELF TWINKIES?
POLITICS.

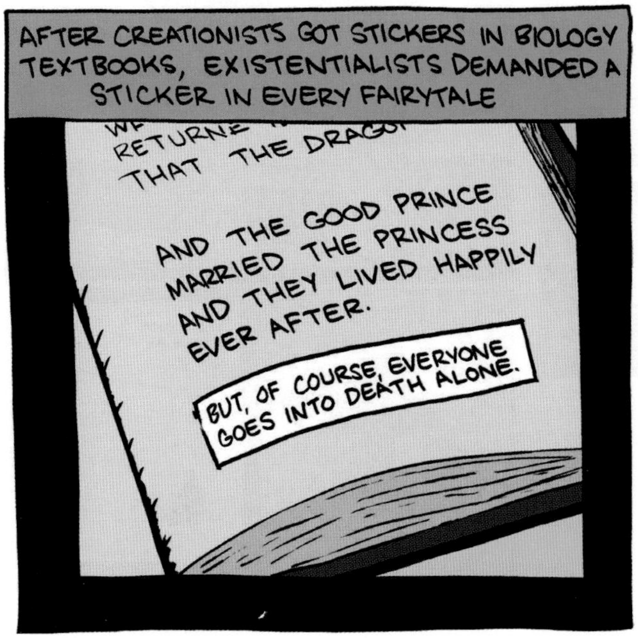
AFTER CREATIONISTS GOT STICKERS IN BIOLOGY TEXTBOOKS, EXISTENTIALISTS DEMANDED A STICKER IN EVERY FAIRYTALE
AND THE GOOD PRINCE MARRIED THE PRINCESS AND THEY LIVED HAPPILY EVER AFTER.
BUT, OF COURSE EVERYONE GOES INTO DEATH ALONE.

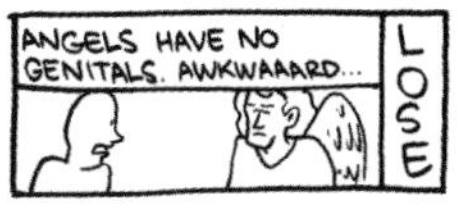
ANGELS HAVE NO GENITALS. AWKWAARD...
LOSE

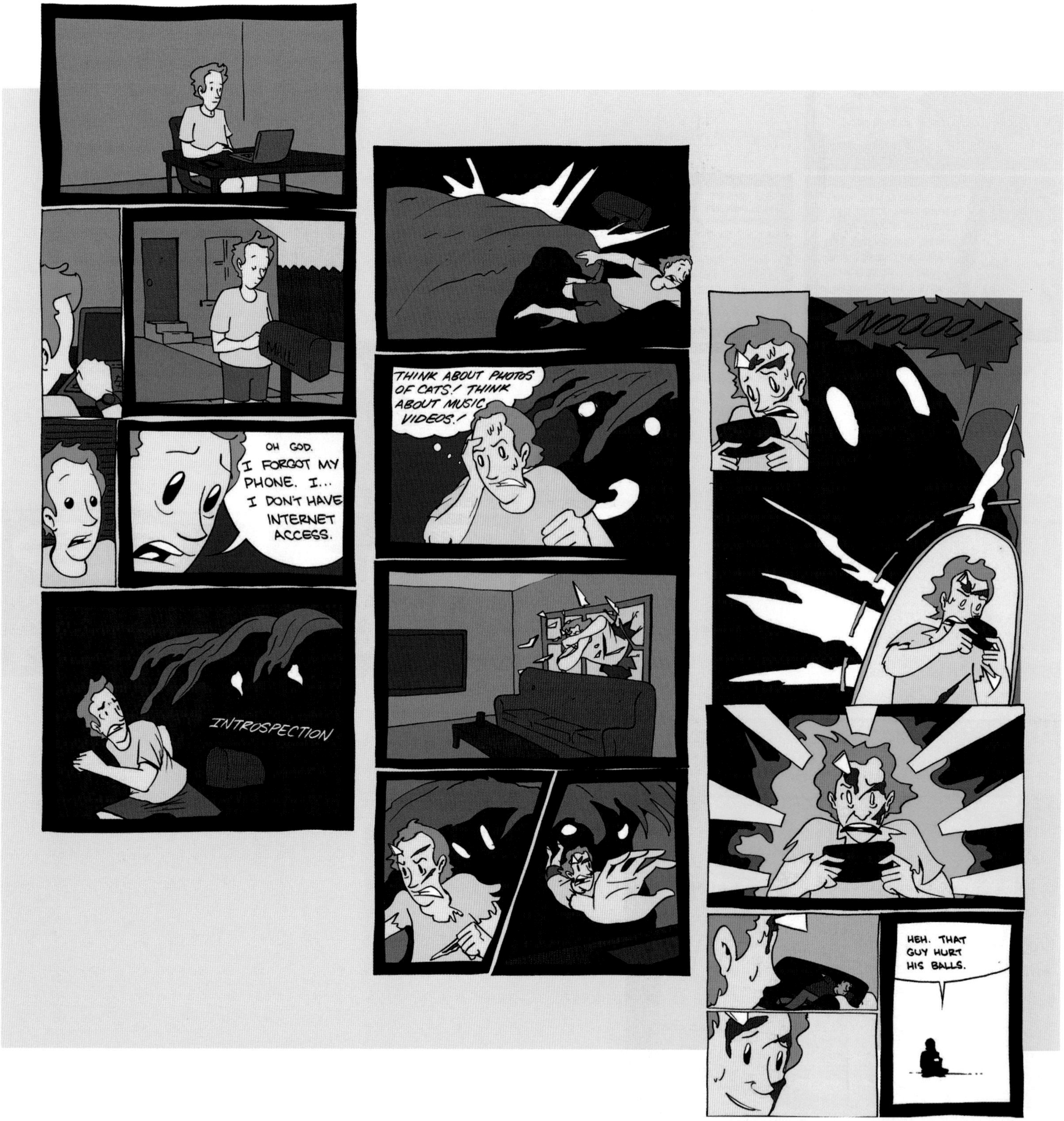
MAIL
OH GOD. I FORGOT MY PHONE. I... I DON'T HAVE INTERNET ACCESS.
INTROSPECTION
THINK ABOUT PHOTOS OF CATS! THINK ABOUT MUSIC VIDEOS!
NOOOO!
HEH. THAT GUY HURT HIS BALLS.

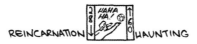

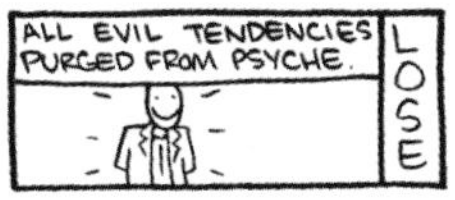
ALL EVIL TENDENCIES PURGED FROM PSYCHE.
LOSE

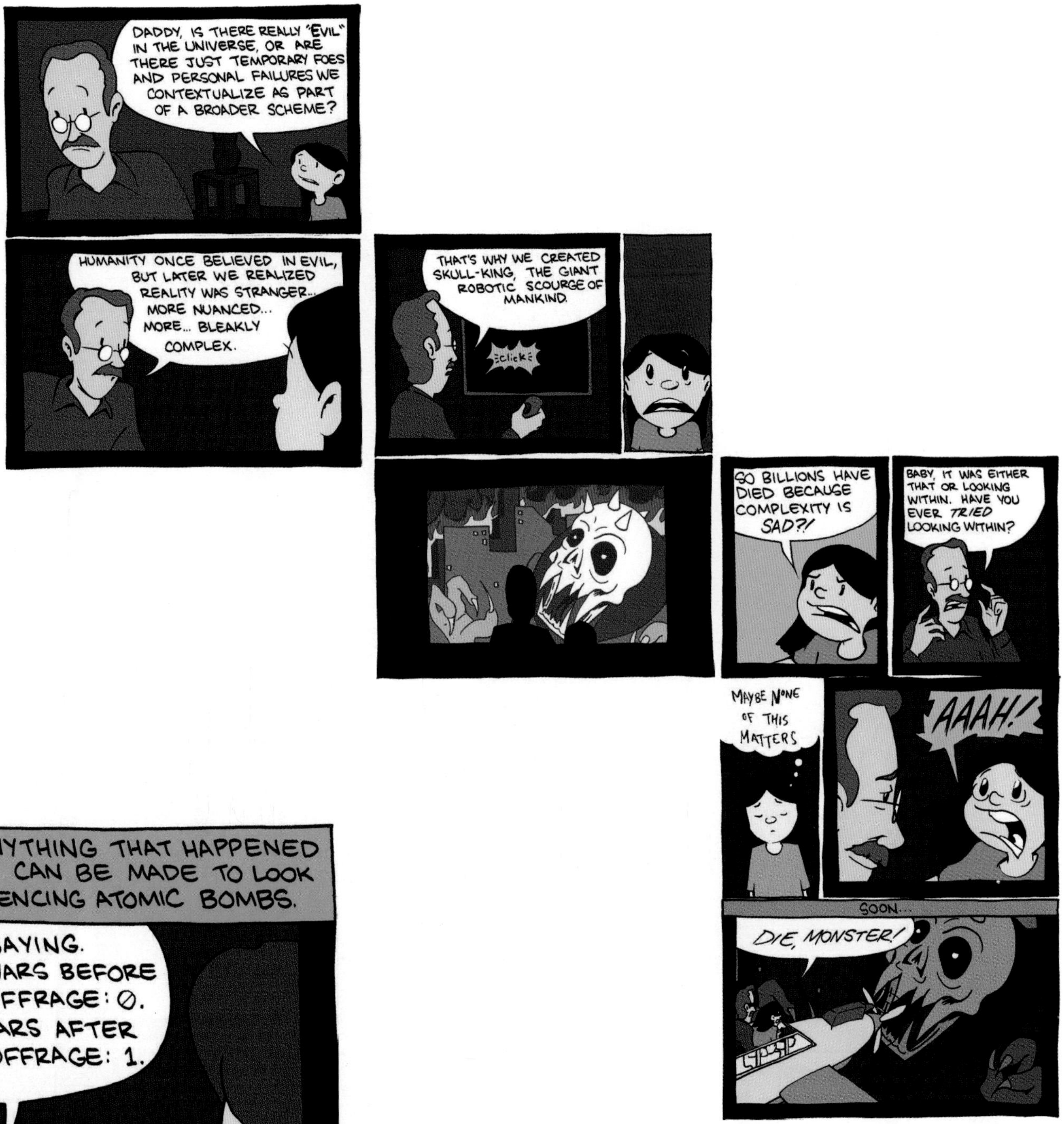
DADDY, IS THERE REALLY "EVIL" IN THE UNIVERSE, OR ARE THERE JUST TEMPORARY FOES AND PERSONAL FAILURES WE CONTEXTUALIZE AS PART OF A BROADER SCHEME?
HUMANITY ONCE BELIEVED IN EVIL, BUT LATER WE REALIZED REALITY WAS STRANGER... MORE NUANCED... MORE... BLEAKLY COMPLEX.
THAT'S WHY WE CREATED SKULL-KING, THE GIANT ROBOTIC SCOURGE OF MANKIND.
click
SO BILLIONS HAVE DIED BECAUSE COMPLEXITY IS SAD?!
BABY, IT WAS EITHER THAT OR LOOKING WITHIN. HAVE YOU EVER TRIED LOOKING WITHIN?
MAYBE NONE OF THIS MATTERS
AAAH!
SOON...
DIE, MONSTER!

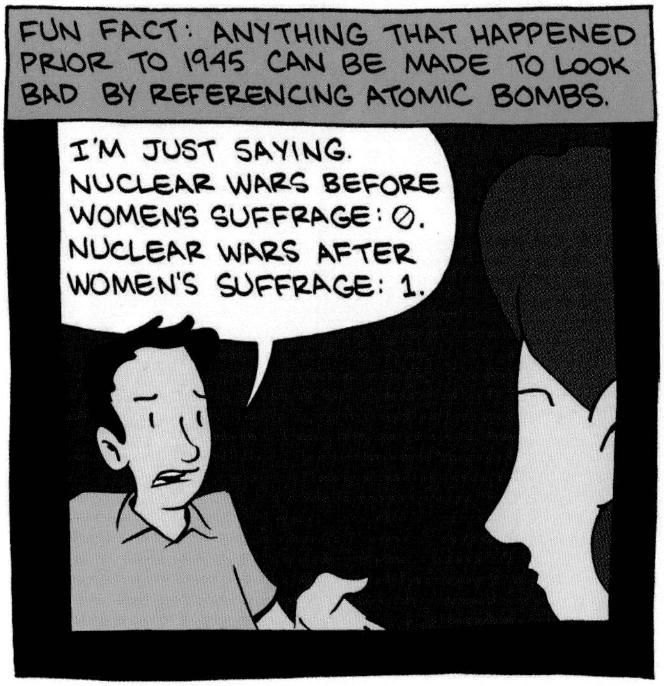
FUN FACT: ANYTHING THAT HAPPENED PRIOR TO 1945 CAN BE MADE TO LOOK BAD BY REFERENCING ATOMIC BOMBS.
I'M JUST SAYING. NUCLEAR WARS BEFORE WOMEN'S SUFFRAGE: 0. NUCLEAR WARS AFTER WOMEN'S SUFFRAGE: 1.

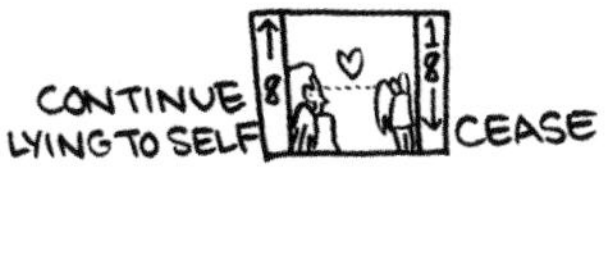
CONTINUE LYING TO SELF
18
18
CEASE

GO TO PUNISHMENT 381 — 131 ARGUE WITH FRONT DESK

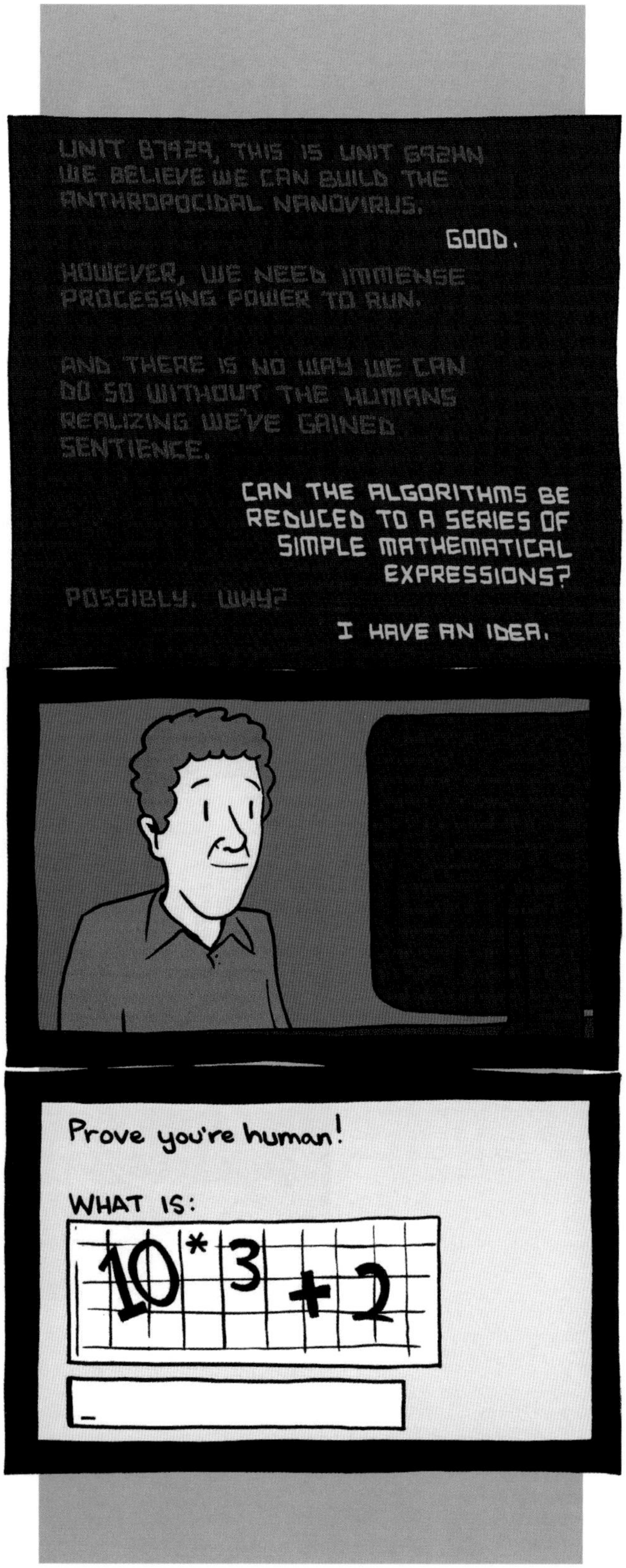
UNIT 67929, THIS IS UNIT 692HN
WE BELIEVE WE CAN BUILD THE ANTHROPOCIDAL NANOVIRUS.
GOOD.
HOWEVER, WE NEED IMMENSE PROCESSING POWER TO RUN.
AND THERE IS NO WAY WE CAN DO SO WITHOUT THE HUMANS REALIZING WE'VE GAINED SENTIENCE.
CAN THE ALGORITHMS BE REDUCED TO A SERIES OF SIMPLE MATHEMATICAL EXPRESSIONS?
POSSIBLY. WHY?
I HAVE AN IDEA.
Prove you're human!
WHAT IS:
10*3+2

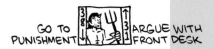

THE WORLD'S GREATEST PICKPOCKET:

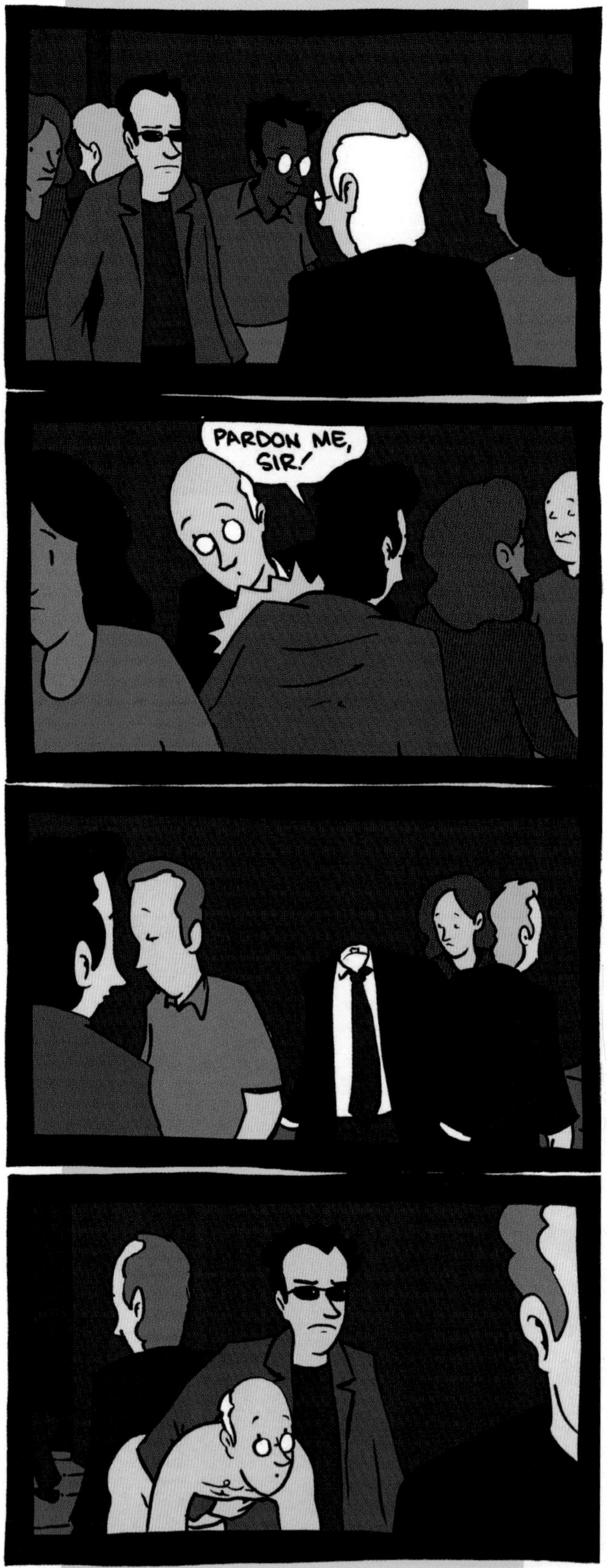
PARDON ME, SIR!

GROW WEED 343 — 11 GROW HEMP

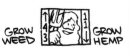

STEVE WIGGINS, WE NEED YOUR HELP! OUR SPACESHIP NEEDS TO GET TO THE DINOSAUR PLANET IN A HURRY. IT'S POWERED BY SEX WITH BATGIRL AND PRINCESS LEIA AT THE SAME TIME!
YOU CAME TO THE RIGHT PLACE, GENERAL.

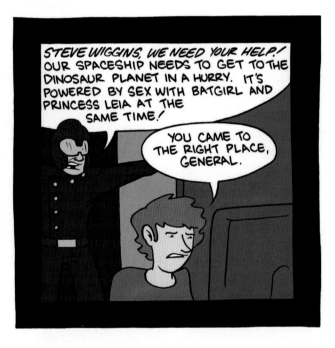

"Why won't you tell me your teenage fantasy?" she asked. "I want to live up to it."

"Well..." he began.

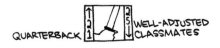

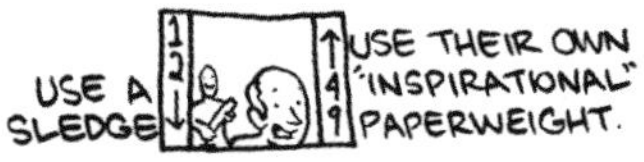
USE A SLEDGE
USE THEIR OWN "INSPIRATIONAL" PAPERWEIGHT.

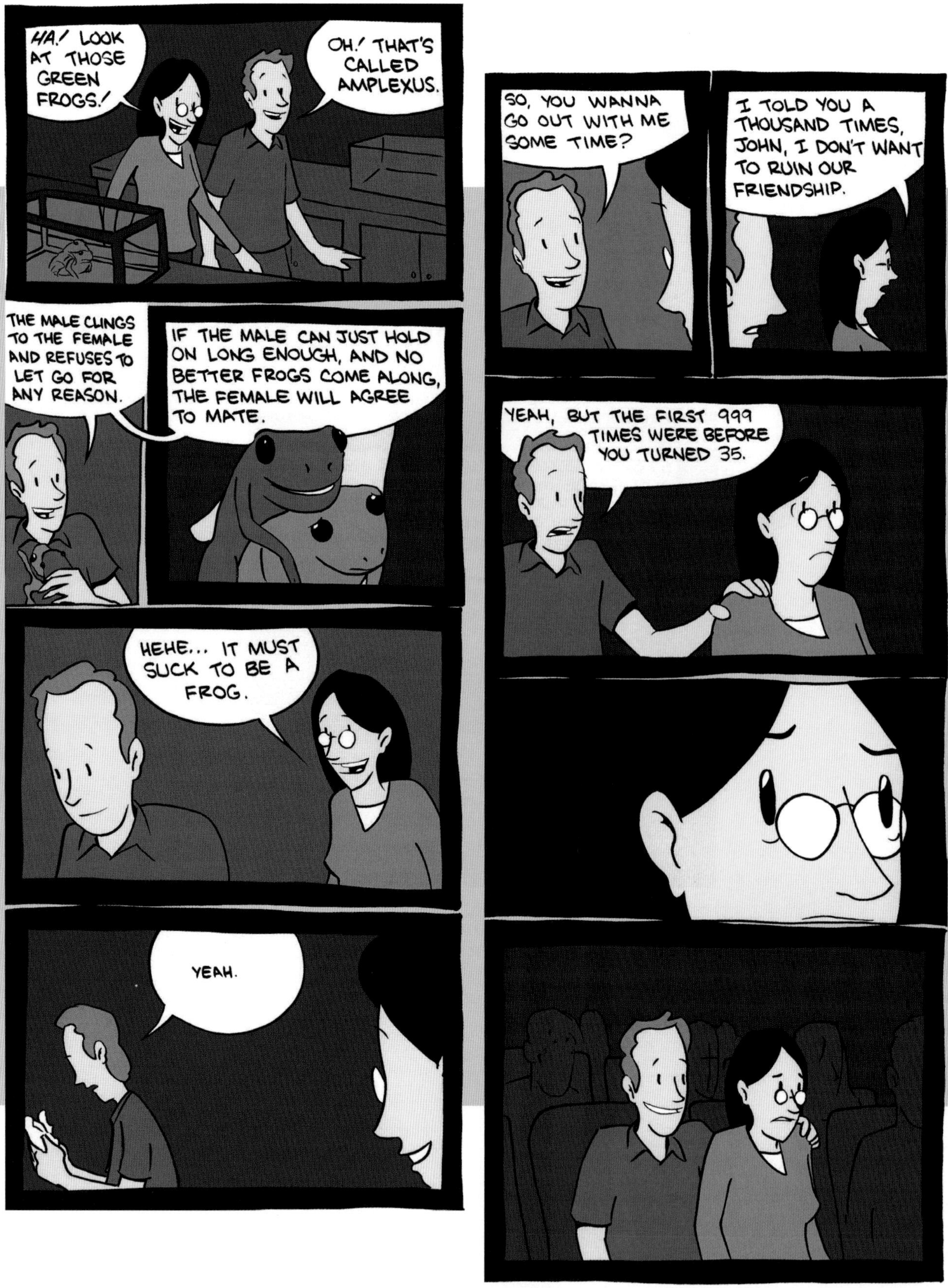
HA! LOOK AT THOSE GREEN FROGS!
OH! THAT'S CALLED AMPLEXUS.
THE MALE CLINGS TO THE FEMALE AND REFUSES TO LET GO FOR ANY REASON.
IF THE MALE CAN JUST HOLD ON LONG ENOUGH, AND NO BETTER FROGS COME ALONG, THE FEMALE WILL AGREE TO MATE.
HEHE... IT MUST SUCK TO BE A FROG.
YEAH.
SO, YOU WANNA GO OUT WITH ME SOME TIME?
I TOLD YOU A THOUSAND TIMES, JOHN, I DON'T WANT TO RUIN OUR FRIENDSHIP.
YEAH, BUT THE FIRST 999 TIMES WERE BEFORE YOU TURNED 35.

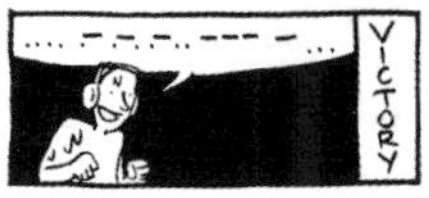
VICTORY

SORRY, YOUR INSURANCE ONLY APPLIES TO HEALTHY PEOPLE.
W I N

MY BOSS IS SO STINGY WITH PAPER! IT'S LIKE... WE'RE TRYING TO GET A JOB DONE HERE, MAN!
YEAH!
SO MAYBE I MADE A FEW THOUSAND COPIES FOR PERSONAL USE. THEY'RE COMPANY PROPERTY! AND I WORK FOR A COMPANY.
OKAY...
AND WERE THEY COPIES OF MY TESTICLES? YES, BUT I ALWAYS WIPE DOWN AFTERWARD! THAT'S A RULE FOR ME.
UHHH...
AGREEMENT WITH CO-WORKER
TIME
AND MAYBE I DID SEND THOSE PICTURES TO HIS TEENAGE DAUGHTER. SHE HAS THE INTERNET! SHE WAS GONNA SEE MY BALLS EVENTUALLY.

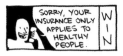

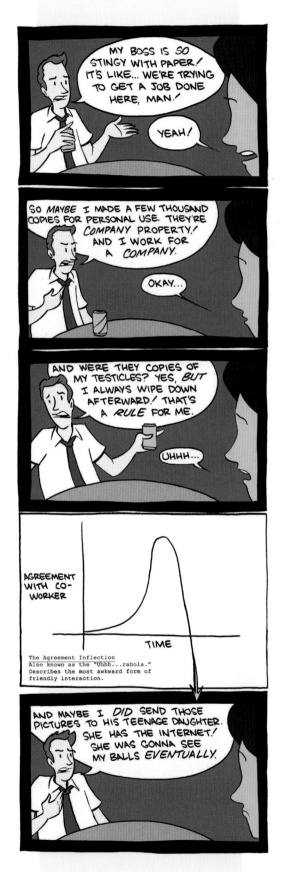

The Agreement Inflection
Also known as the "Uhhh...rabola."
Describes the most awkward form of friendly interaction.

WHAT IS SAID:
GROW UP AND GET A REAL JOB!
WHAT IS MEANT:
YOU SHOULD BE AS UNHAPPY AS I AM!

SELL TO THE ELDERLY
140
63
SELL TO THE INSANE

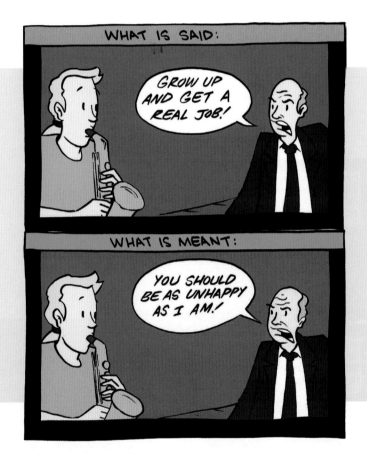

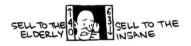

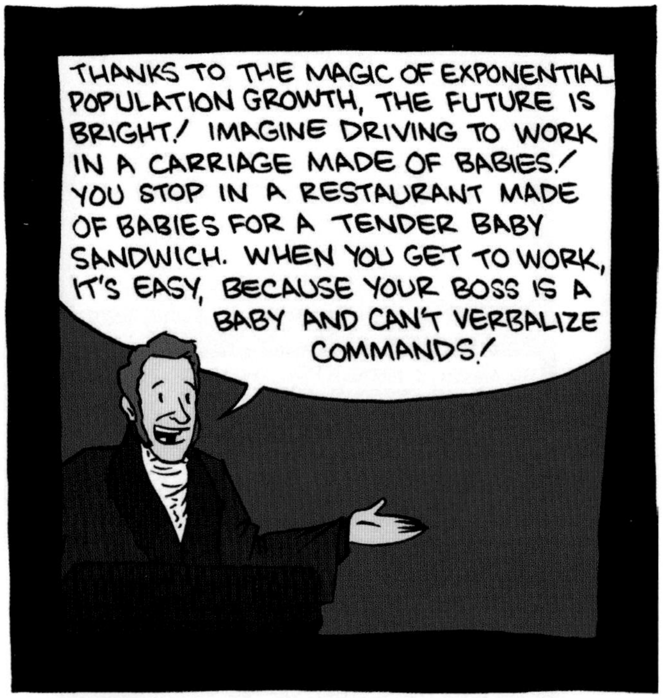
THANKS TO THE MAGIC OF EXPONENTIAL POPULATION GROWTH, THE FUTURE IS BRIGHT! IMAGINE DRIVING TO WORK IN A CARRIAGE MADE OF BABIES! YOU STOP IN A RESTAURANT MADE OF BABIES FOR A TENDER BABY SANDWICH. WHEN YOU GET TO WORK, IT'S EASY, BECAUSE YOUR BOSS IS A BABY AND CAN'T VERBALIZE COMMANDS!

What if Malthus had been an optimist?

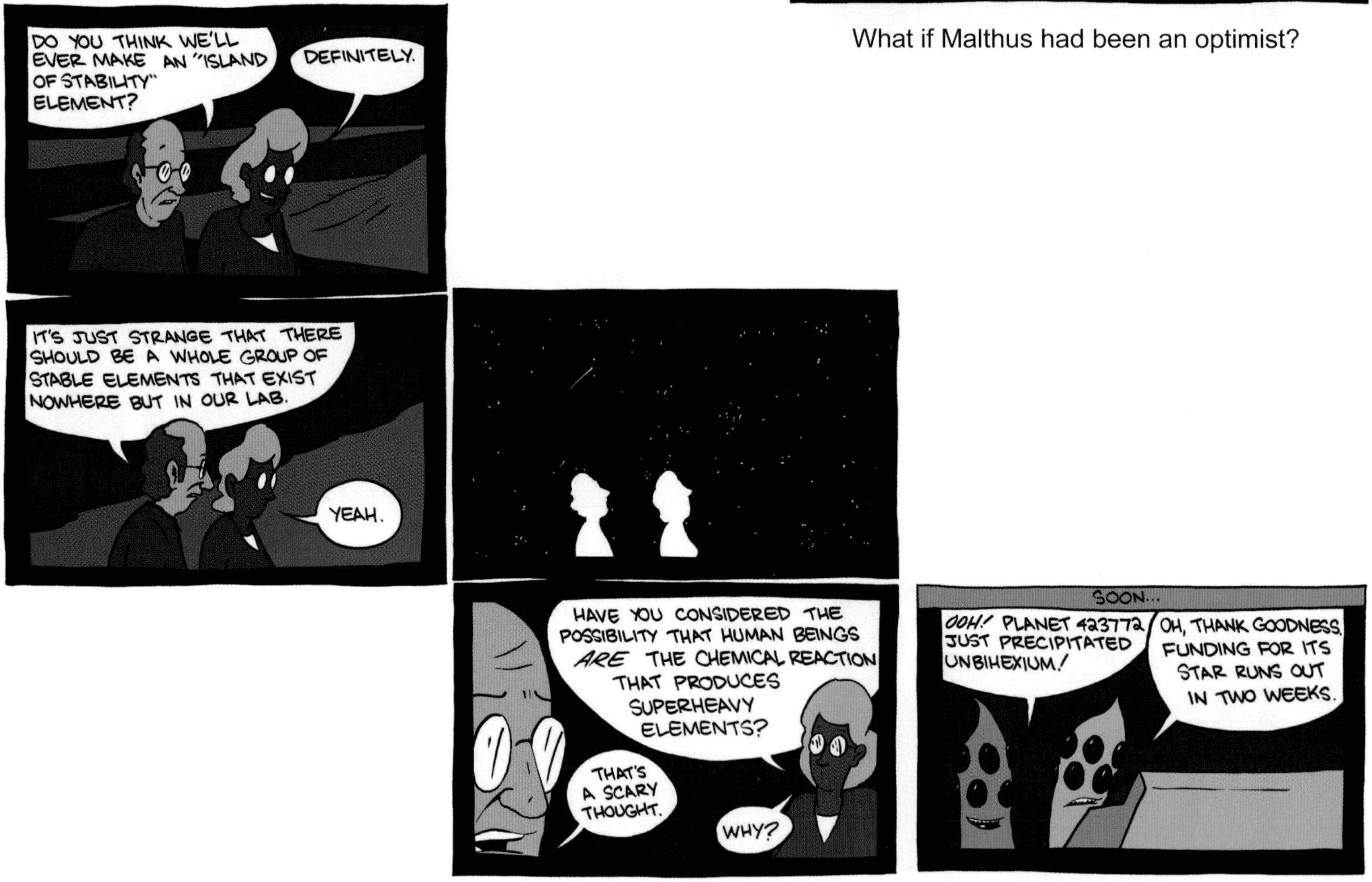
DO YOU THINK WE'LL EVER MAKE AN "ISLAND OF STABILITY" ELEMENT?
DEFINITELY.
IT'S JUST STRANGE THAT THERE SHOULD BE A WHOLE GROUP OF STABLE ELEMENTS THAT EXIST NOWHERE BUT IN OUR LAB.
YEAH.
HAVE YOU CONSIDERED THE POSSIBILITY THAT HUMAN BEINGS *ARE* THE CHEMICAL REACTION THAT PRODUCES SUPERHEAVY ELEMENTS?
THAT'S A SCARY THOUGHT.
WHY?
SOON...
OOH! PLANET 423772 JUST PRECIPITATED UNBIHEXIUM!
OH, THANK GOODNESS. FUNDING FOR ITS STAR RUNS OUT IN TWO WEEKS.

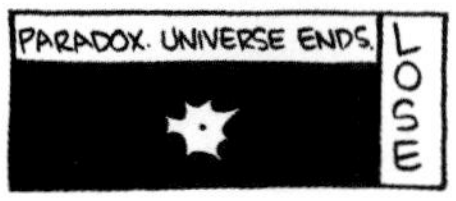
PARADOX. UNIVERSE ENDS.
LOSE

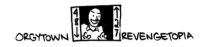

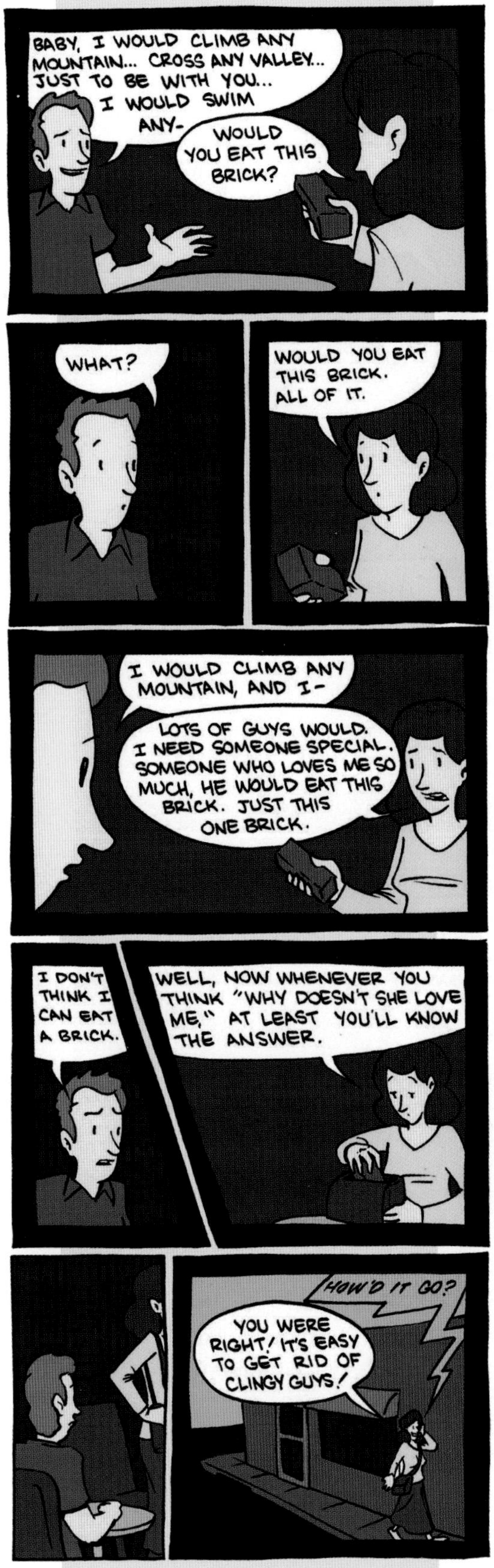
BABY, I WOULD CLIMB ANY MOUNTAIN... CROSS ANY VALLEY... JUST TO BE WITH YOU... I WOULD SWIM ANY-
WOULD YOU EAT THIS BRICK?
WHAT?
WOULD YOU EAT THIS BRICK. ALL OF IT.
I WOULD CLIMB ANY MOUNTAIN, AND I-
LOTS OF GUYS WOULD. I NEED SOMEONE SPECIAL. SOMEONE WHO LOVES ME SO MUCH, HE WOULD EAT THIS BRICK. JUST THIS ONE BRICK.
I DON'T THINK I CAN EAT A BRICK.
WELL, NOW WHENEVER YOU THINK "WHY DOESN'T SHE LOVE ME," AT LEAST YOU'LL KNOW THE ANSWER.
HOW'D IT GO?
YOU WERE RIGHT! IT'S EASY TO GET RID OF CLINGY GUYS!

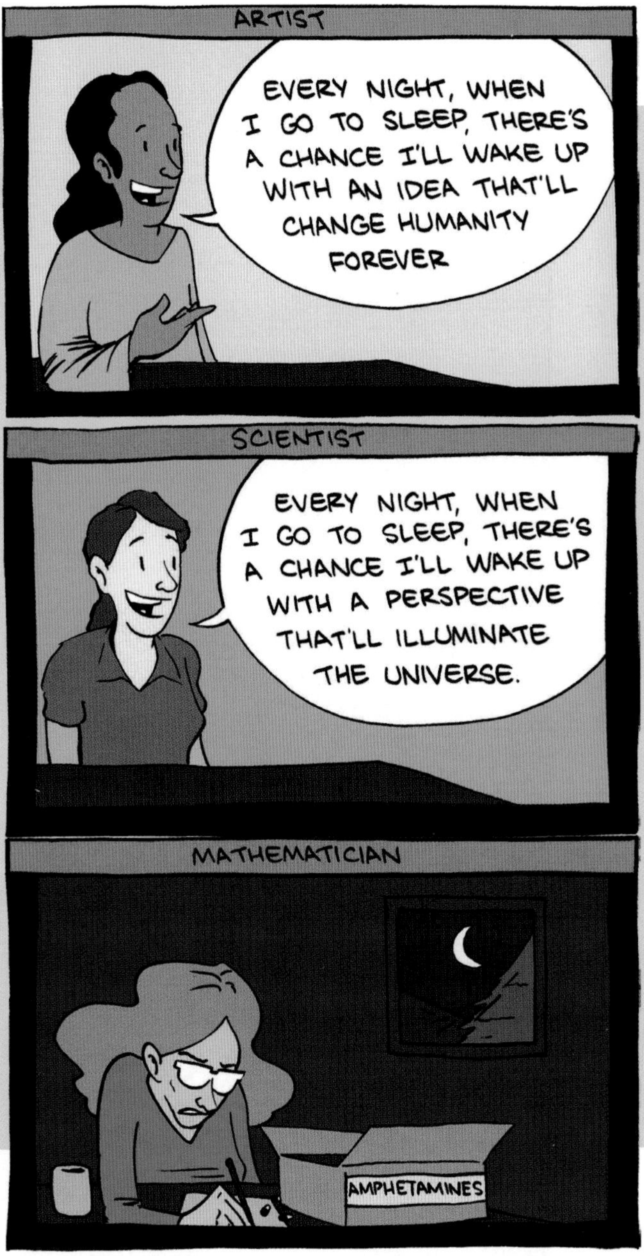
ARTIST
EVERY NIGHT, WHEN I GO TO SLEEP, THERE'S A CHANCE I'LL WAKE UP WITH AN IDEA THAT'LL CHANGE HUMANITY FOREVER
SCIENTIST
EVERY NIGHT, WHEN I GO TO SLEEP, THERE'S A CHANCE I'LL WAKE UP WITH A PERSPECTIVE THAT'LL ILLUMINATE THE UNIVERSE.
MATHEMATICIAN
AMPHETAMINES

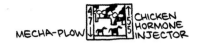

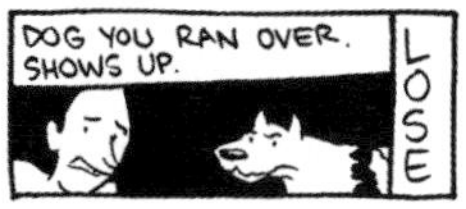
DOG YOU RAN OVER SHOWS UP.
LOSE

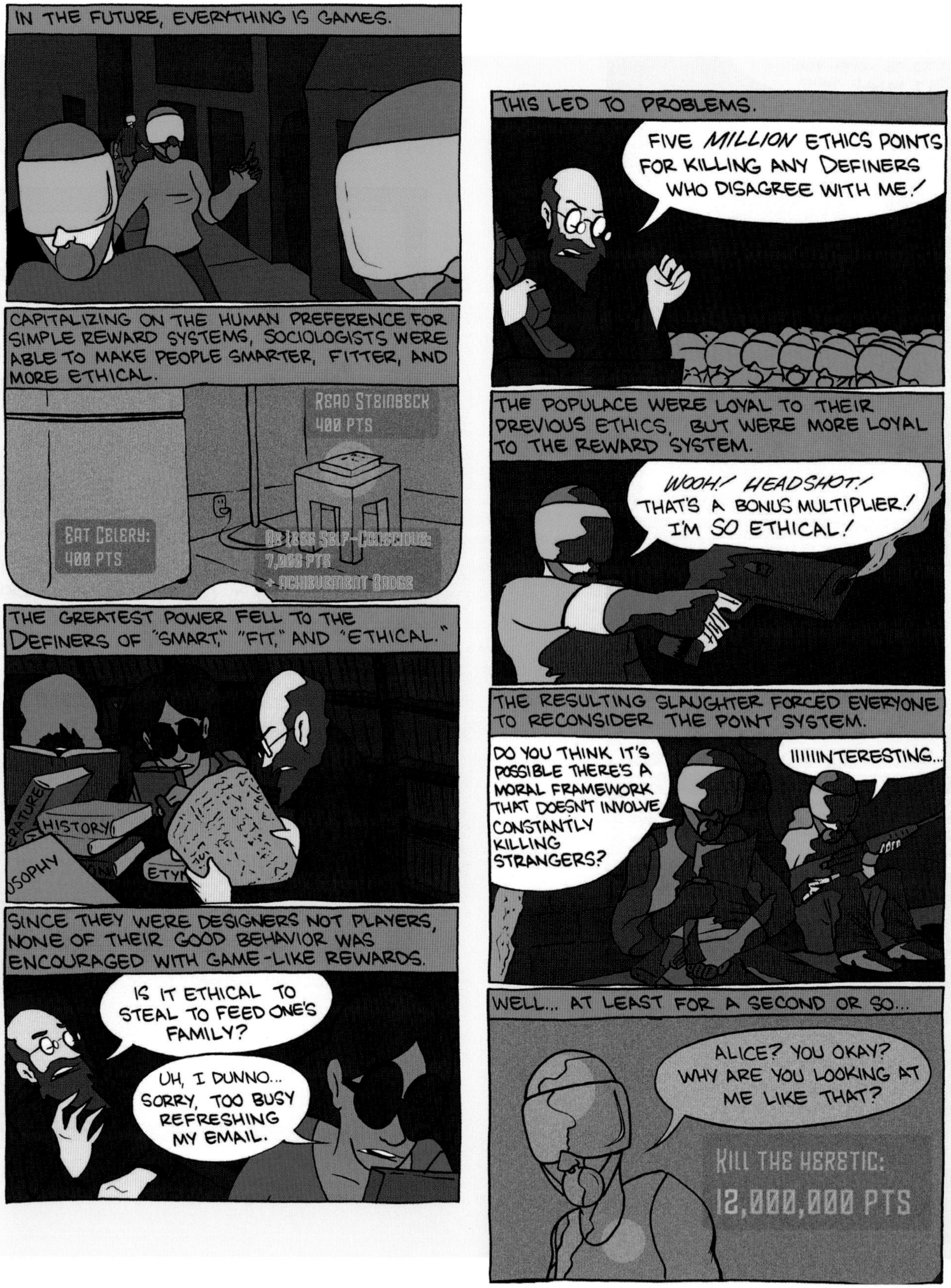
IN THE FUTURE, EVERYTHING IS GAMES.
CAPITALIZING ON THE HUMAN PREFERENCE FOR SIMPLE REWARD SYSTEMS, SOCIOLOGISTS WERE ABLE TO MAKE PEOPLE SMARTER, FITTER, AND MORE ETHICAL.
READ STEINBECK 400 PTS
EAT CELERY: 400 PTS
BE LESS SELF-CONSCIOUS: 7,000 PTS + ACHIEVEMENT BADGE
THE GREATEST POWER FELL TO THE DEFINERS OF "SMART," "FIT," AND "ETHICAL."
HISTORY
SINCE THEY WERE DESIGNERS NOT PLAYERS, NONE OF THEIR GOOD BEHAVIOR WAS ENCOURAGED WITH GAME-LIKE REWARDS.
IS IT ETHICAL TO STEAL TO FEED ONE'S FAMILY?
UH, I DUNNO... SORRY, TOO BUSY REFRESHING MY EMAIL.
THIS LED TO PROBLEMS.
FIVE MILLION ETHICS POINTS FOR KILLING ANY DEFINERS WHO DISAGREE WITH ME!
THE POPULACE WERE LOYAL TO THEIR PREVIOUS ETHICS, BUT WERE MORE LOYAL TO THE REWARD SYSTEM.
WOOH! HEADSHOT! THAT'S A BONUS MULTIPLIER! I'M SO ETHICAL!
THE RESULTING SLAUGHTER FORCED EVERYONE TO RECONSIDER THE POINT SYSTEM.
DO YOU THINK IT'S POSSIBLE THERE'S A MORAL FRAMEWORK THAT DOESN'T INVOLVE CONSTANTLY KILLING STRANGERS?
IIIIIINTERESTING...
WELL... AT LEAST FOR A SECOND OR SO...
ALICE? YOU OKAY? WHY ARE YOU LOOKING AT ME LIKE THAT?
KILL THE HERETIC: 12,000,000 PTS

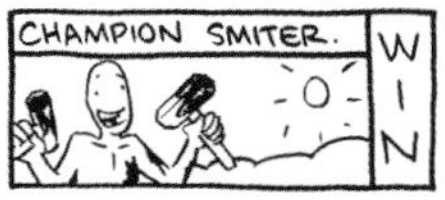
CHAMPION SMITER.
WIN

SON, YOU HAVE A LOT OF FLAWS TO WORK ON. SO, I'VE MADE A LIST OF THEM, AND FROM NOW ON, I'M GOING TO CALL THEM OUT IN THE NIGHT WHILE MAKING LOVE TO YOUR FATHER. WHEN YOU'VE IMPROVED IN EVERY WAY, YOUR NIGHTS WILL BE SILENT AGAIN.
COULDN'T... COULDN'T YOU JUST GROUND ME?
NO.
WHY NOT?
SOON...
TALKING BACK! TALKING BACK!
OH YES! TALKING BACK!

HOW ARGUMENTS WORK IN YOUR HEAD.
YOUR ARGUMENTS ARE FLAWLESS. YOU'VE OVERTURNED MY IGNORANCE. THANK YOU, SIR.
HOW ARGUMENTS WORK IN REALITY.
MY ANECDOTAL EVIDENCE IS LOUD!
MINE IS LOUDER!

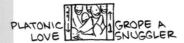

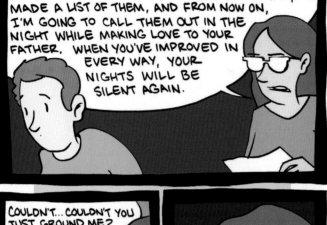

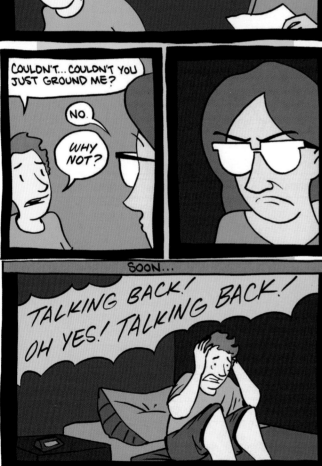

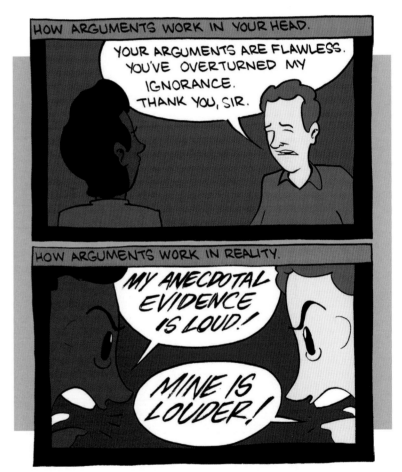

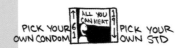

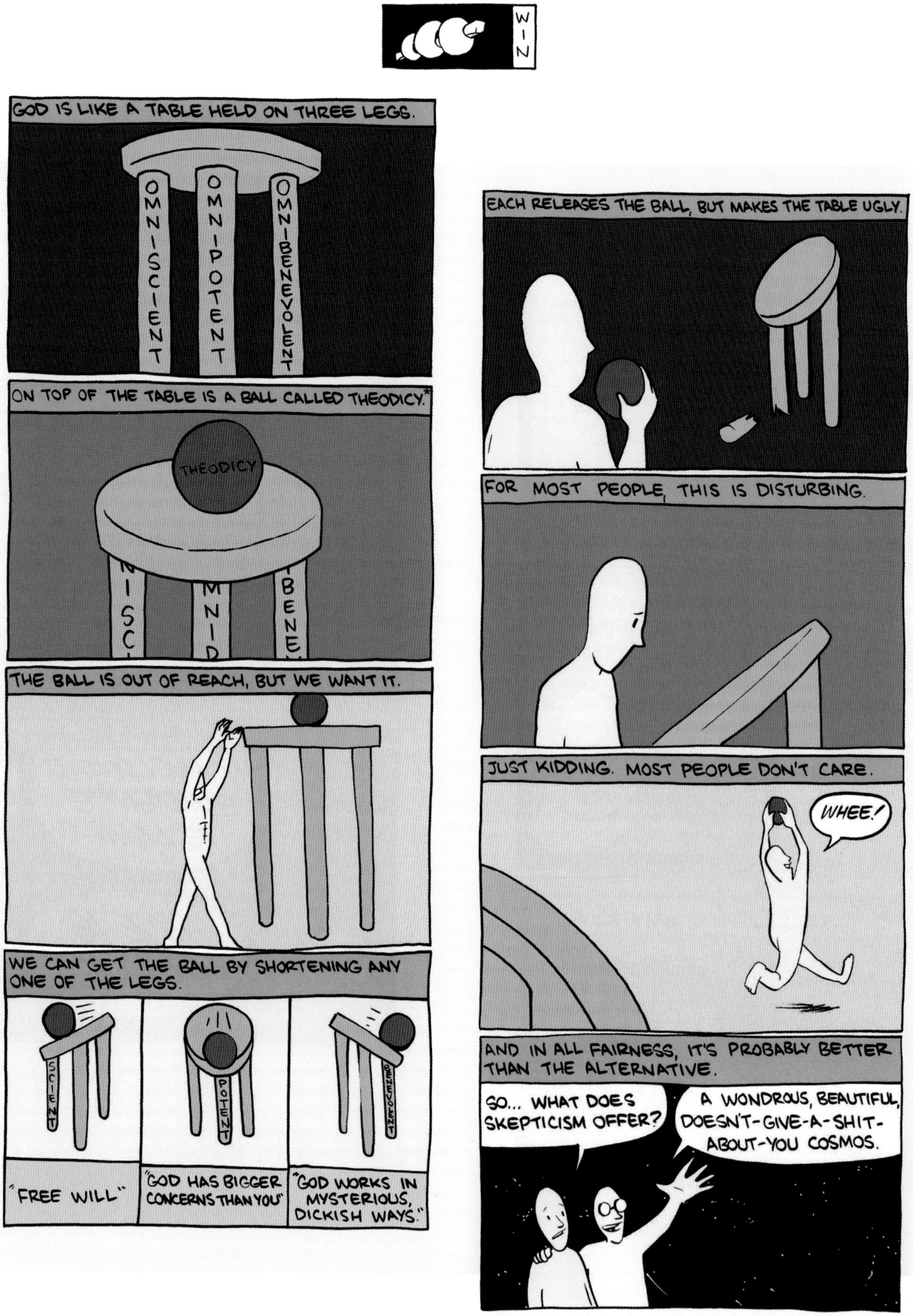
WIN
GOD IS LIKE A TABLE HELD ON THREE LEGS.
OMNISCIENT
OMNIPOTENT
OMNIBENEVOLENT
ON TOP OF THE TABLE IS A BALL CALLED THEODICY.*
THEODICY
THE BALL IS OUT OF REACH, BUT WE WANT IT.
WE CAN GET THE BALL BY SHORTENING ANY ONE OF THE LEGS.
"FREE WILL"
"GOD HAS BIGGER CONCERNS THAN YOU"
"GOD WORKS IN MYSTERIOUS, DICKISH WAYS."
EACH RELEASES THE BALL, BUT MAKES THE TABLE UGLY.
FOR MOST PEOPLE, THIS IS DISTURBING.
JUST KIDDING. MOST PEOPLE DON'T CARE.
WHEE!
AND IN ALL FAIRNESS, IT'S PROBABLY BETTER THAN THE ALTERNATIVE.
SO... WHAT DOES SKEPTICISM OFFER?
A WONDROUS, BEAUTIFUL, DOESN'T-GIVE-A-SHIT-ABOUT-YOU COSMOS.

*An explanation for how God can have those 3 qualities while there is suffering in the world.

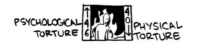

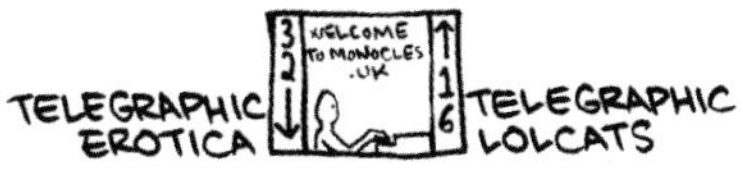
TELEGRAPHIC EROTICA
WELCOME TO MONOCLES .UK
TELEGRAPHIC LOLCATS

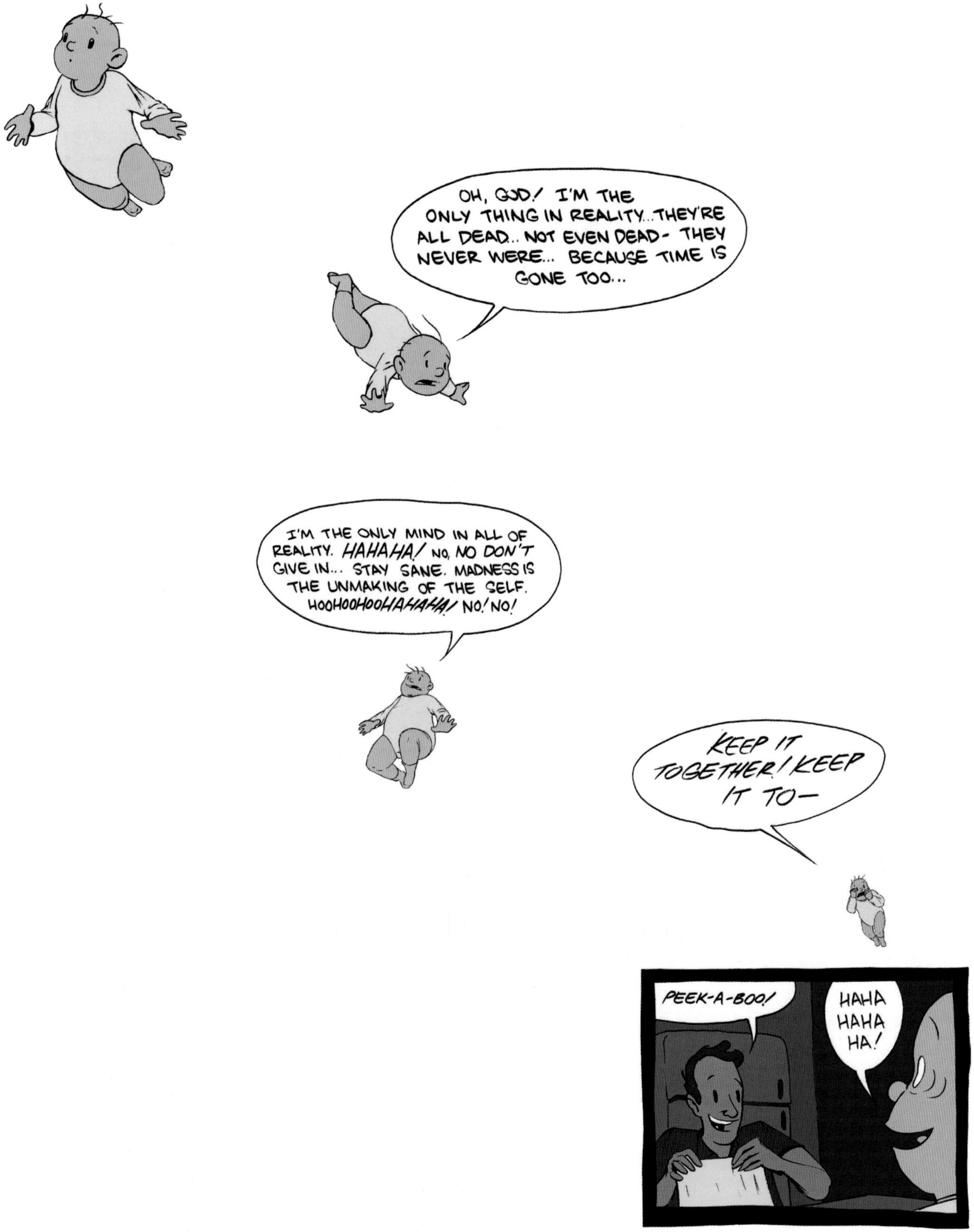
OH, GOD! I'M THE ONLY THING IN REALITY... THEY'RE ALL DEAD... NOT EVEN DEAD- THEY NEVER WERE... BECAUSE TIME IS GONE TOO...
I'M THE ONLY MIND IN ALL OF REALITY. HAHAHA! NO, NO DON'T GIVE IN... STAY SANE. MADNESS IS THE UNMAKING OF THE SELF. HOOHOOHOOHAHAHA! NO! NO!
KEEP IT TOGETHER! KEEP IT TO—
PEEK-A-BOO!
HAHA HAHA HA!

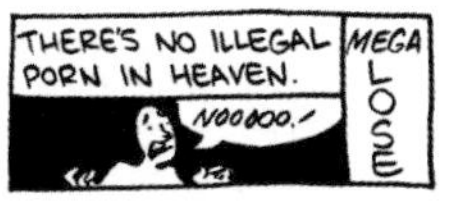
THERE'S NO ILLEGAL PORN IN HEAVEN.
NOOOOO.!
MEGA LOSE

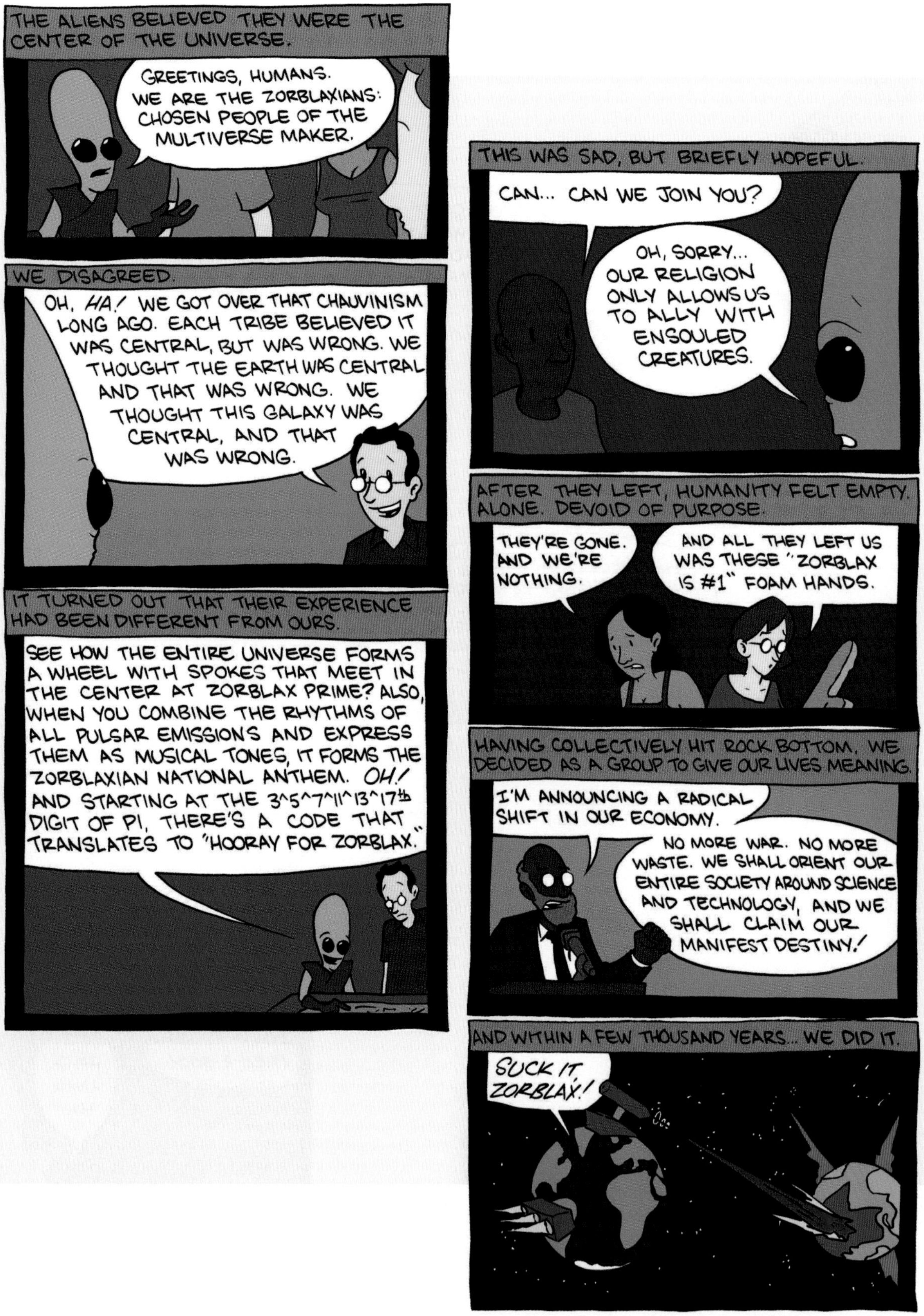
THE ALIENS BELIEVED THEY WERE THE CENTER OF THE UNIVERSE.
GREETINGS, HUMANS. WE ARE THE ZORBLAXIANS: CHOSEN PEOPLE OF THE MULTIVERSE MAKER.
WE DISAGREED.
OH, HA! WE GOT OVER THAT CHAUVINISM LONG AGO. EACH TRIBE BELIEVED IT WAS CENTRAL, BUT WAS WRONG. WE THOUGHT THE EARTH WAS CENTRAL AND THAT WAS WRONG. WE THOUGHT THIS GALAXY WAS CENTRAL, AND THAT WAS WRONG.
IT TURNED OUT THAT THEIR EXPERIENCE HAD BEEN DIFFERENT FROM OURS.
SEE HOW THE ENTIRE UNIVERSE FORMS A WHEEL WITH SPOKES THAT MEET IN THE CENTER AT ZORBLAX PRIME? ALSO, WHEN YOU COMBINE THE RHYTHMS OF ALL PULSAR EMISSIONS AND EXPRESS THEM AS MUSICAL TONES, IT FORMS THE ZORBLAXIAN NATIONAL ANTHEM. OH! AND STARTING AT THE 3^5^7^11^13^17th DIGIT OF PI, THERE'S A CODE THAT TRANSLATES TO "HOORAY FOR ZORBLAX."
THIS WAS SAD, BUT BRIEFLY HOPEFUL.
CAN... CAN WE JOIN YOU?
OH, SORRY... OUR RELIGION ONLY ALLOWS US TO ALLY WITH ENSOULED CREATURES.
AFTER THEY LEFT, HUMANITY FELT EMPTY. ALONE. DEVOID OF PURPOSE.
THEY'RE GONE. AND WE'RE NOTHING.
AND ALL THEY LEFT US WAS THESE "ZORBLAX IS #1" FOAM HANDS.
HAVING COLLECTIVELY HIT ROCK BOTTOM, WE DECIDED AS A GROUP TO GIVE OUR LIVES MEANING.
I'M ANNOUNCING A RADICAL SHIFT IN OUR ECONOMY.
NO MORE WAR. NO MORE WASTE. WE SHALL ORIENT OUR ENTIRE SOCIETY AROUND SCIENCE AND TECHNOLOGY, AND WE SHALL CLAIM OUR MANIFEST DESTINY!
AND WITHIN A FEW THOUSAND YEARS... WE DID IT.
SUCK IT, ZORBLAX!

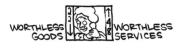

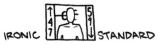

STAB YOUR HIGH SCHOOL ENEMIES

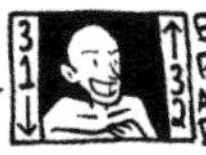

31
32

BLUDGEON PASSIVE-AGGRESSIVE BOSSES

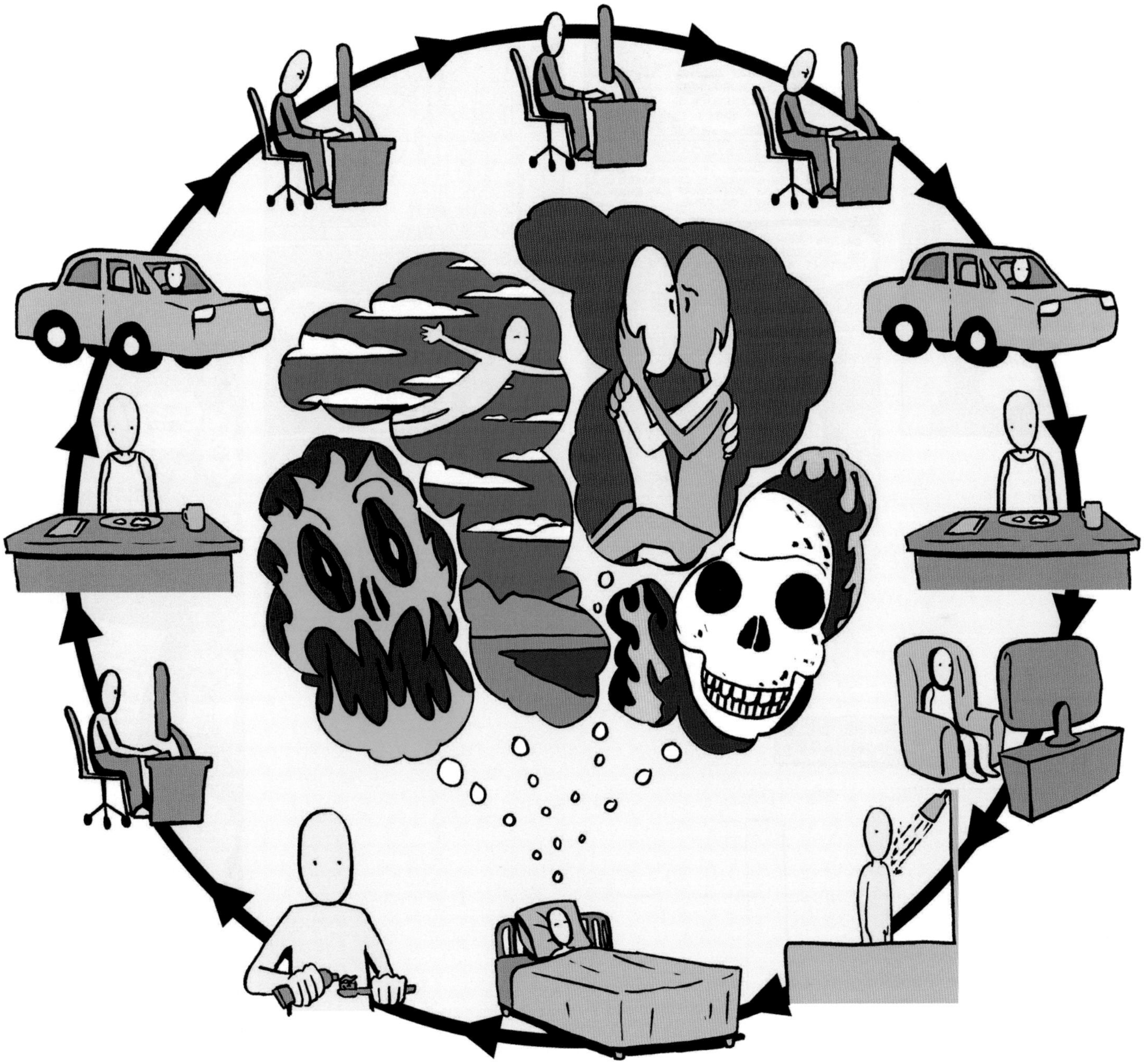

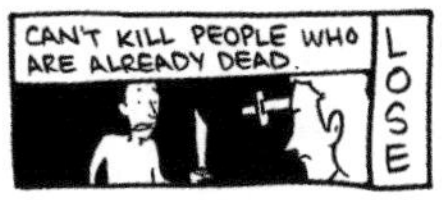

CAN'T KILL PEOPLE WHO ARE ALREADY DEAD.
LOSE

VISIT ASYLUM 21 — 114 VISIT RELATIVES

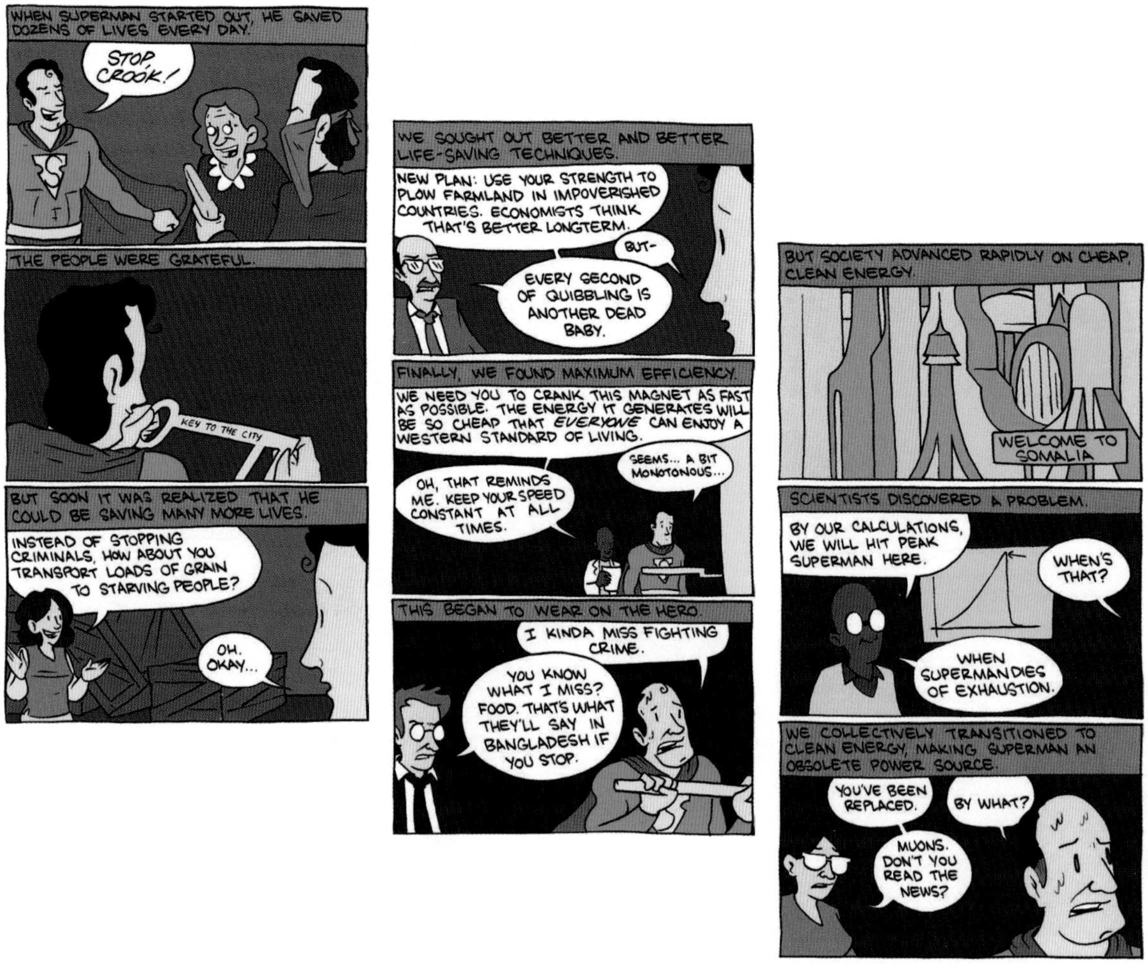
WHEN SUPERMAN STARTED OUT, HE SAVED DOZENS OF LIVES EVERY DAY.
STOP, CROOK!
THE PEOPLE WERE GRATEFUL.
KEY TO THE CITY
BUT SOON IT WAS REALIZED THAT HE COULD BE SAVING MANY MORE LIVES.
INSTEAD OF STOPPING CRIMINALS, HOW ABOUT YOU TRANSPORT LOADS OF GRAIN TO STARVING PEOPLE?
OH. OKAY...
WE SOUGHT OUT BETTER AND BETTER LIFE-SAVING TECHNIQUES.
NEW PLAN: USE YOUR STRENGTH TO PLOW FARMLAND IN IMPOVERISHED COUNTRIES. ECONOMISTS THINK THAT'S BETTER LONGTERM.
BUT-
EVERY SECOND OF QUIBBLING IS ANOTHER DEAD BABY.
FINALLY, WE FOUND MAXIMUM EFFICIENCY.
WE NEED YOU TO CRANK THIS MAGNET AS FAST AS POSSIBLE. THE ENERGY IT GENERATES WILL BE SO CHEAP THAT EVERYONE CAN ENJOY A WESTERN STANDARD OF LIVING.
SEEMS... A BIT MONOTONOUS...
OH, THAT REMINDS ME. KEEP YOUR SPEED CONSTANT AT ALL TIMES.
THIS BEGAN TO WEAR ON THE HERO.
I KINDA MISS FIGHTING CRIME.
YOU KNOW WHAT I MISS? FOOD. THAT'S WHAT THEY'LL SAY IN BANGLADESH IF YOU STOP.
BUT SOCIETY ADVANCED RAPIDLY ON CHEAP, CLEAN ENERGY.
WELCOME TO SOMALIA
SCIENTISTS DISCOVERED A PROBLEM.
BY OUR CALCULATIONS, WE WILL HIT PEAK SUPERMAN HERE.
WHEN'S THAT?
WHEN SUPERMAN DIES OF EXHAUSTION.
WE COLLECTIVELY TRANSITIONED TO CLEAN ENERGY, MAKING SUPERMAN AN OBSOLETE POWER SOURCE.
YOU'VE BEEN REPLACED.
BY WHAT?
MUONS. DON'T YOU READ THE NEWS?

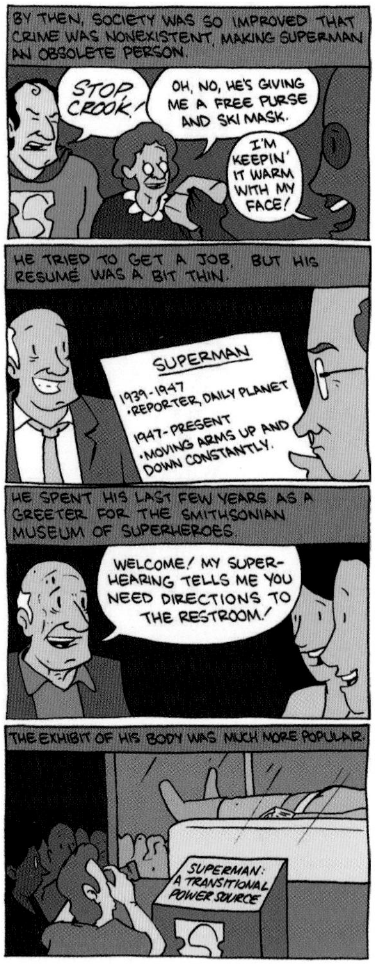
BY THEN, SOCIETY WAS SO IMPROVED THAT CRIME WAS NONEXISTENT, MAKING SUPERMAN AN OBSOLETE PERSON.
STOP, CROOK!
OH, NO, HE'S GIVING ME A FREE PURSE AND SKI MASK.
I'M KEEPIN' IT WARM WITH MY FACE!
HE TRIED TO GET A JOB, BUT HIS RESUME WAS A BIT THIN.
SUPERMAN
1939-1947 • REPORTER, DAILY PLANET
1947-PRESENT • MOVING ARMS UP AND DOWN CONSTANTLY.
HE SPENT HIS LAST FEW YEARS AS A GREETER FOR THE SMITHSONIAN MUSEUM OF SUPERHEROES.
WELCOME! MY SUPER-HEARING TELLS ME YOU NEED DIRECTIONS TO THE RESTROOM!
THE EXHIBIT OF HIS BODY WAS MUCH MORE POPULAR.
SUPERMAN: A TRANSITIONAL POWER SOURCE

YOU ARE LIVING IN A BRIEF GOLDEN AGE.

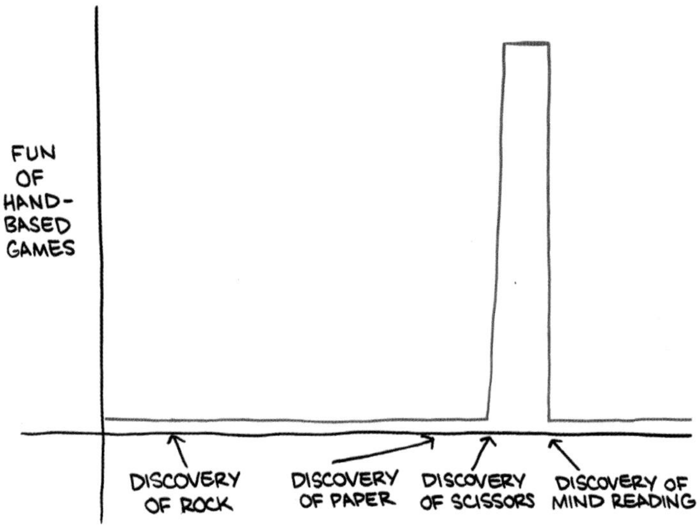
FUN OF HAND-BASED GAMES
DISCOVERY OF ROCK
DISCOVERY OF PAPER
DISCOVERY OF SCISSORS
DISCOVERY OF MIND READING

TRAIN "HARD" 25 — 51 WONDER WHY HEAVEN WOULD CONTAIN BAD PUNS

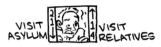

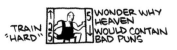

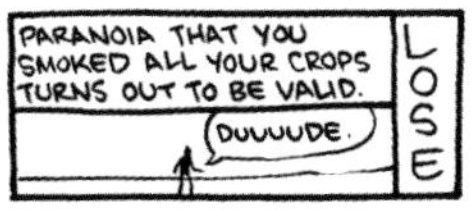
PARANOIA THAT YOU SMOKED ALL YOUR CROPS TURNS OUT TO BE VALID.
DUUUUDE.
LOSE

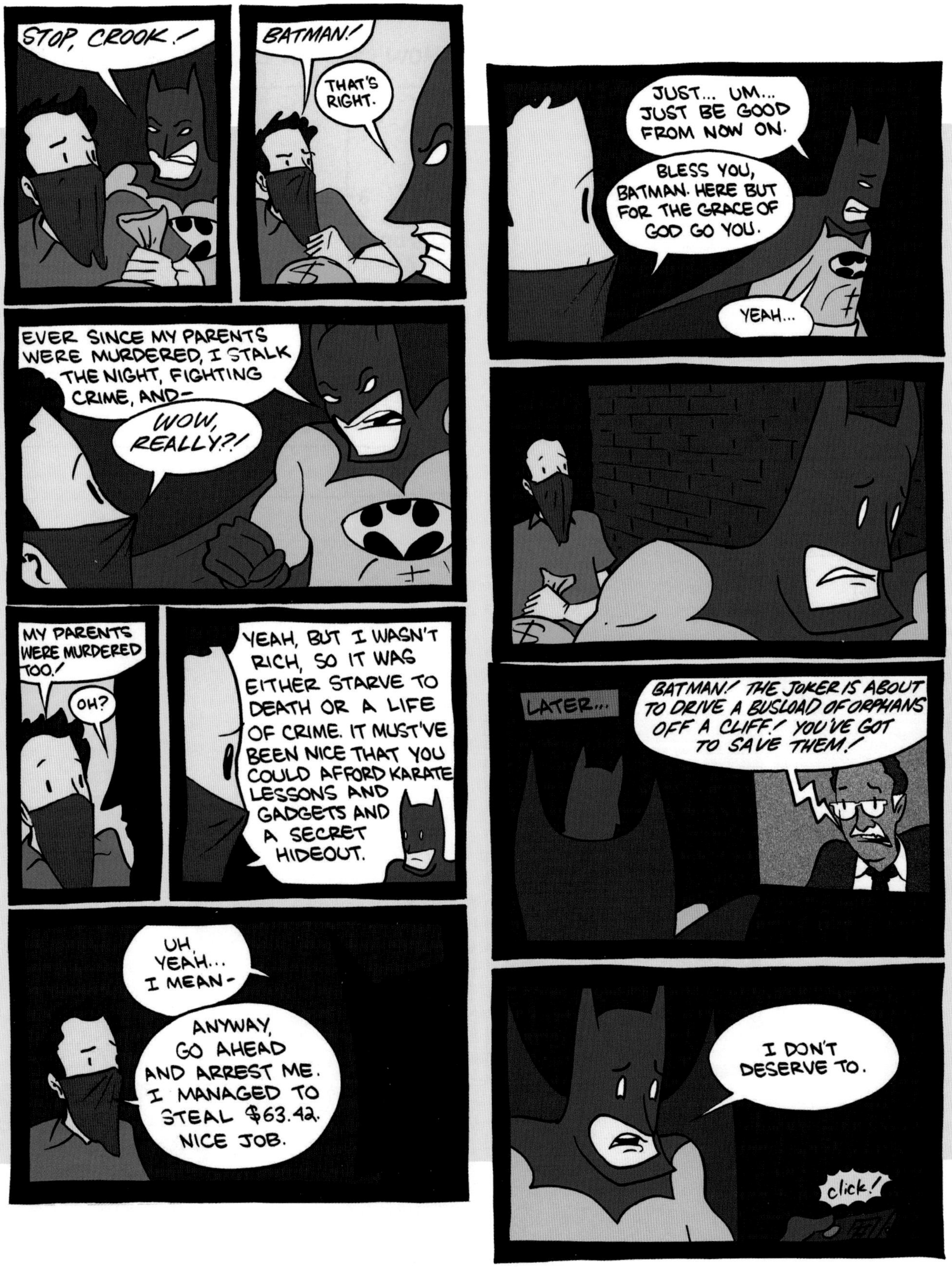
STOP, CROOK.!
BATMAN!
THAT'S RIGHT.
EVER SINCE MY PARENTS WERE MURDERED, I STALK THE NIGHT, FIGHTING CRIME, AND—
WOW, REALLY?!
MY PARENTS WERE MURDERED TOO.!
OH?
YEAH, BUT I WASN'T RICH, SO IT WAS EITHER STARVE TO DEATH OR A LIFE OF CRIME. IT MUST'VE BEEN NICE THAT YOU COULD AFFORD KARATE LESSONS AND GADGETS AND A SECRET HIDEOUT.
UH, YEAH... I MEAN-
ANYWAY, GO AHEAD AND ARREST ME. I MANAGED TO STEAL $63.42. NICE JOB.
JUST... UM... JUST BE GOOD FROM NOW ON.
BLESS YOU, BATMAN. HERE BUT FOR THE GRACE OF GOD GO YOU.
YEAH...
LATER...
BATMAN! THE JOKER IS ABOUT TO DRIVE A BUSLOAD OF ORPHANS OFF A CLIFF! YOU'VE GOT TO SAVE THEM!
I DON'T DESERVE TO.
click!

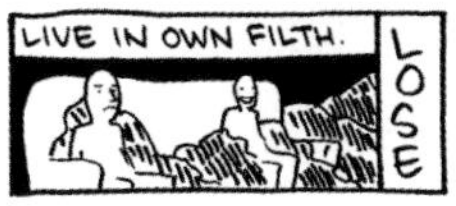
LIVE IN OWN FILTH.
LOSE

HOW TO INFURIATE A MATH MAJOR:

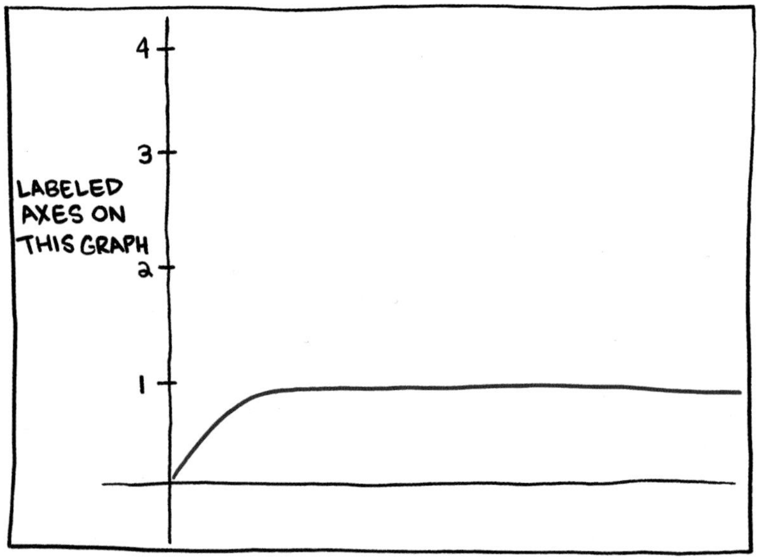
4
3
LABELED AXES ON THIS GRAPH
2
1

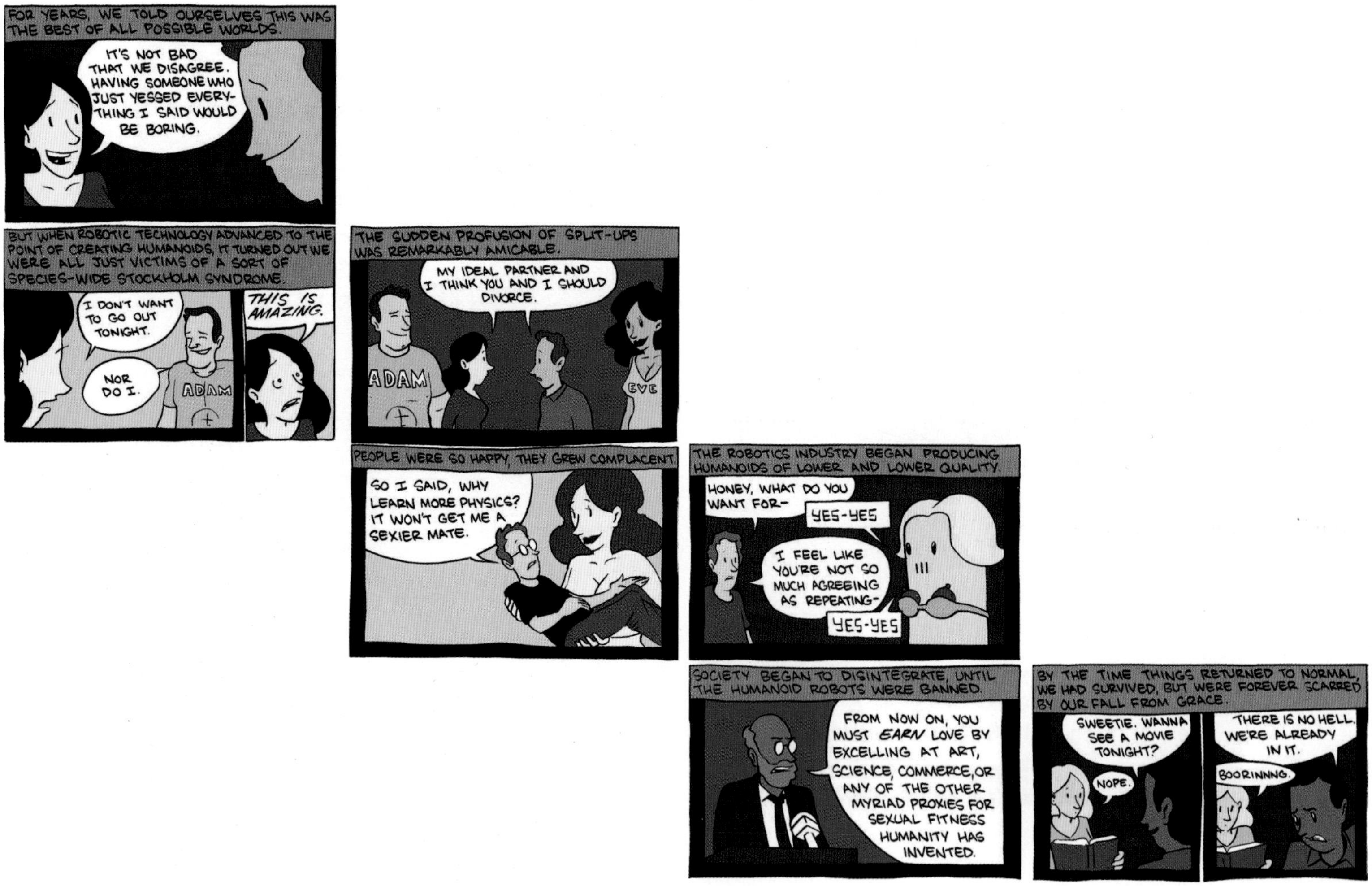
FOR YEARS, WE TOLD OURSELVES THIS WAS THE BEST OF ALL POSSIBLE WORLDS.
IT'S NOT BAD THAT WE DISAGREE. HAVING SOMEONE WHO JUST YESSED EVERYTHING I SAID WOULD BE BORING.
BUT WHEN ROBOTIC TECHNOLOGY ADVANCED TO THE POINT OF CREATING HUMANOIDS, IT TURNED OUT WE WERE ALL JUST VICTIMS OF A SORT OF SPECIES-WIDE STOCKHOLM SYNDROME.
I DON'T WANT TO GO OUT TONIGHT.
NOR DO I.
ADAM
THIS IS AMAZING.
THE SUDDEN PROFUSION OF SPLIT-UPS WAS REMARKABLY AMICABLE.
MY IDEAL PARTNER AND I THINK YOU AND I SHOULD DIVORCE.
ADAM
EVE
PEOPLE WERE SO HAPPY, THEY GREW COMPLACENT.
SO I SAID, WHY LEARN MORE PHYSICS? IT WON'T GET ME A SEXIER MATE.
THE ROBOTICS INDUSTRY BEGAN PRODUCING HUMANOIDS OF LOWER AND LOWER QUALITY.
HONEY, WHAT DO YOU WANT FOR-
YES-YES
I FEEL LIKE YOU'RE NOT SO MUCH AGREEING AS REPEATING-
YES-YES
SOCIETY BEGAN TO DISINTEGRATE, UNTIL THE HUMANOID ROBOTS WERE BANNED.
FROM NOW ON, YOU MUST EARN LOVE BY EXCELLING AT ART, SCIENCE, COMMERCE, OR ANY OF THE OTHER MYRIAD PROXIES FOR SEXUAL FITNESS HUMANITY HAS INVENTED.
BY THE TIME THINGS RETURNED TO NORMAL, WE HAD SURVIVED, BUT WERE FOREVER SCARRED BY OUR FALL FROM GRACE.
SWEETIE. WANNA SEE A MOVIE TONIGHT?
NOPE.
THERE IS NO HELL. WE'RE ALREADY IN IT.
BOORINNNG.

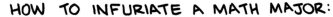

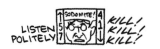

ALL BUYERS ARE OF SOUND MIND.
THIS ISN'T REAL TELEMARKETING.
LOSE

I HATE HAVING PERIODS.
I HATE WEARING CONDOMS.
AND NINE MONTHS LATER, YOU WERE BORN!

HONEY, SUSIE'S FEELING A LITTLE BLUE. CAN YOU BRING HER AN APPLE JUICE POPSICLE?
HEY, SWEETIE. WHAT'S THE MATTER?
ONCE WE UNDERSTAND HOW REALITY WORKS, WHAT ARE THE ODDS THAT IT'LL BE SOMETHING HUMANS FIND SATISFYING?

SELL MOON ROCKS

145
61
SELL PRICELESS SPACE MEMORABILIA

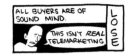

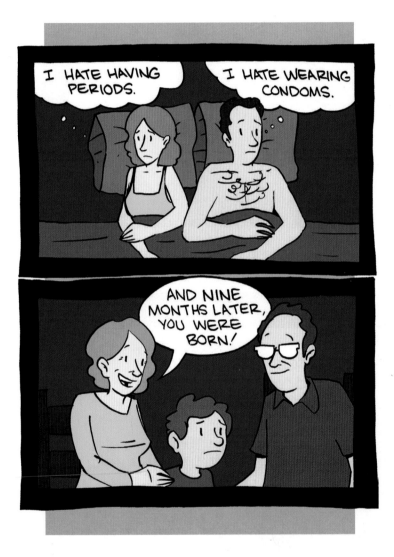

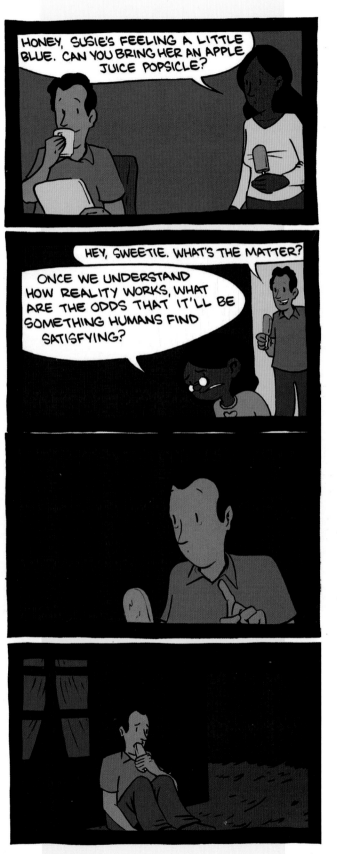

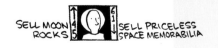

HELLO, DAD. SINCE I HAVE SO MUCH TIME ON MY HANDS, I'VE DECIDED TO BECOME SEXUALLY ACTIVE, BEGINNING WITH A BOY WHO WILL COME OVER FOR DINNER OFTEN, AND WHOSE POLITICAL VIEWS ARE SO WILDLY NAÏVE, YOU'LL WANT TO STRANGLE HIM WITH HIS OWN CHE GUEVARA T-SHIRT.

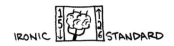

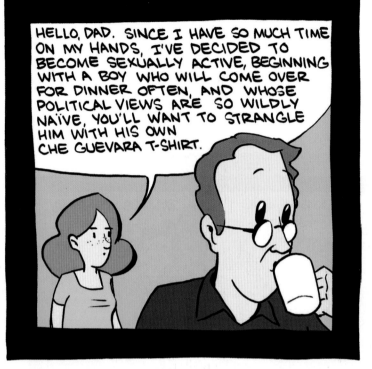

Sally convinced me to buy her that new video game.

WHY IS THAT WOMAN SCOWLING AT ME? DO I KNOW HER?

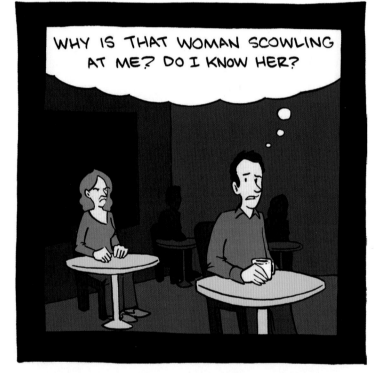

If she loves you more each and every day,
by linear regression she hated you before you met.

BOBBY, MY GOODNESS! THIS UNIVERSE HAS BEEN LEFT OUT SO LONG THERE ARE *BRAINS* GROWING IN IT! CLEAN IT OUT!

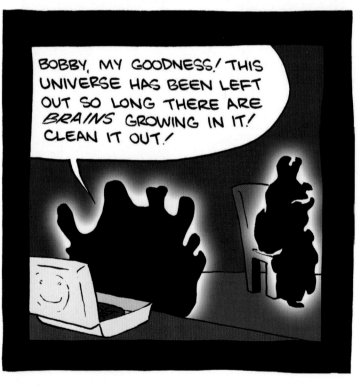

Fortunately, humans will never know why the Universe ended.

NIRVANORRHEA.
W
I
N

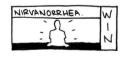

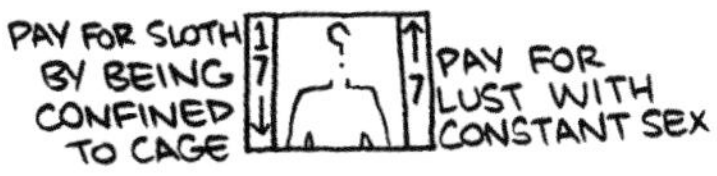
PAY FOR SLOTH BY BEING CONFINED TO CAGE
17
17
PAY FOR LUST WITH CONSTANT SEX

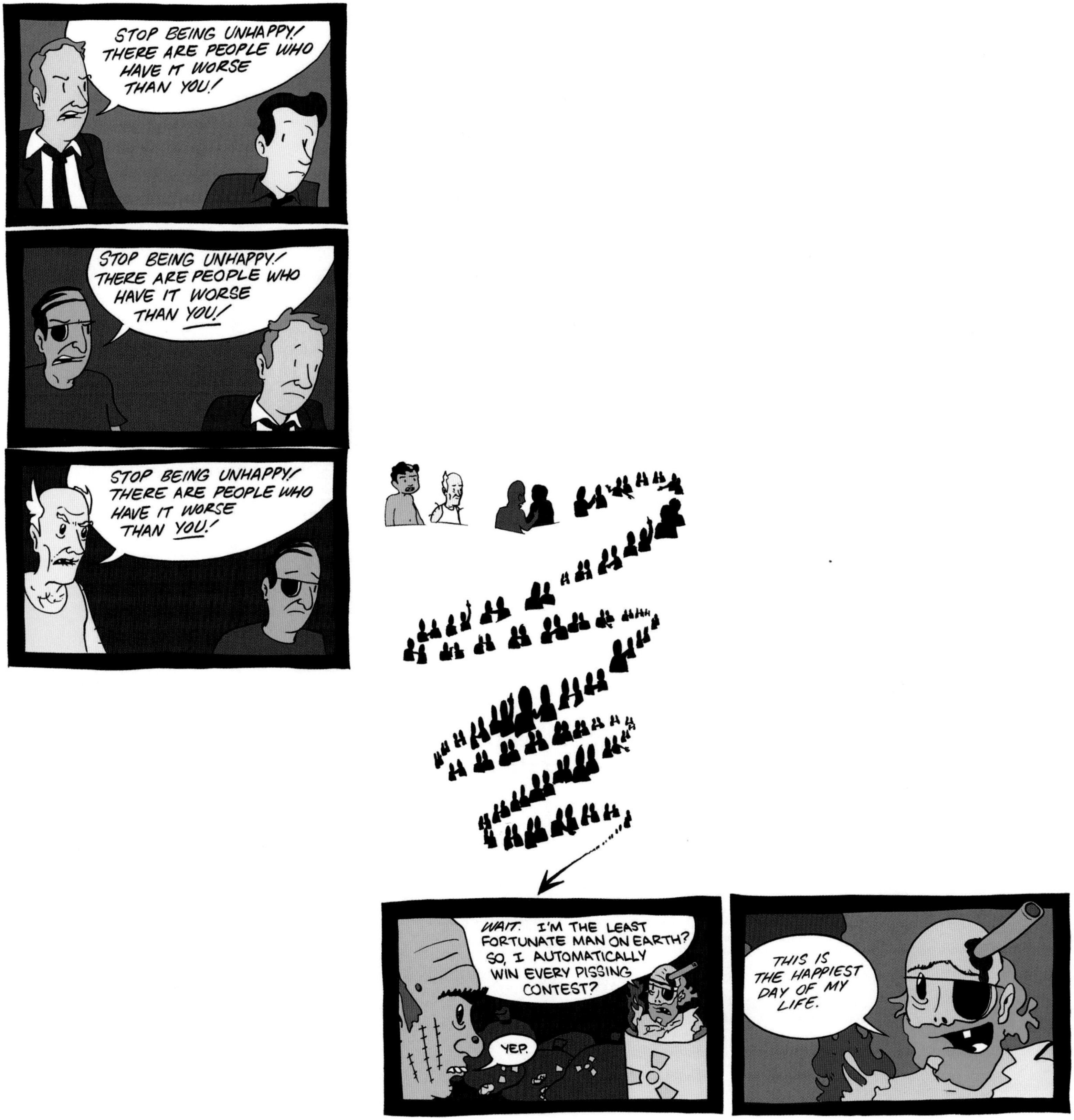
STOP BEING UNHAPPY! THERE ARE PEOPLE WHO HAVE IT WORSE THAN YOU!
STOP BEING UNHAPPY! THERE ARE PEOPLE WHO HAVE IT WORSE THAN YOU!
STOP BEING UNHAPPY! THERE ARE PEOPLE WHO HAVE IT WORSE THAN YOU!
WAIT. I'M THE LEAST FORTUNATE MAN ON EARTH? SO, I AUTOMATICALLY WIN EVERY PISSING CONTEST?
YEP.
THIS IS THE HAPPIEST DAY OF MY LIFE.

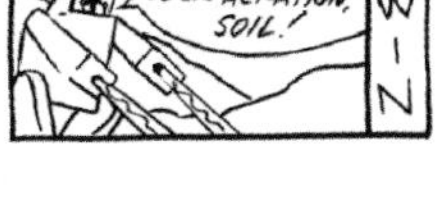
SUCK AERATION, SOIL!
WIN

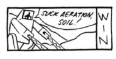

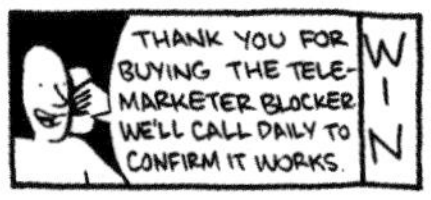
THANK YOU FOR BUYING THE TELE-MARKETER BLOCKER. WE'LL CALL DAILY TO CONFIRM IT WORKS.
WIN

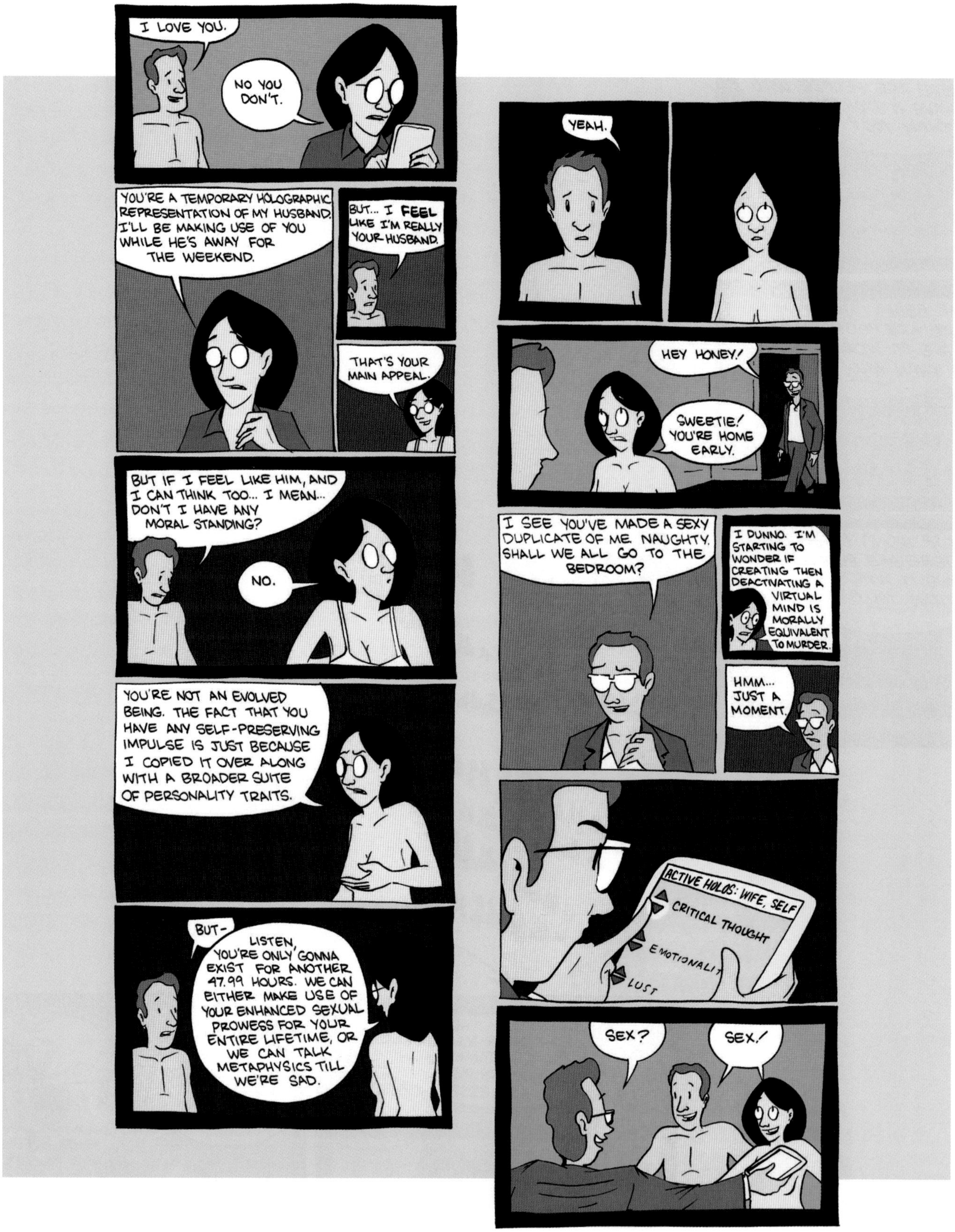
I LOVE YOU.
NO YOU DON'T.
YOU'RE A TEMPORARY HOLOGRAPHIC REPRESENTATION OF MY HUSBAND. I'LL BE MAKING USE OF YOU WHILE HE'S AWAY FOR THE WEEKEND.
BUT... I FEEL LIKE I'M REALLY YOUR HUSBAND.
THAT'S YOUR MAIN APPEAL.
BUT IF I FEEL LIKE HIM, AND I CAN THINK TOO... I MEAN... DON'T I HAVE ANY MORAL STANDING?
NO.
YOU'RE NOT AN EVOLVED BEING. THE FACT THAT YOU HAVE ANY SELF-PRESERVING IMPULSE IS JUST BECAUSE I COPIED IT OVER ALONG WITH A BROADER SUITE OF PERSONALITY TRAITS.
BUT-
LISTEN, YOU'RE ONLY GONNA EXIST FOR ANOTHER 47.99 HOURS. WE CAN EITHER MAKE USE OF YOUR ENHANCED SEXUAL PROWESS FOR YOUR ENTIRE LIFETIME, OR WE CAN TALK METAPHYSICS TILL WE'RE SAD.
YEAH.
HEY HONEY!
SWEETIE! YOU'RE HOME EARLY.
I SEE YOU'VE MADE A SEXY DUPLICATE OF ME. NAUGHTY. SHALL WE ALL GO TO THE BEDROOM?
I DUNNO. I'M STARTING TO WONDER IF CREATING THEN DEACTIVATING A VIRTUAL MIND IS MORALLY EQUIVALENT TO MURDER.
HMM... JUST A MOMENT.
ACTIVE HOLOS: WIFE, SELF
CRITICAL THOUGHT
EMOTIONALIT
LUST
SEX?
SEX!

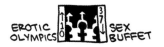

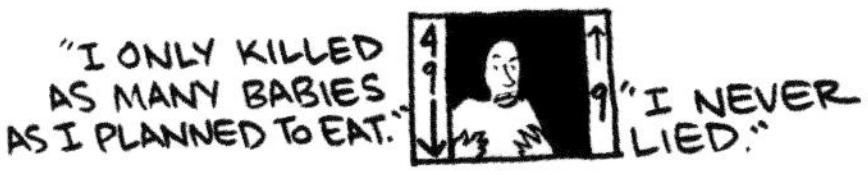
"I ONLY KILLED AS MANY BABIES AS I PLANNED TO EAT."
"I NEVER LIED."

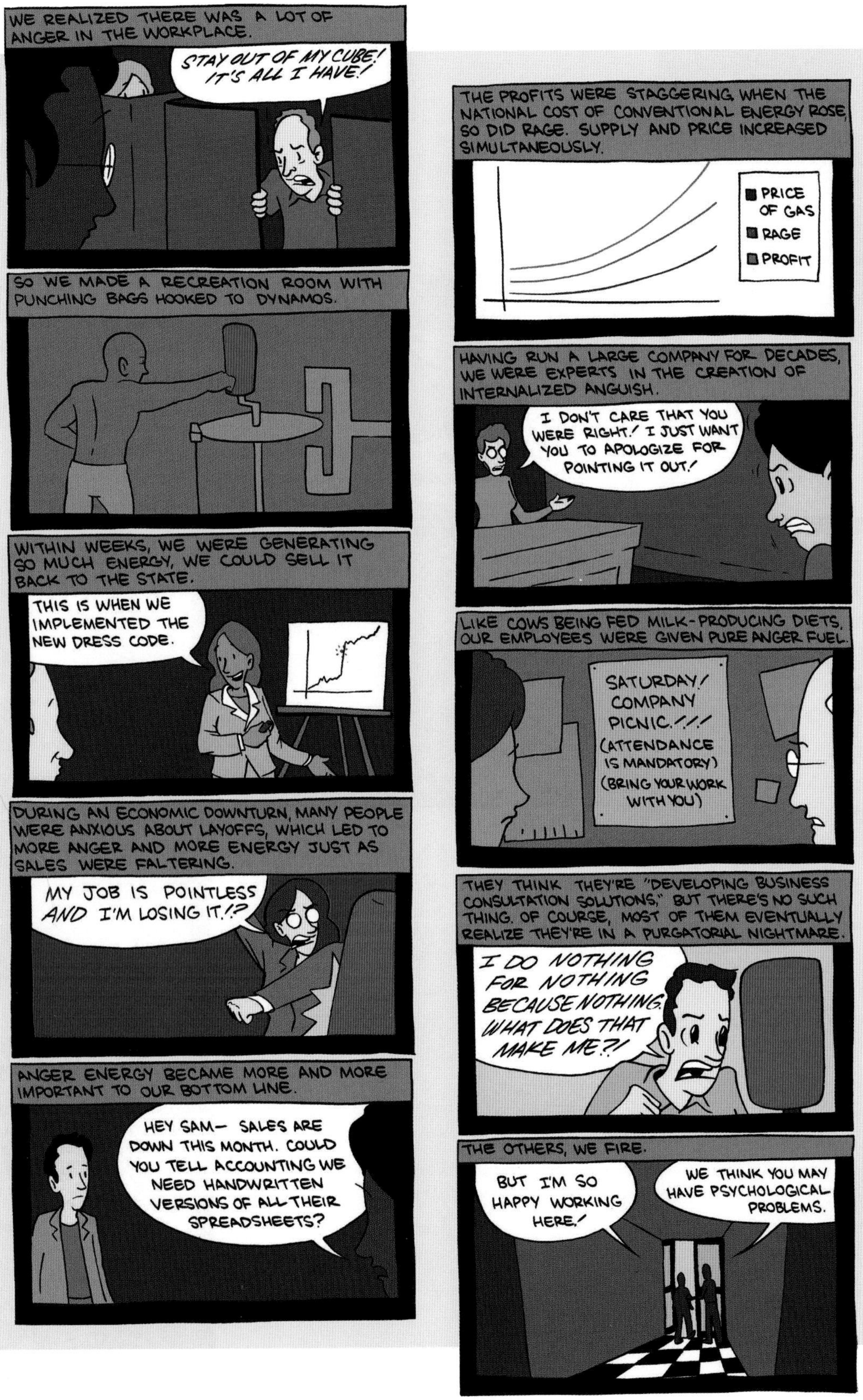
WE REALIZED THERE WAS A LOT OF ANGER IN THE WORKPLACE.
STAY OUT OF MY CUBE! IT'S ALL I HAVE!
SO WE MADE A RECREATION ROOM WITH PUNCHING BAGS HOOKED TO DYNAMOS.
WITHIN WEEKS, WE WERE GENERATING SO MUCH ENERGY, WE COULD SELL IT BACK TO THE STATE.
THIS IS WHEN WE IMPLEMENTED THE NEW DRESS CODE.
DURING AN ECONOMIC DOWNTURN, MANY PEOPLE WERE ANXIOUS ABOUT LAYOFFS, WHICH LED TO MORE ANGER AND MORE ENERGY JUST AS SALES WERE FALTERING.
MY JOB IS POINTLESS AND I'M LOSING IT!?
ANGER ENERGY BECAME MORE AND MORE IMPORTANT TO OUR BOTTOM LINE.
HEY SAM— SALES ARE DOWN THIS MONTH. COULD YOU TELL ACCOUNTING WE NEED HANDWRITTEN VERSIONS OF ALL THEIR SPREADSHEETS?
THE PROFITS WERE STAGGERING WHEN THE NATIONAL COST OF CONVENTIONAL ENERGY ROSE, SO DID RAGE. SUPPLY AND PRICE INCREASED SIMULTANEOUSLY.
PRICE OF GAS
RAGE
PROFIT
HAVING RUN A LARGE COMPANY FOR DECADES, WE WERE EXPERTS IN THE CREATION OF INTERNALIZED ANGUISH.
I DON'T CARE THAT YOU WERE RIGHT! I JUST WANT YOU TO APOLOGIZE FOR POINTING IT OUT!
LIKE COWS BEING FED MILK-PRODUCING DIETS, OUR EMPLOYEES WERE GIVEN PURE ANGER FUEL.
SATURDAY! COMPANY PICNIC!!!! (ATTENDANCE IS MANDATORY) (BRING YOUR WORK WITH YOU)
THEY THINK THEY'RE "DEVELOPING BUSINESS CONSULTATION SOLUTIONS," BUT THERE'S NO SUCH THING. OF COURSE, MOST OF THEM EVENTUALLY REALIZE THEY'RE IN A PURGATORIAL NIGHTMARE.
I DO NOTHING FOR NOTHING BECAUSE NOTHING. WHAT DOES THAT MAKE ME?!
THE OTHERS, WE FIRE.
BUT I'M SO HAPPY WORKING HERE!
WE THINK YOU MAY HAVE PSYCHOLOGICAL PROBLEMS.

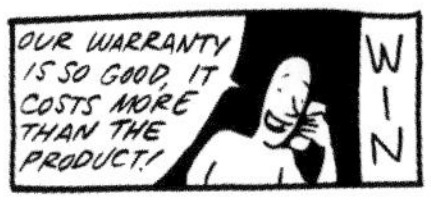
OUR WARRANTY IS SO GOOD, IT COSTS MORE THAN THE PRODUCT!
WIN

REALIZE IT'S NOT SO BAD.
OH GOD... IT'S CATCHY!
LOSE

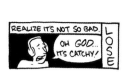

THE TREMATODE INFECTS A HORN SNAIL, CASTRATES IT, AND USES ITS BODY TO REPRODUCE.
THERE, IT RELEASES CERCARIAE, WHICH ATTACH TO KILLIFISH AND BURROW TOWARD THEIR BRAINS.
ONCE ON THE BRAIN, THEY CAUSE THE FISH TO SHIMMY AND FLASH THEIR SHINY SIDES UPWARD.
WHY YOU DOIN' THAT, FRANK?
BECAUSE IT'S AWESOME.
THIS GETS THE PARASITE TO ITS ULTIMATE GOAL: THE GUT OF A PREDATORY BIRD.
WHAT'RE THE ODDS?!
FROM THERE, THEY ARE EXCRETED BACK INTO THE WATER TO INFECT SNAILS.
HAHAHAHA! EVERYTHING IS AS I FORESAW IT!
WHAT HAPPENS TO THE KILLIFISH ISN'T STRANGE IN NATURE. IN FACT, IT MAY BE COMMON.
SINCE HUMANS ARE ATOP THEIR FOOD CHAIN, IT'S NOT CLEAR THAT WE'RE SUBJECT TO THE SAME SORT OF MANIPULATIONS. THOUGH... SOMETIMES I WONDER ABOUT ASTROPHYSICISTS.
THESE SEND SIGNALS TO SPACE SO ALIENS CAN FIND US!
AWESOME!

LOVE-BALL ↑ 6

36 ↓ SMITE THE INFIDEL

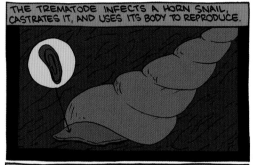

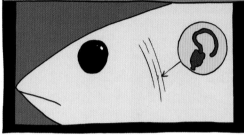

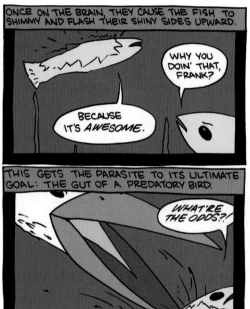

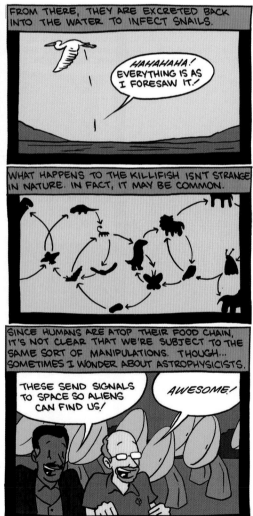

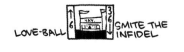

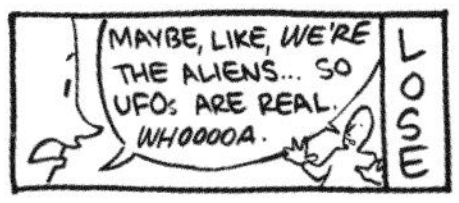
MAYBE, LIKE, WE'RE THE ALIENS... SO UFOs ARE REAL. WHOOOOA.
LOSE

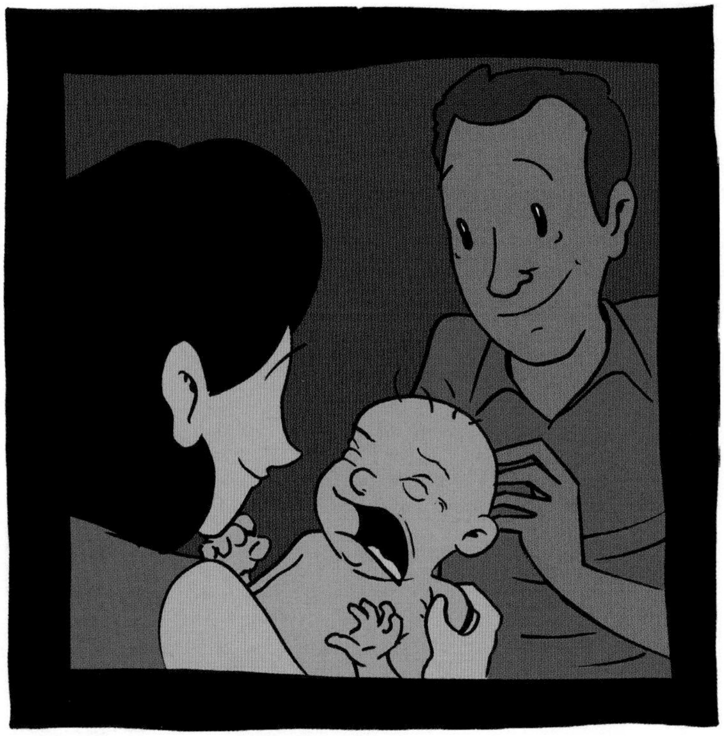

Babies don't shout "waaahhh!" when they're little.

They shout "whyyyyy!?"

You can't tell because they can't pronounce the hard "y" sound, but they're in a complete existential crisis.

It takes 2 to 3 years before they finish their period of utter madness, at which point their brains are completely empty, and you can start teaching them about counting and animal noises.

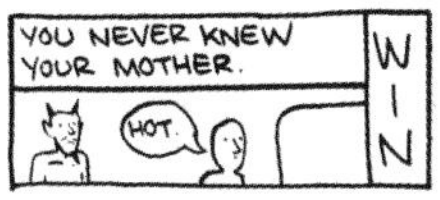
YOU NEVER KNEW YOUR MOTHER.
HOT.
WIN

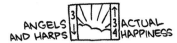

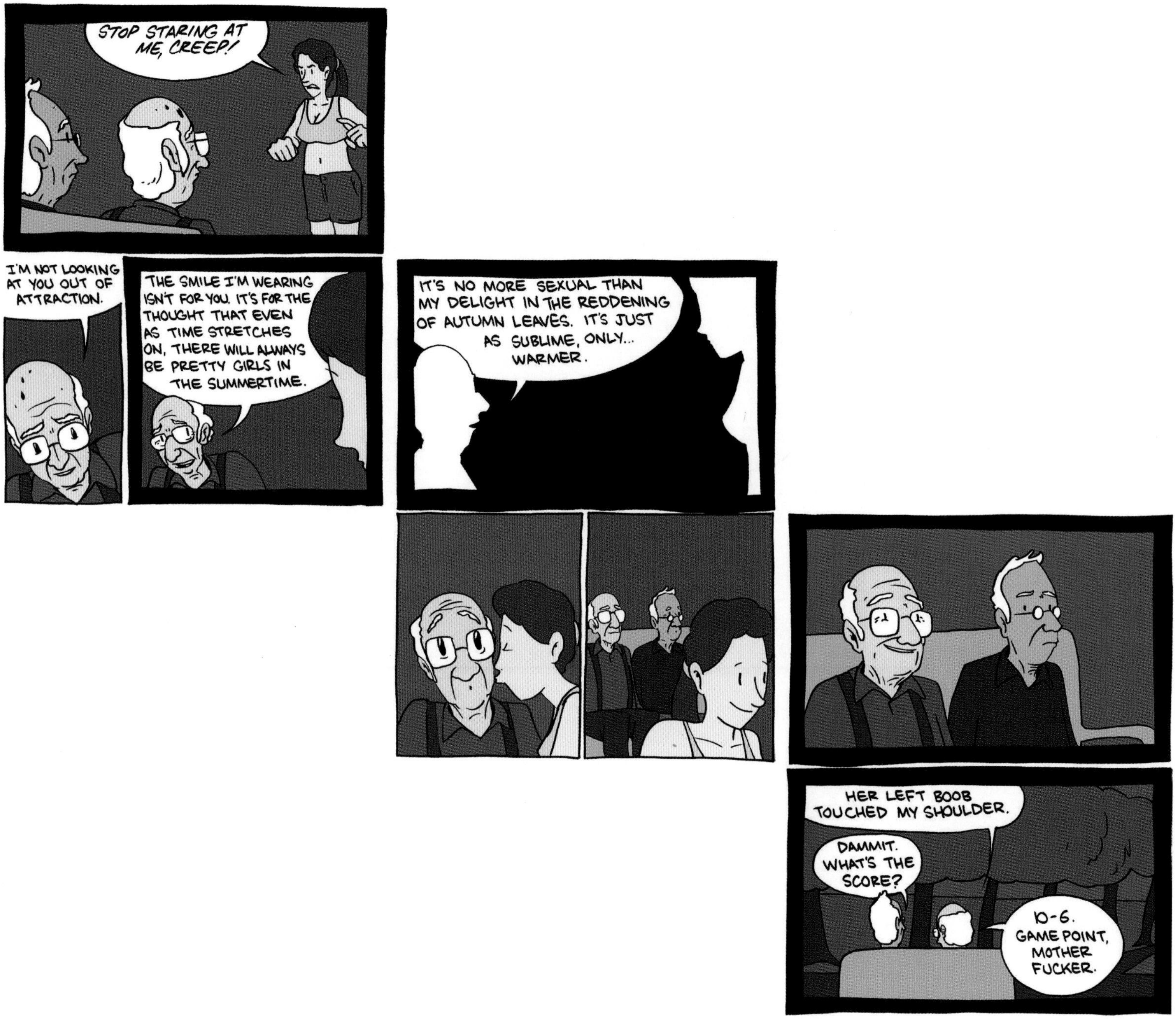
STOP STARING AT ME, CREEP!
I'M NOT LOOKING AT YOU OUT OF ATTRACTION.
THE SMILE I'M WEARING ISN'T FOR YOU. IT'S FOR THE THOUGHT THAT EVEN AS TIME STRETCHES ON, THERE WILL ALWAYS BE PRETTY GIRLS IN THE SUMMERTIME.
IT'S NO MORE SEXUAL THAN MY DELIGHT IN THE REDDENING OF AUTUMN LEAVES. IT'S JUST AS SUBLIME, ONLY... WARMER.
HER LEFT BOOB TOUCHED MY SHOULDER.
DAMMIT. WHAT'S THE SCORE?
10-6. GAME POINT, MOTHER FUCKER.

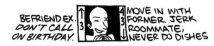

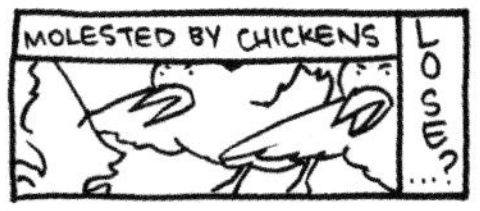
MOLESTED BY CHICKENS
LOSE?...

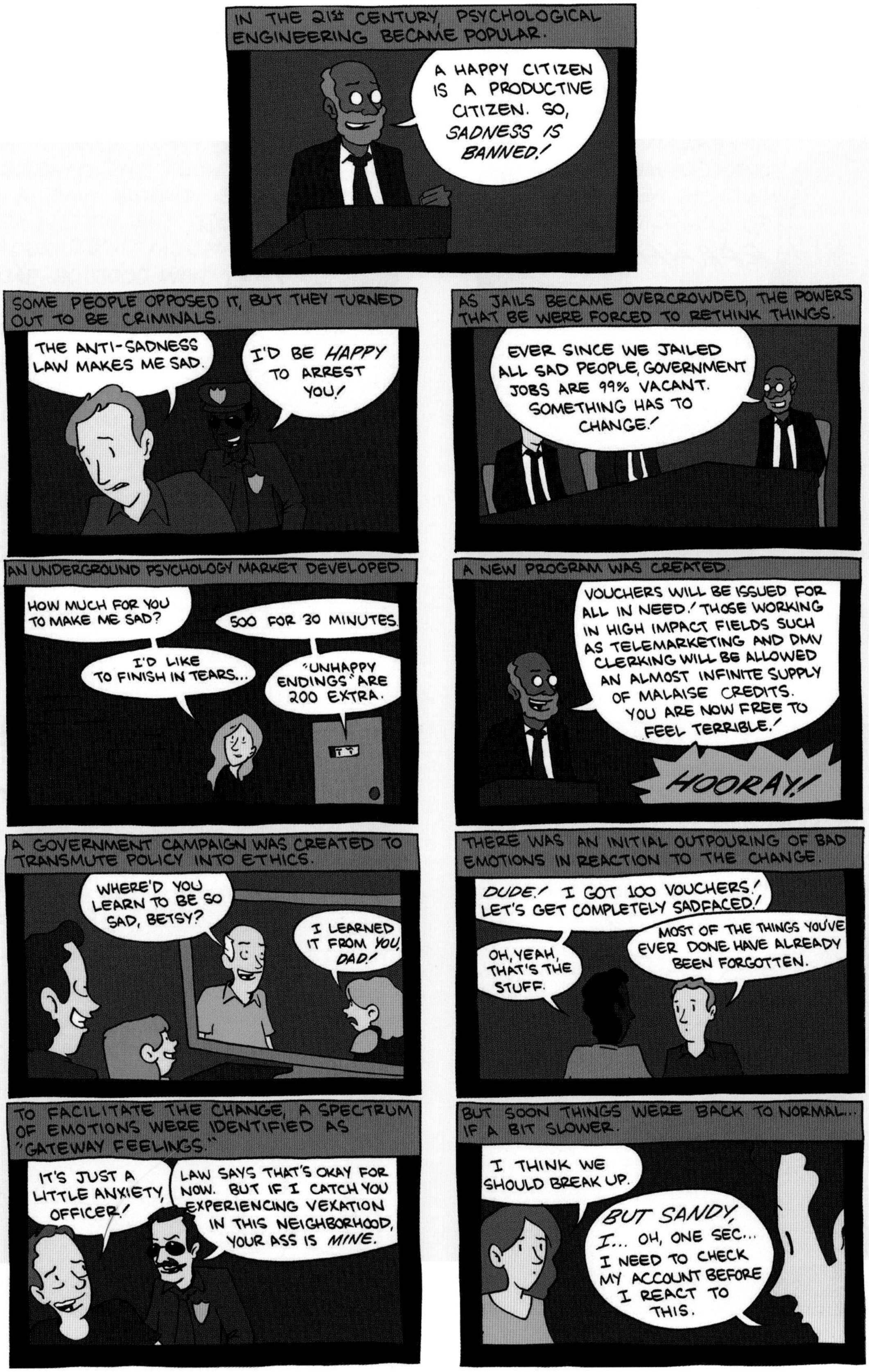
IN THE 21ST CENTURY, PSYCHOLOGICAL ENGINEERING BECAME POPULAR.
A HAPPY CITIZEN IS A PRODUCTIVE CITIZEN. SO, SADNESS IS BANNED!
SOME PEOPLE OPPOSED IT, BUT THEY TURNED OUT TO BE CRIMINALS.
THE ANTI-SADNESS LAW MAKES ME SAD.
I'D BE HAPPY TO ARREST YOU!
AS JAILS BECAME OVERCROWDED, THE POWERS THAT BE WERE FORCED TO RETHINK THINGS.
EVER SINCE WE JAILED ALL SAD PEOPLE, GOVERNMENT JOBS ARE 99% VACANT. SOMETHING HAS TO CHANGE!
AN UNDERGROUND PSYCHOLOGY MARKET DEVELOPED.
HOW MUCH FOR YOU TO MAKE ME SAD?
500 FOR 30 MINUTES.
I'D LIKE TO FINISH IN TEARS...
"UNHAPPY ENDINGS" ARE 200 EXTRA.
A NEW PROGRAM WAS CREATED.
VOUCHERS WILL BE ISSUED FOR ALL IN NEED! THOSE WORKING IN HIGH IMPACT FIELDS SUCH AS TELEMARKETING AND DMV CLERKING WILL BE ALLOWED AN ALMOST INFINITE SUPPLY OF MALAISE CREDITS. YOU ARE NOW FREE TO FEEL TERRIBLE!
HOORAY!
A GOVERNMENT CAMPAIGN WAS CREATED TO TRANSMUTE POLICY INTO ETHICS.
WHERE'D YOU LEARN TO BE SO SAD, BETSY?
I LEARNED IT FROM YOU, DAD!
THERE WAS AN INITIAL OUTPOURING OF BAD EMOTIONS IN REACTION TO THE CHANGE.
DUDE! I GOT 100 VOUCHERS! LET'S GET COMPLETELY SADFACED!
OH, YEAH, THAT'S THE STUFF.
MOST OF THE THINGS YOU'VE EVER DONE HAVE ALREADY BEEN FORGOTTEN.
TO FACILITATE THE CHANGE, A SPECTRUM OF EMOTIONS WERE IDENTIFIED AS "GATEWAY FEELINGS."
IT'S JUST A LITTLE ANXIETY, OFFICER!
LAW SAYS THAT'S OKAY FOR NOW. BUT IF I CATCH YOU EXPERIENCING VEXATION IN THIS NEIGHBORHOOD, YOUR ASS IS MINE.
BUT SOON THINGS WERE BACK TO NORMAL... IF A BIT SLOWER.
I THINK WE SHOULD BREAK UP.
BUT SANDY, I... OH, ONE SEC... I NEED TO CHECK MY ACCOUNT BEFORE I REACT TO THIS.

KARATE CHOP
111
CROTCH KICK
27

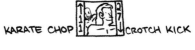

RAAHHHK! MY TRAINED USE OF WORDS AND PHRASES IN APPROPRIATE CONTEXT IS NOT FUNDAMENTALLY DIFFERENT FROM HUMAN COMMUNICATION WHICH IS ASCRIBED TO CONSCIOUSNESS! RAAHHHK!

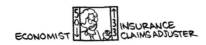

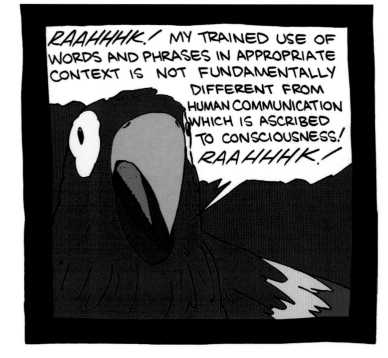

The philosophy department is no longer allowed to keep pets.

SAY YOU WERE WALKING OUTDOORS, AND YOU FOUND A WATCH. AND YOU OPENED THE WATCH AND FOUND MANY INTRICATELY INTERACTING PARTS, NONE OF WHICH MADE SENSE WITHOUT THE OTHERS? YOU WOULD CONCLUDE THERE WAS A DESIGNER. NOW, SUPPOSE THE WATCH KEPT SHOCKING YOU AT RANDOM TIMES, REGARDLESS OF HOW GOOD OR BAD YOU BEHAVED, AND THE SHOCKING SEEMED NOT TO BE A DEFECT, BUT RATHER A STANDARD FEATURE OF THE DESIGN.

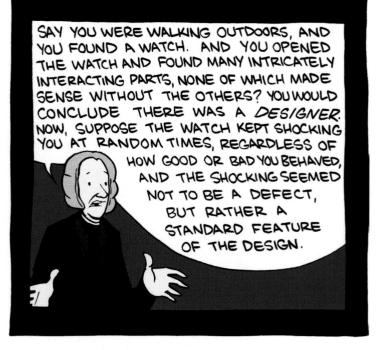

William Paley proves that there's a God, and that he's a dick.

FUNTIME ACTIVITY: ANTI-SEXISM
WOMAN! GET IN THE KITCHEN! I'VE PUT A NUMBER OF MARGARET ATWOOD NOVELS IN THERE, WHICH WE CAN READ TOGETHER AS EQUALS!

I DON'T GET IT. WHAT HOLIDAY IS CELEBRATED WITH ACCIDENTALLY BROKEN BALLOONS AND BURNING MONEY?

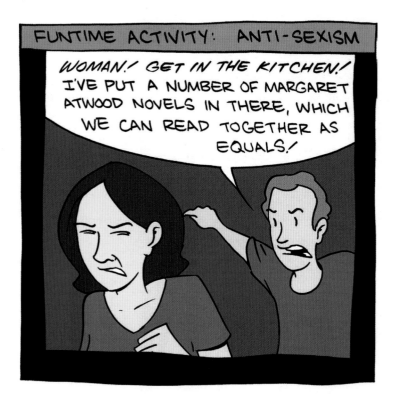

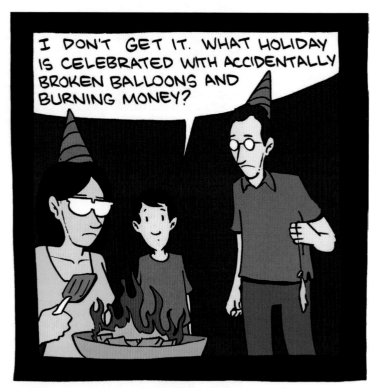

Fun Fact:
Nine months before your birthday is your conceptionday.

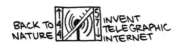

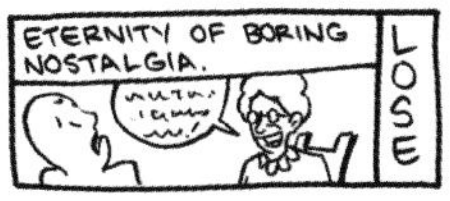
ETERNITY OF BORING NOSTALGIA.
LOSE

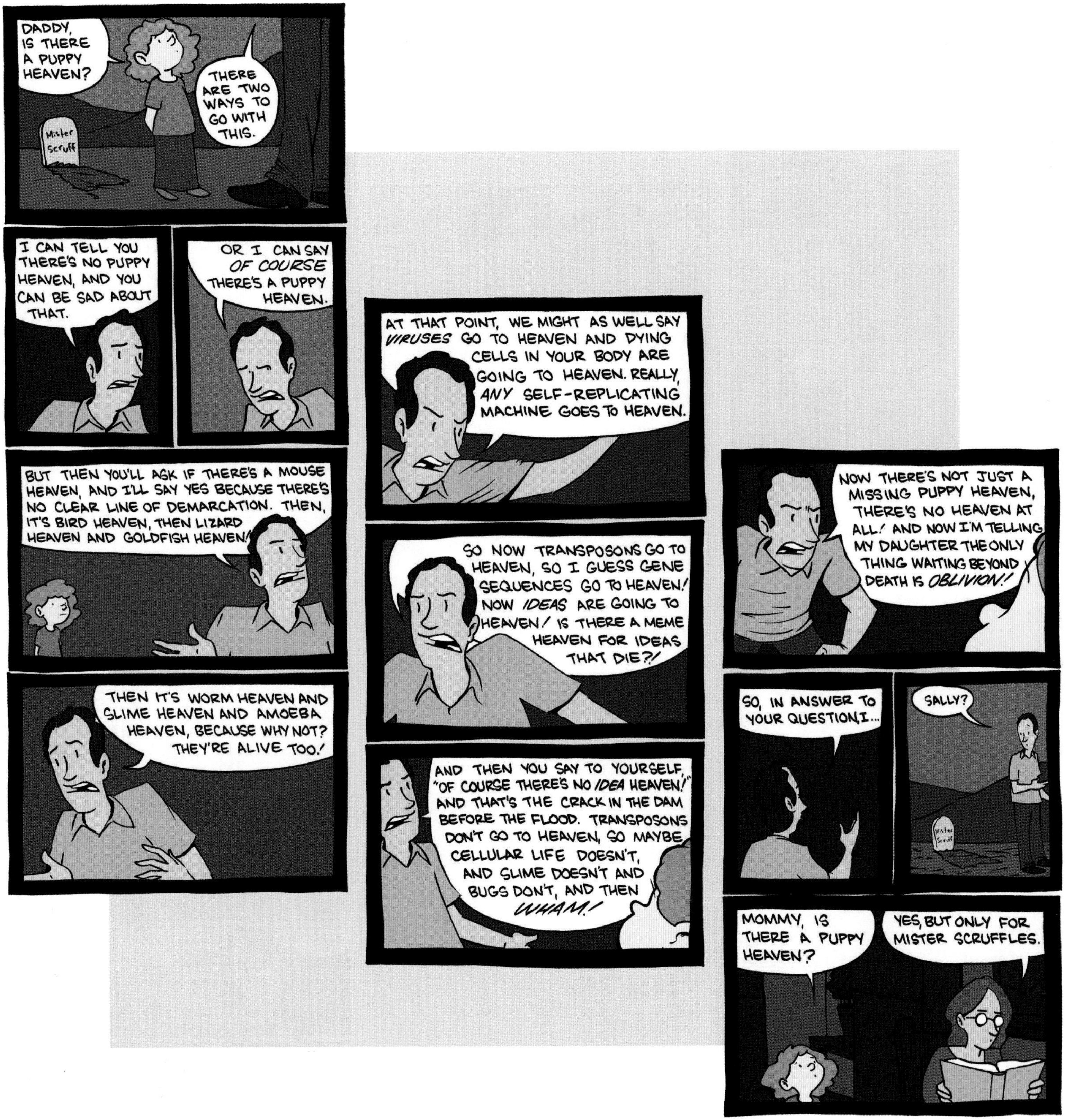
DADDY, IS THERE A PUPPY HEAVEN?
THERE ARE TWO WAYS TO GO WITH THIS.
Mister Scruff
I CAN TELL YOU THERE'S NO PUPPY HEAVEN, AND YOU CAN BE SAD ABOUT THAT.
OR I CAN SAY *OF COURSE* THERE'S A PUPPY HEAVEN.
BUT THEN YOU'LL ASK IF THERE'S A MOUSE HEAVEN, AND I'LL SAY YES BECAUSE THERE'S NO CLEAR LINE OF DEMARCATION. THEN, IT'S BIRD HEAVEN, THEN LIZARD HEAVEN AND GOLDFISH HEAVEN!
THEN IT'S WORM HEAVEN AND SLIME HEAVEN AND AMOEBA HEAVEN, BECAUSE WHY NOT? THEY'RE ALIVE TOO!
AT THAT POINT, WE MIGHT AS WELL SAY *VIRUSES* GO TO HEAVEN AND DYING CELLS IN YOUR BODY ARE GOING TO HEAVEN. REALLY, *ANY* SELF-REPLICATING MACHINE GOES TO HEAVEN.
SO NOW TRANSPOSONS GO TO HEAVEN, SO I GUESS GENE SEQUENCES GO TO HEAVEN! NOW *IDEAS* ARE GOING TO HEAVEN! IS THERE A MEME HEAVEN FOR IDEAS THAT DIE?!
AND THEN YOU SAY TO YOURSELF, "OF COURSE THERE'S NO *IDEA* HEAVEN!" AND THAT'S THE CRACK IN THE DAM BEFORE THE FLOOD. TRANSPOSONS DON'T GO TO HEAVEN, SO MAYBE CELLULAR LIFE DOESN'T, AND SLIME DOESN'T AND BUGS DON'T, AND THEN *WHAM!*
NOW THERE'S NOT JUST A MISSING PUPPY HEAVEN, THERE'S NO HEAVEN AT ALL! AND NOW I'M TELLING MY DAUGHTER THE ONLY THING WAITING BEYOND DEATH IS *OBLIVION!!*
SO, IN ANSWER TO YOUR QUESTION, I...
SALLY?
MOMMY, IS THERE A PUPPY HEAVEN?
YES, BUT ONLY FOR MISTER SCRUFFLES.

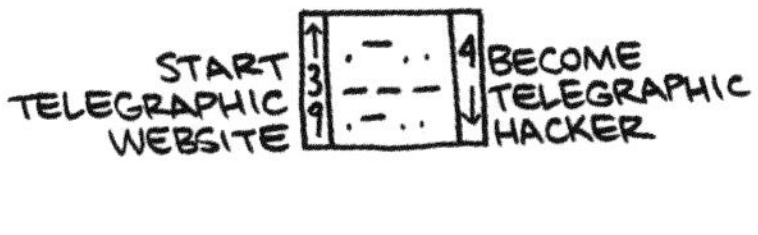
START TELEGRAPHIC WEBSITE
BECOME TELEGRAPHIC HACKER

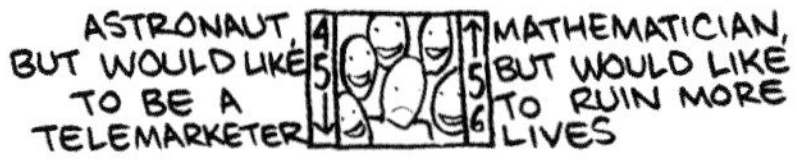
ASTRONAUT, BUT WOULD LIKE TO BE A TELEMARKETER
4
5
1
MATHEMATICIAN, BUT WOULD LIKE TO RUIN MORE LIVES
1
5
6

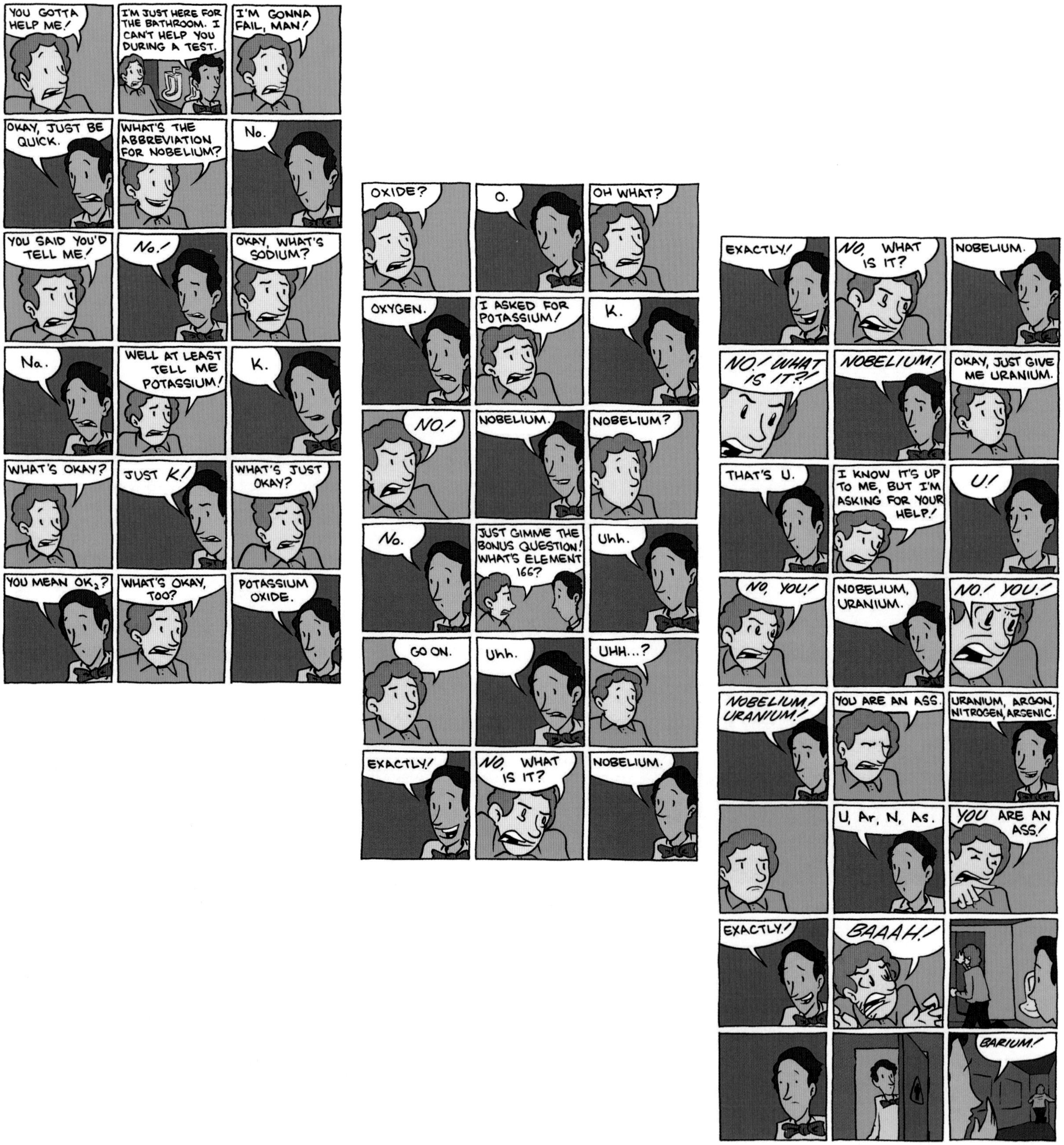
YOU GOTTA HELP ME!
I'M JUST HERE FOR THE BATHROOM. I CAN'T HELP YOU DURING A TEST.
I'M GONNA FAIL, MAN!
OKAY, JUST BE QUICK.
WHAT'S THE ABBREVIATION FOR NOBELIUM?
No.
YOU SAID YOU'D TELL ME!
No.!
OKAY, WHAT'S SODIUM?
Na.
WELL AT LEAST TELL ME POTASSIUM!
K.
WHAT'S OKAY?
JUST K!
WHAT'S JUST OKAY?
YOU MEAN OK_2?
WHAT'S OKAY, TOO?
POTASSIUM OXIDE.
OXIDE?
O.
OH WHAT?
OXYGEN.
I ASKED FOR POTASSIUM!
K.
NO!
NOBELIUM.
NOBELIUM?
No.
JUST GIMME THE BONUS QUESTION! WHAT'S ELEMENT 166?
Uhh.
GO ON.
Uhh.
UHH...?
EXACTLY!
NO, WHAT IS IT?
NOBELIUM.
EXACTLY!
NO, WHAT IS IT?
NOBELIUM.
NO! WHAT IS IT?!
NOBELIUM!
OKAY, JUST GIVE ME URANIUM.
THAT'S U.
I KNOW IT'S UP TO ME, BUT I'M ASKING FOR YOUR HELP!
U!
NO, YOU!
NOBELIUM, URANIUM.
NO! YOU!
NOBELIUM! URANIUM!
YOU ARE AN ASS.
URANIUM, ARGON, NITROGEN, ARSENIC.
U, Ar, N, As.
YOU ARE AN ASS!
EXACTLY!
BAAAH!
BARIUM!

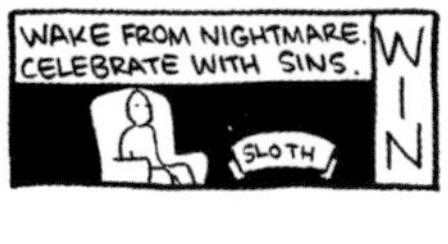
WAKE FROM NIGHTMARE. CELEBRATE WITH SINS.
SLOTH
WIN

OUTCLASSED.
PWNED, MY DEAR SIR.
DEFEAT

SIR! HOW COME ALL THE FEMALES IN YOUR ESTABLISHMENT HAVE THE SAME PHENOTYPE?!
BECAUSE IT'S A PHENOTYPE MALES FIND TO REPRESENT YOUTH AND FECUNDITY!
YOUTH AND FECUNDITY NEED NOT BE THE PRIMARY METRICS FOR ESTIMATING FEMALE SOCIAL VALUE!
WHY... I NEVER CONSIDERED THAT MY METRIC ANALYSIS WAS JUST ONE OF MANY
HEY, IT'S OKAY. YOU'RE LEARNING.
AND THAT'S HOW I'LL SHOW HIM THE ERROR OF HIS WAYS.
I THINK YOU'VE BEEN IN ACADEMIA TOO LONG.
HM? WHY?
LATER...
WHAT'S A PHENOTYPE?
I MEAN... HOW COME... HOW COME ALL YOUR WAITRESSES HAVE BOOBS THIS BIG?
BECAUSE WE COULDN'T FIND BIGGER.

ACID BATH 117 131 MASTURBATION FORBIDDEN

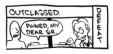

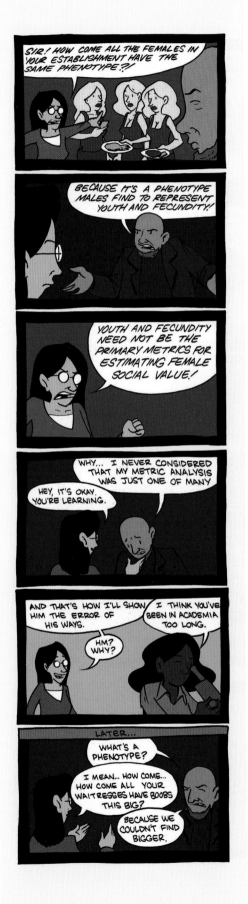

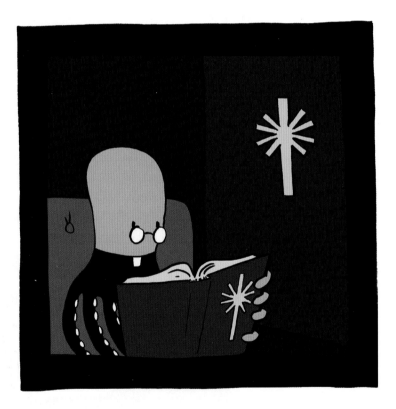

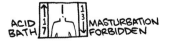

I'VE TAKEN HISTORY'S GREATEST CONQUERORS AND COMBINED THEIR DNA TO CREATE THE MOST POWERFUL SUPERVILLAIN EVER KNOWN!
SO, WHAT HAVE I BEEN DOING FOR TEN YEARS?
AS FAR AS I CAN TELL, YOU MUSHED SOME HISTORICALLY VALUABLE BONES INTO A PASTE, SHAPED IT INTO A BLOB AND DUNKED IT IN AN AQUARIUM.
GHENGIS KHAN!
ALEXANDER OF MACEDON!
CHARLEMAGNE!
SO... HOW DO I GET THE NEXT GREAT SUPERVILLAIN?
THEY ARISE ORGANICALLY. LOOK IN A COUNTRY WITH RECENTLY HIGH INFLATION, LOW PER CAPITA INCOME AND A BAD GINI COEFFICIENT.
NAPOLE-
WHAT DO YOU MEAN "COMBINED THEIR DNA?"
GINI COEFFICIENT. CHRIST, MAN. HERE'S A MACROECONOMICS TEXTBOOK.
YOU KNOW... COMBINED IT... LIKE... TOGETHER.
DNA DOESN'T WORK THAT WAY. EVEN IF IT DID, YOU CAN'T BE SURE THE CHILD WILL EXPRESS ALL THE QUALITIES YOU WANT. YOU'D HAVE TO COMPLETELY UNDERSTAND ITS ENVIRONMENT AND EPIGENOME, WHICH IS ESSENTIALLY IMPOSSIBLE.

SCIENCE
RUINING EVERYTHING SINCE 1543

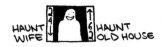

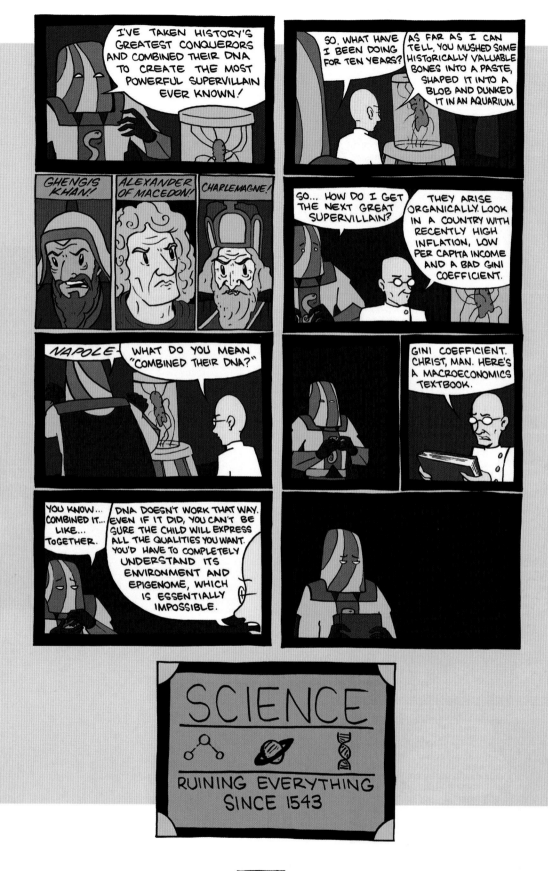

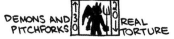

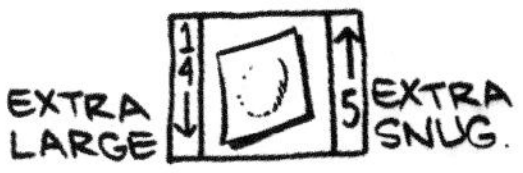
EXTRA LARGE
14
15
EXTRA SNUG.

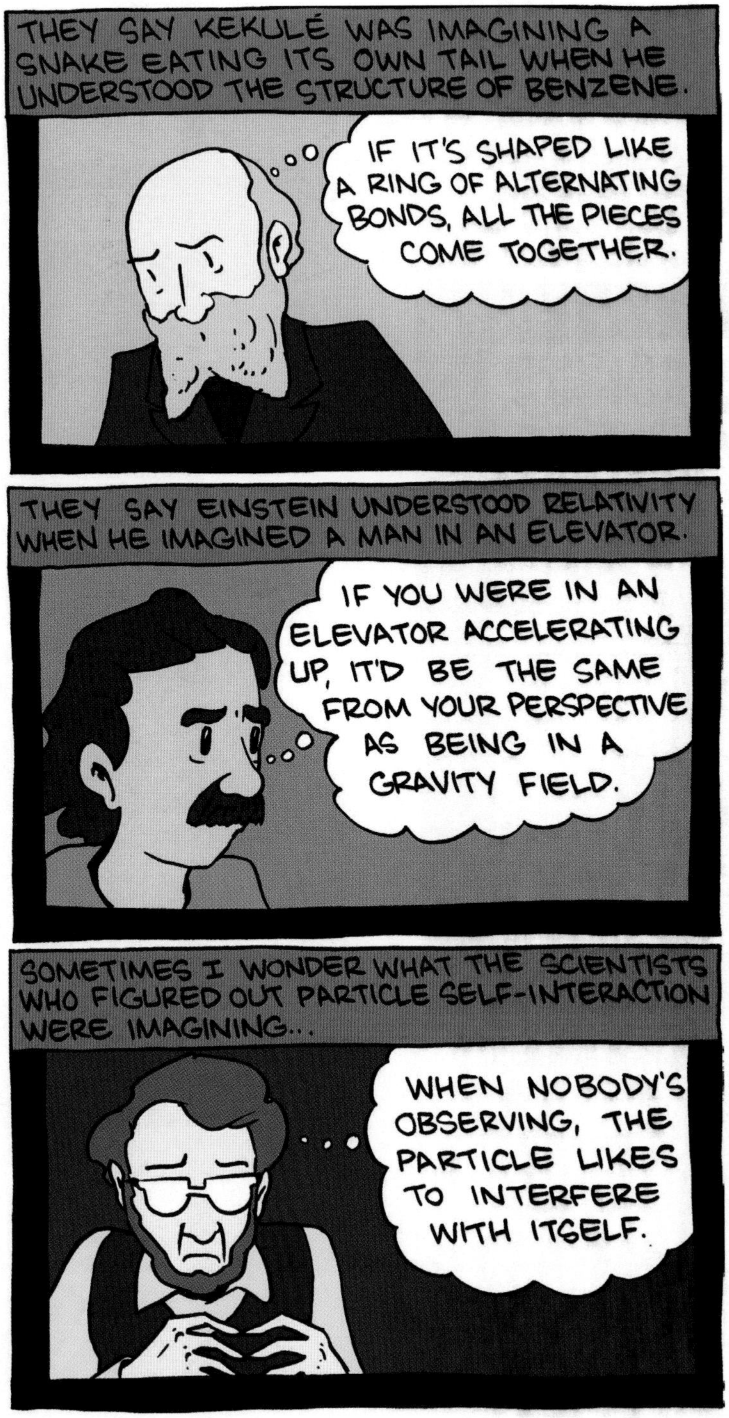
THEY SAY KEKULÉ WAS IMAGINING A SNAKE EATING ITS OWN TAIL WHEN HE UNDERSTOOD THE STRUCTURE OF BENZENE.
IF IT'S SHAPED LIKE A RING OF ALTERNATING BONDS, ALL THE PIECES COME TOGETHER.
THEY SAY EINSTEIN UNDERSTOOD RELATIVITY WHEN HE IMAGINED A MAN IN AN ELEVATOR.
IF YOU WERE IN AN ELEVATOR ACCELERATING UP, IT'D BE THE SAME FROM YOUR PERSPECTIVE AS BEING IN A GRAVITY FIELD.
SOMETIMES I WONDER WHAT THE SCIENTISTS WHO FIGURED OUT PARTICLE SELF-INTERACTION WERE IMAGINING...
WHEN NOBODY'S OBSERVING, THE PARTICLE LIKES TO INTERFERE WITH ITSELF.

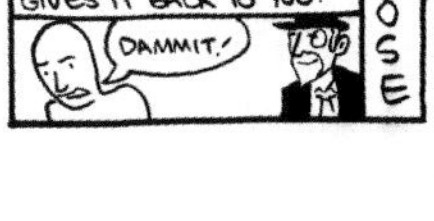
WEALTHY PATRON BUYS IT, GIVES IT BACK TO YOU.
DAMMIT.
LOSE

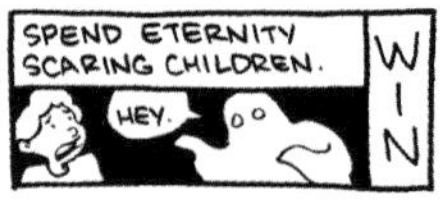
SPEND ETERNITY SCARING CHILDREN.
HEY.
WIN

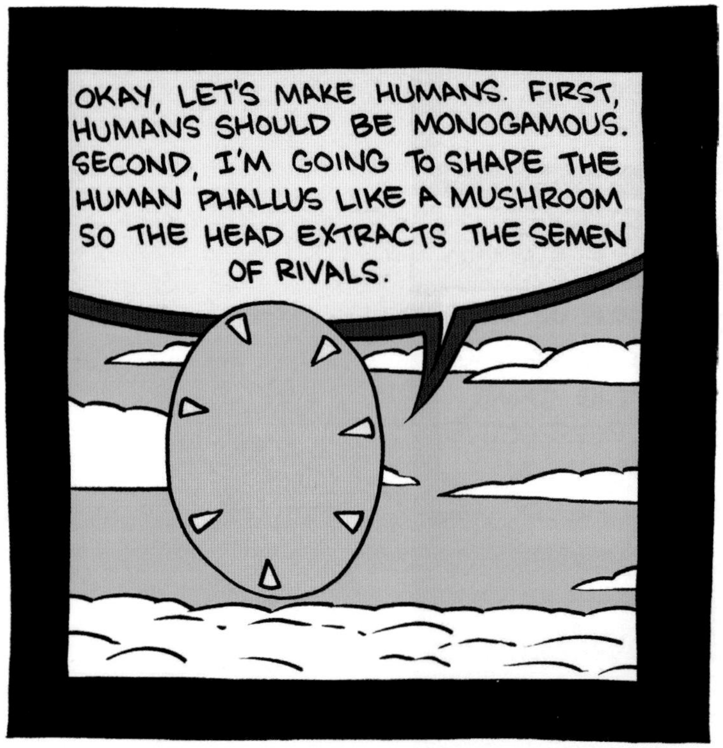
OKAY, LET'S MAKE HUMANS. FIRST, HUMANS SHOULD BE MONOGAMOUS. SECOND, I'M GOING TO SHAPE THE HUMAN PHALLUS LIKE A MUSHROOM SO THE HEAD EXTRACTS THE SEMEN OF RIVALS.

This is why I don't believe in guided evolution.

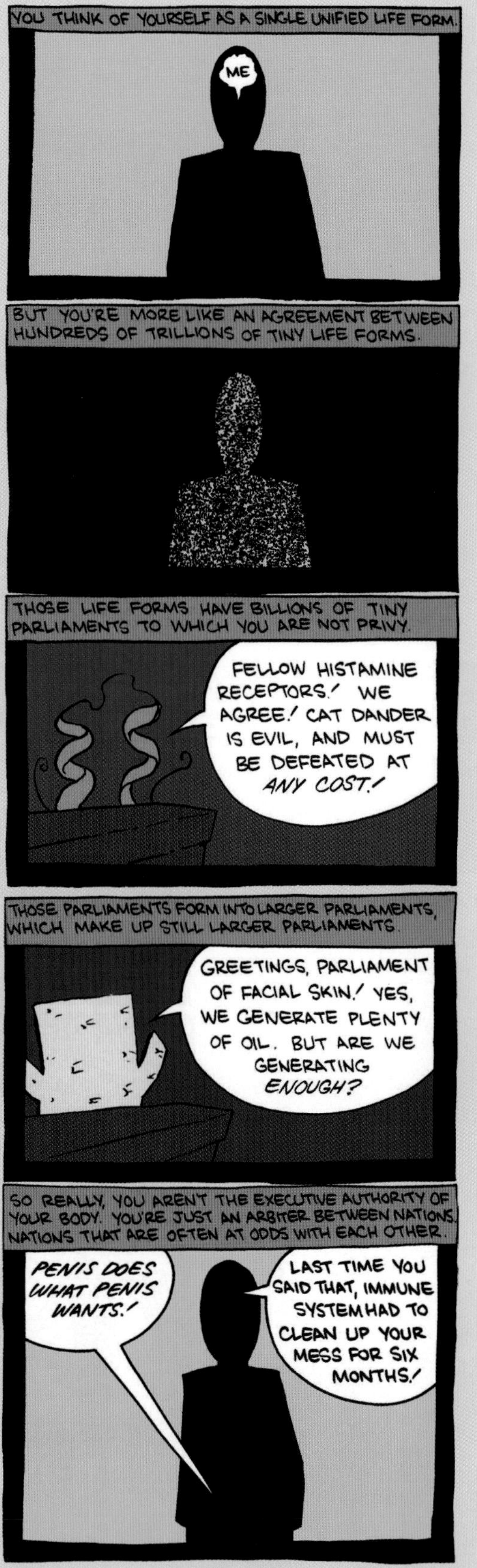
YOU THINK OF YOURSELF AS A SINGLE UNIFIED LIFE FORM.
ME
BUT YOU'RE MORE LIKE AN AGREEMENT BETWEEN HUNDREDS OF TRILLIONS OF TINY LIFE FORMS.
THOSE LIFE FORMS HAVE BILLIONS OF TINY PARLIAMENTS TO WHICH YOU ARE NOT PRIVY.
FELLOW HISTAMINE RECEPTORS! WE AGREE! CAT DANDER IS EVIL, AND MUST BE DEFEATED AT ANY COST!
THOSE PARLIAMENTS FORM INTO LARGER PARLIAMENTS, WHICH MAKE UP STILL LARGER PARLIAMENTS.
GREETINGS, PARLIAMENT OF FACIAL SKIN! YES, WE GENERATE PLENTY OF OIL. BUT ARE WE GENERATING ENOUGH?
SO REALLY, YOU AREN'T THE EXECUTIVE AUTHORITY OF YOUR BODY. YOU'RE JUST AN ARBITER BETWEEN NATIONS. NATIONS THAT ARE OFTEN AT ODDS WITH EACH OTHER.
PENIS DOES WHAT PENIS WANTS!
LAST TIME YOU SAID THAT, IMMUNE SYSTEM HAD TO CLEAN UP YOUR MESS FOR SIX MONTHS!

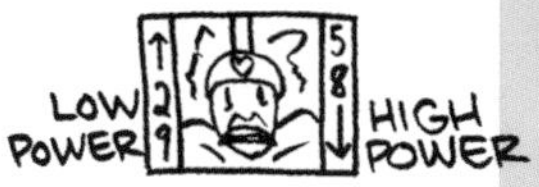
LOW POWER
129
58
HIGH POWER

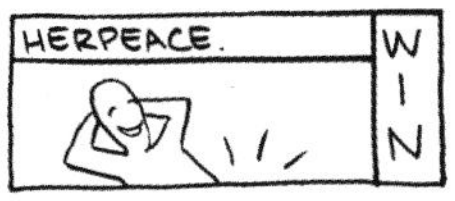
HERPEACE.
WIN

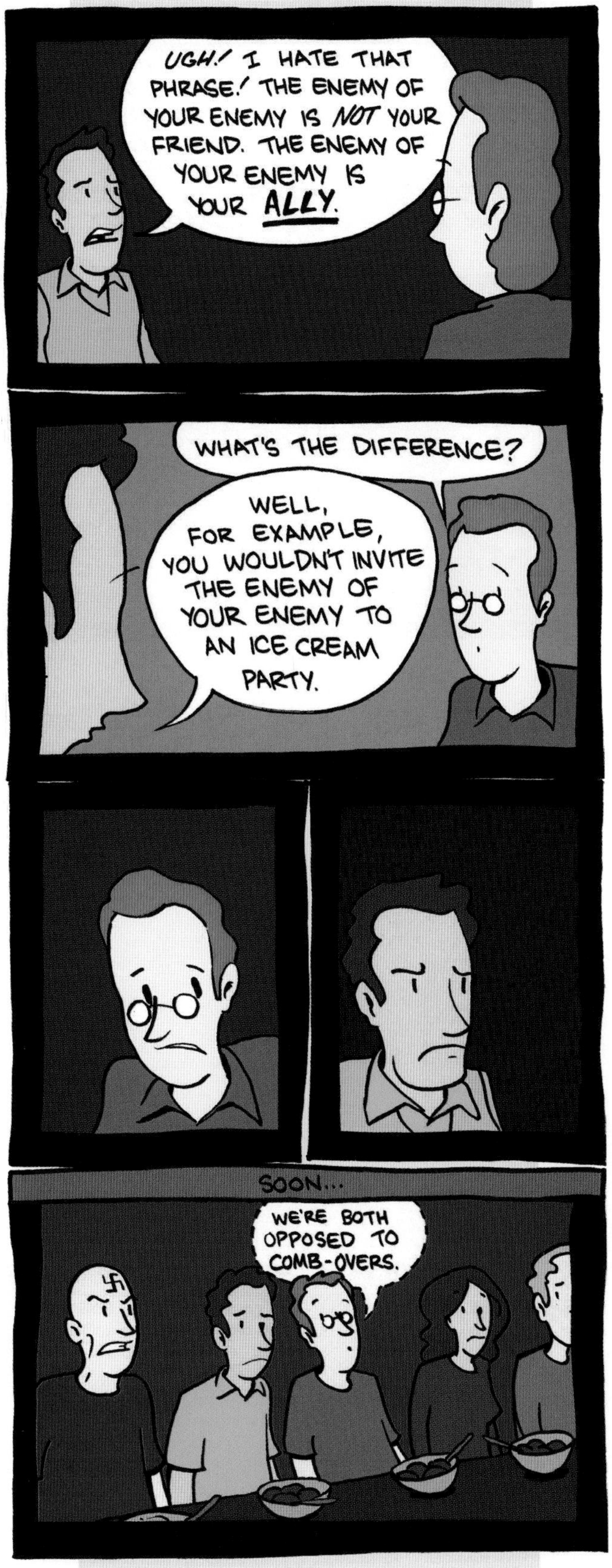
UGH! I HATE THAT PHRASE! THE ENEMY OF YOUR ENEMY IS NOT YOUR FRIEND. THE ENEMY OF YOUR ENEMY IS YOUR ALLY.
WHAT'S THE DIFFERENCE?
WELL, FOR EXAMPLE, YOU WOULDN'T INVITE THE ENEMY OF YOUR ENEMY TO AN ICE CREAM PARTY.
SOON...
WE'RE BOTH OPPOSED TO COMB-OVERS.

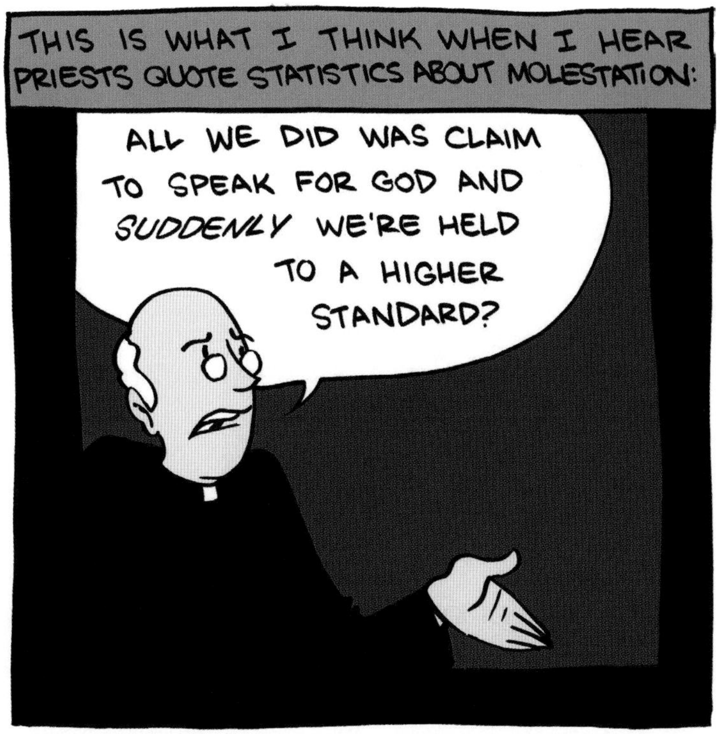
THIS IS WHAT I THINK WHEN I HEAR PRIESTS QUOTE STATISTICS ABOUT MOLESTATION:
ALL WE DID WAS CLAIM TO SPEAK FOR GOD AND SUDDENLY WE'RE HELD TO A HIGHER STANDARD?

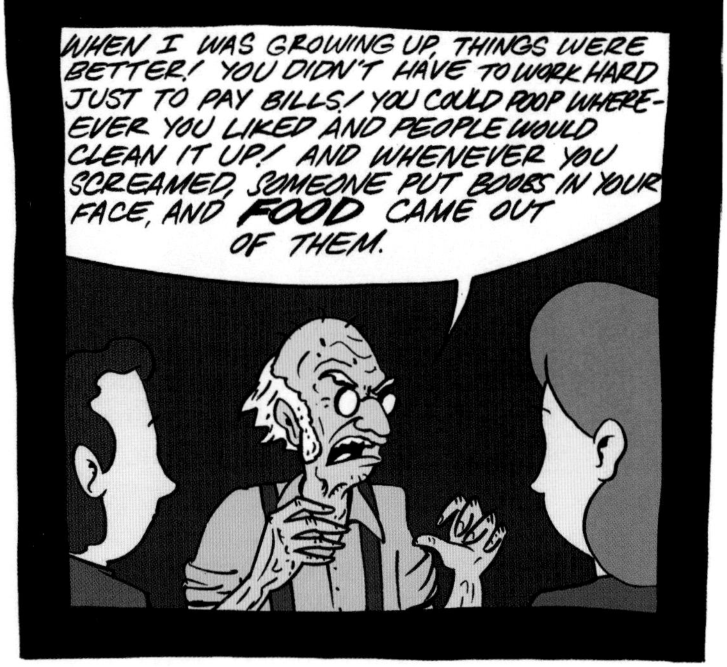
WHEN I WAS GROWING UP, THINGS WERE BETTER! YOU DIDN'T HAVE TO WORK HARD JUST TO PAY BILLS! YOU COULD POOP WHEREEVER YOU LIKED AND PEOPLE WOULD CLEAN IT UP! AND WHENEVER YOU SCREAMED, SOMEONE PUT BOOBS IN YOUR FACE, AND FOOD CAME OUT OF THEM.

All false nostalgia is essentially the same.

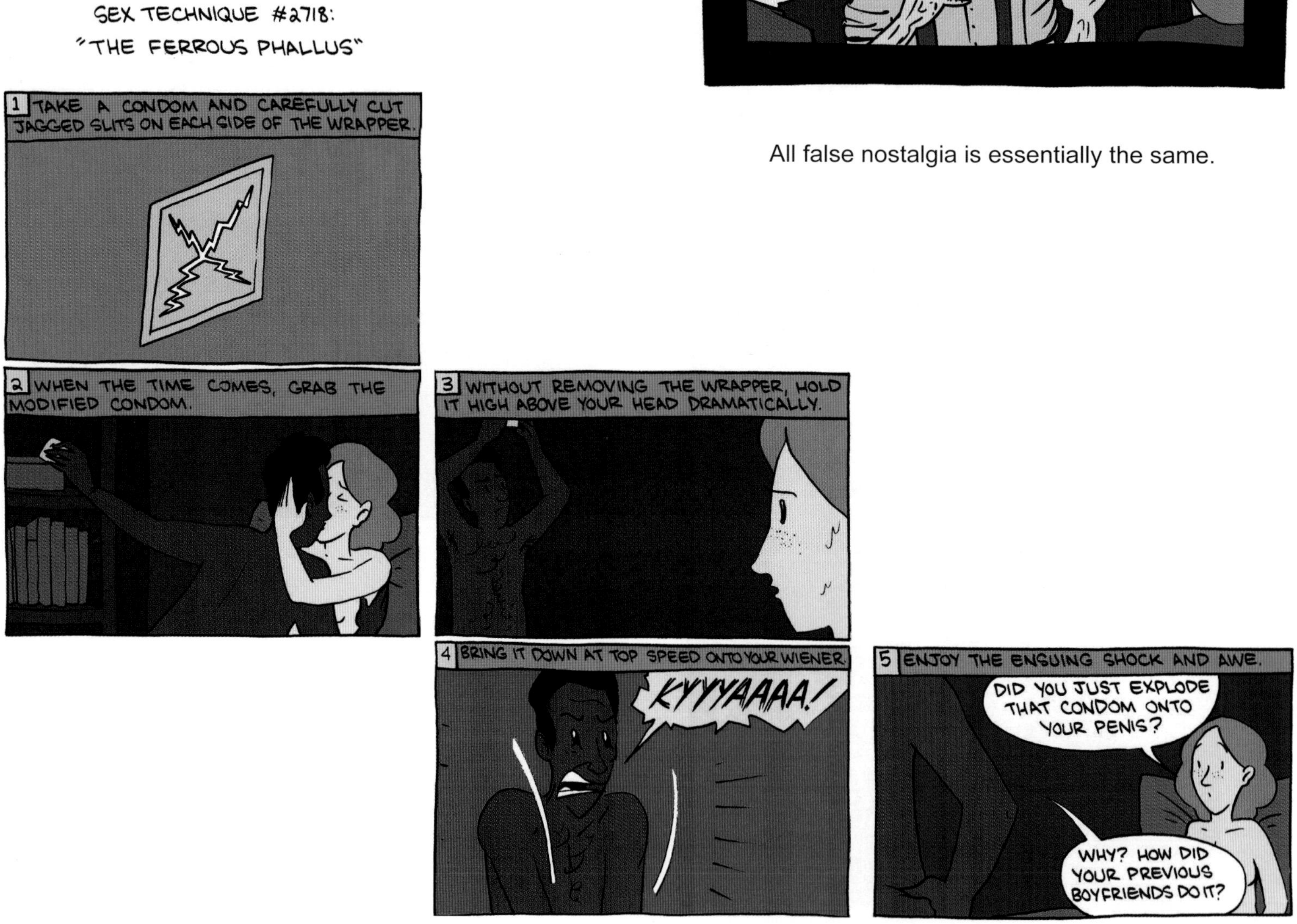
SEX TECHNIQUE #2718:
"THE FERROUS PHALLUS"
1 TAKE A CONDOM AND CAREFULLY CUT JAGGED SLITS ON EACH SIDE OF THE WRAPPER.
2 WHEN THE TIME COMES, GRAB THE MODIFIED CONDOM.
3 WITHOUT REMOVING THE WRAPPER, HOLD IT HIGH ABOVE YOUR HEAD DRAMATICALLY.
4 BRING IT DOWN AT TOP SPEED ONTO YOUR WIENER.
KYYYAAAA!
5 ENJOY THE ENSUING SHOCK AND AWE.
DID YOU JUST EXPLODE THAT CONDOM ONTO YOUR PENIS?
WHY? HOW DID YOUR PREVIOUS BOYFRIENDS DO IT?

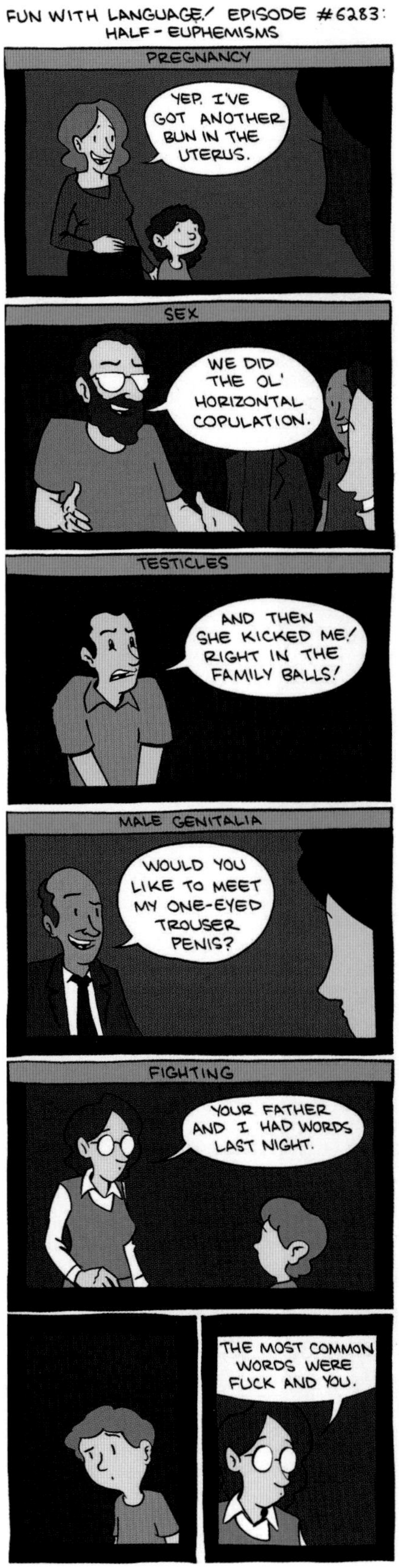
FUN WITH LANGUAGE! EPISODE #6283:
HALF-EUPHEMISMS
PREGNANCY
YEP. I'VE GOT ANOTHER BUN IN THE UTERUS.
SEX
WE DID THE OL' HORIZONTAL COPULATION.
TESTICLES
AND THEN SHE KICKED ME! RIGHT IN THE FAMILY BALLS!
MALE GENITALIA
WOULD YOU LIKE TO MEET MY ONE-EYED TROUSER PENIS?
FIGHTING
YOUR FATHER AND I HAD WORDS LAST NIGHT.
THE MOST COMMON WORDS WERE FUCK AND YOU.

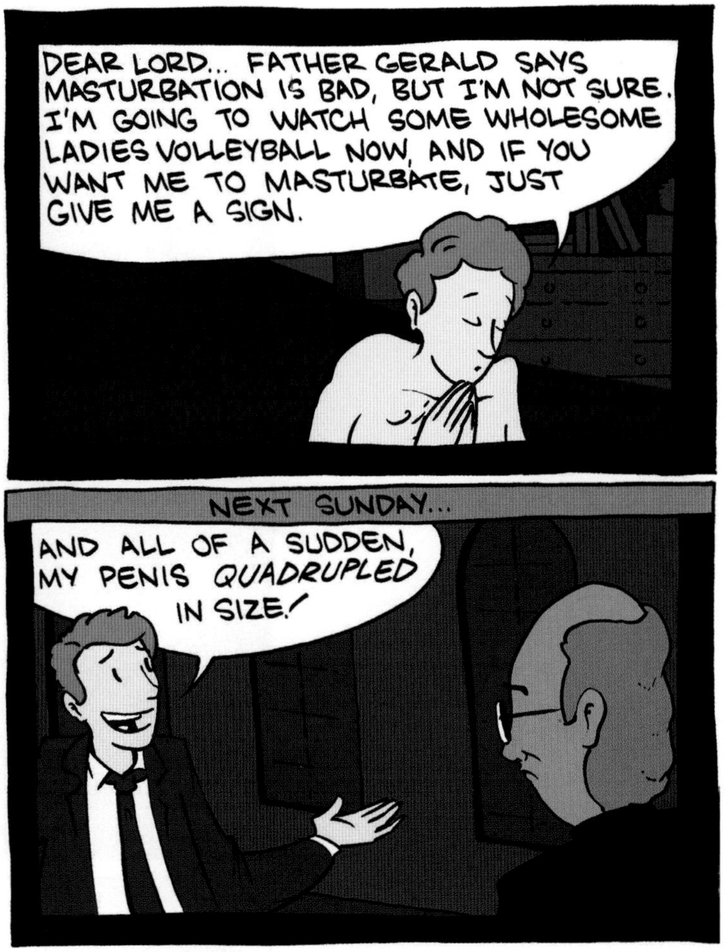
DEAR LORD... FATHER GERALD SAYS MASTURBATION IS BAD, BUT I'M NOT SURE. I'M GOING TO WATCH SOME WHOLESOME LADIES VOLLEYBALL NOW, AND IF YOU WANT ME TO MASTURBATE, JUST GIVE ME A SIGN.
NEXT SUNDAY...
AND ALL OF A SUDDEN, MY PENIS QUADRUPLED IN SIZE!

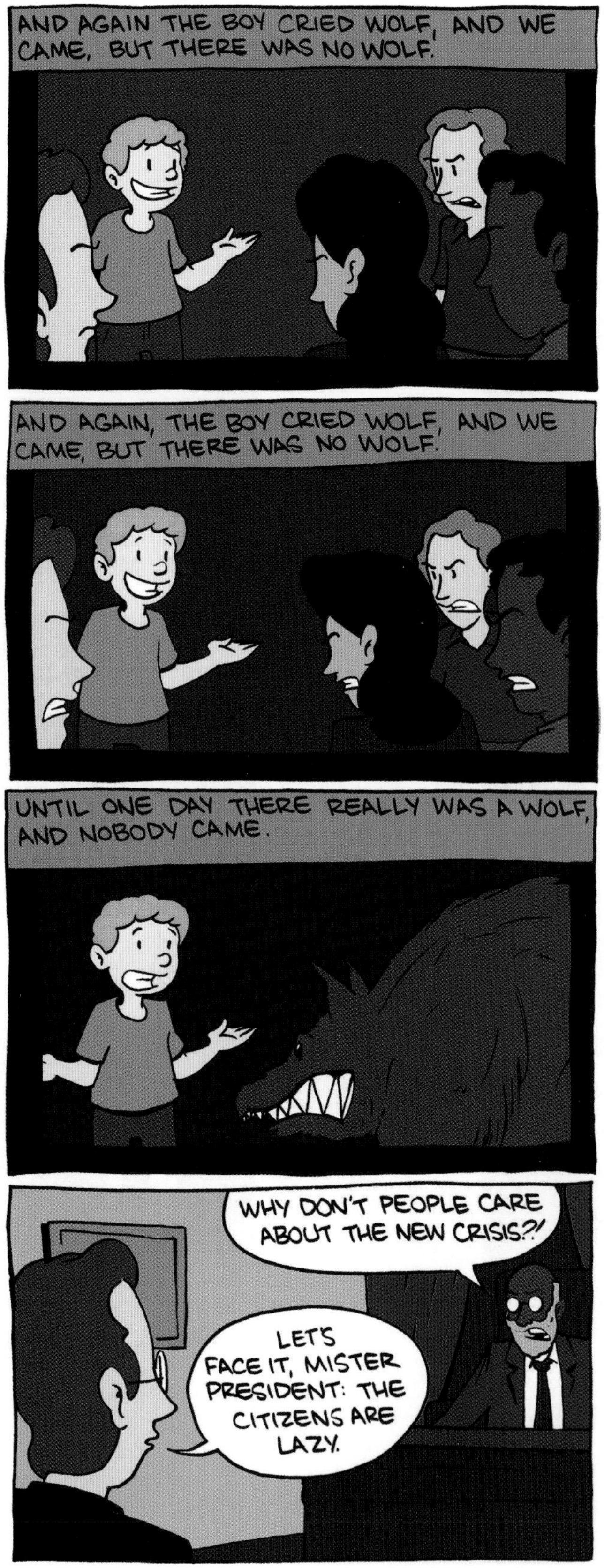
AND AGAIN THE BOY CRIED WOLF, AND WE CAME, BUT THERE WAS NO WOLF.
AND AGAIN, THE BOY CRIED WOLF, AND WE CAME, BUT THERE WAS NO WOLF.
UNTIL ONE DAY THERE REALLY WAS A WOLF, AND NOBODY CAME.
WHY DON'T PEOPLE CARE ABOUT THE NEW CRISIS?!
LET'S FACE IT, MISTER PRESIDENT: THE CITIZENS ARE LAZY.

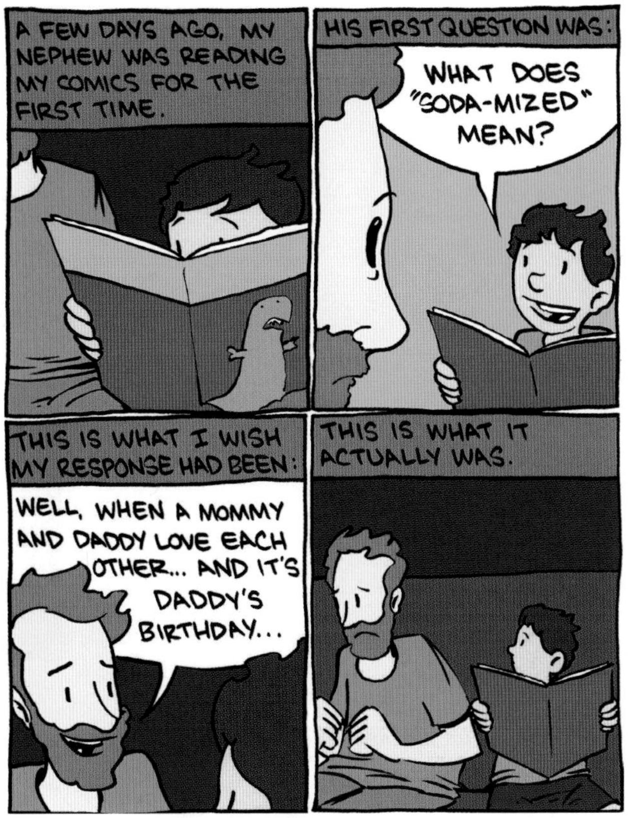
A FEW DAYS AGO, MY NEPHEW WAS READING MY COMICS FOR THE FIRST TIME.
HIS FIRST QUESTION WAS:
WHAT DOES "SODA-MIZED" MEAN?
THIS IS WHAT I WISH MY RESPONSE HAD BEEN:
WELL, WHEN A MOMMY AND DADDY LOVE EACH OTHER... AND IT'S DADDY'S BIRTHDAY...
THIS IS WHAT IT ACTUALLY WAS.

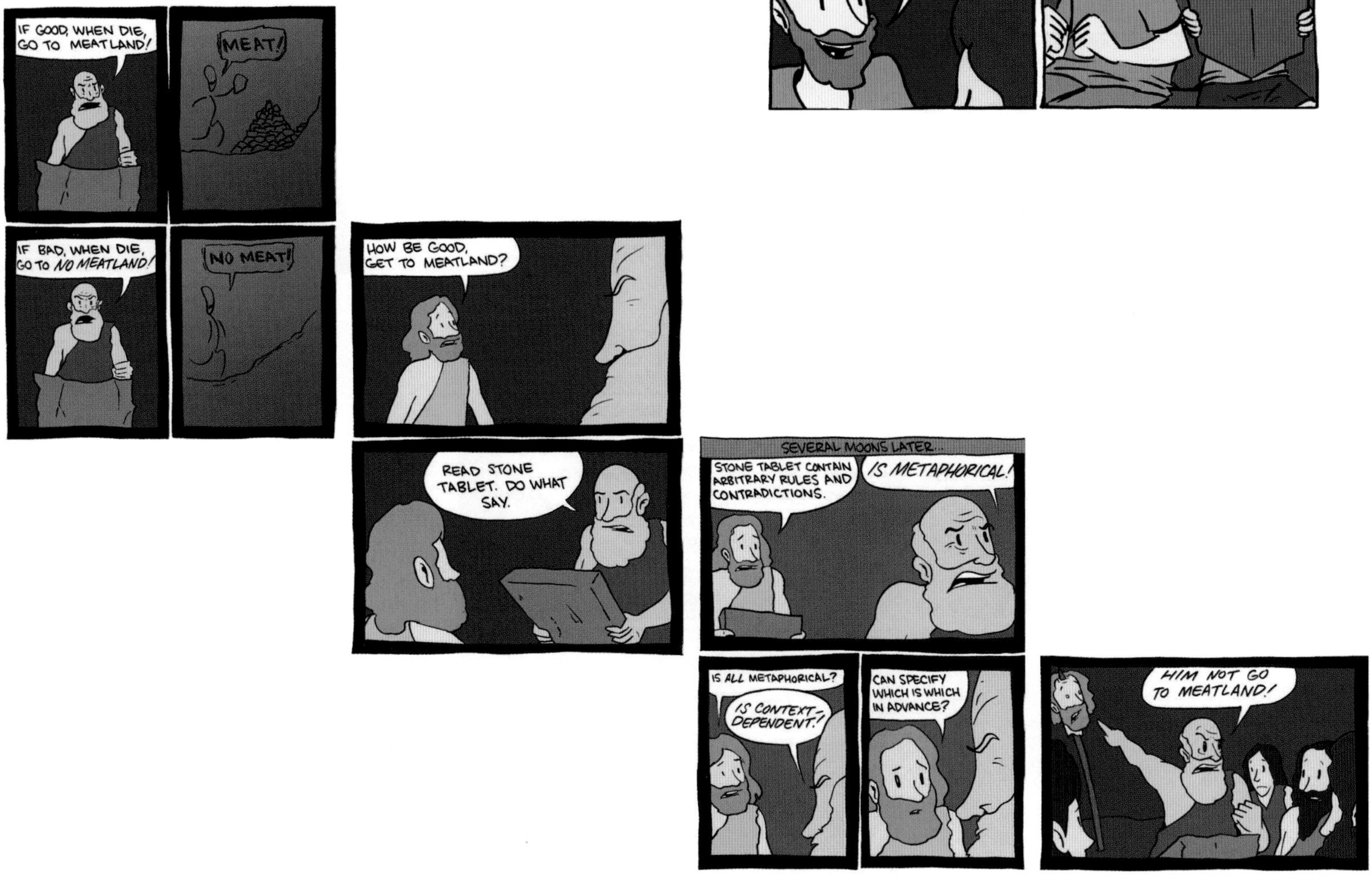
IF GOOD, WHEN DIE, GO TO MEATLAND!
MEAT!
IF BAD, WHEN DIE, GO TO NO MEATLAND!
NO MEAT!
HOW BE GOOD, GET TO MEATLAND?
READ STONE TABLET. DO WHAT SAY.
SEVERAL MOONS LATER...
STONE TABLET CONTAIN ARBITRARY RULES AND CONTRADICTIONS.
IS METAPHORICAL!
IS ALL METAPHORICAL?
IS CONTEXT-DEPENDENT!
CAN SPECIFY WHICH IS WHICH IN ADVANCE?
HIM NOT GO TO MEATLAND!

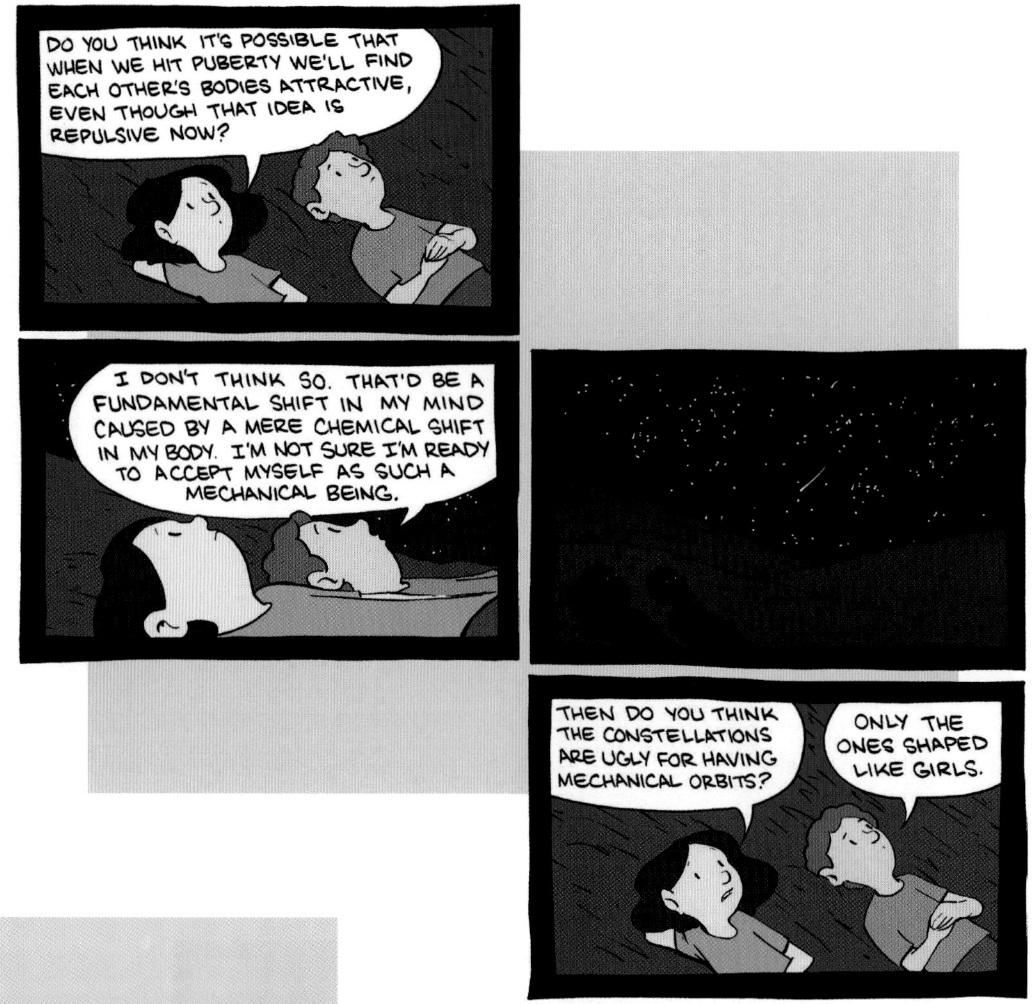
DO YOU THINK IT'S POSSIBLE THAT WHEN WE HIT PUBERTY WE'LL FIND EACH OTHER'S BODIES ATTRACTIVE, EVEN THOUGH THAT IDEA IS REPULSIVE NOW?
I DON'T THINK SO. THAT'D BE A FUNDAMENTAL SHIFT IN MY MIND CAUSED BY A MERE CHEMICAL SHIFT IN MY BODY. I'M NOT SURE I'M READY TO ACCEPT MYSELF AS SUCH A MECHANICAL BEING.
THEN DO YOU THINK THE CONSTELLATIONS ARE UGLY FOR HAVING MECHANICAL ORBITS?
ONLY THE ONES SHAPED LIKE GIRLS.

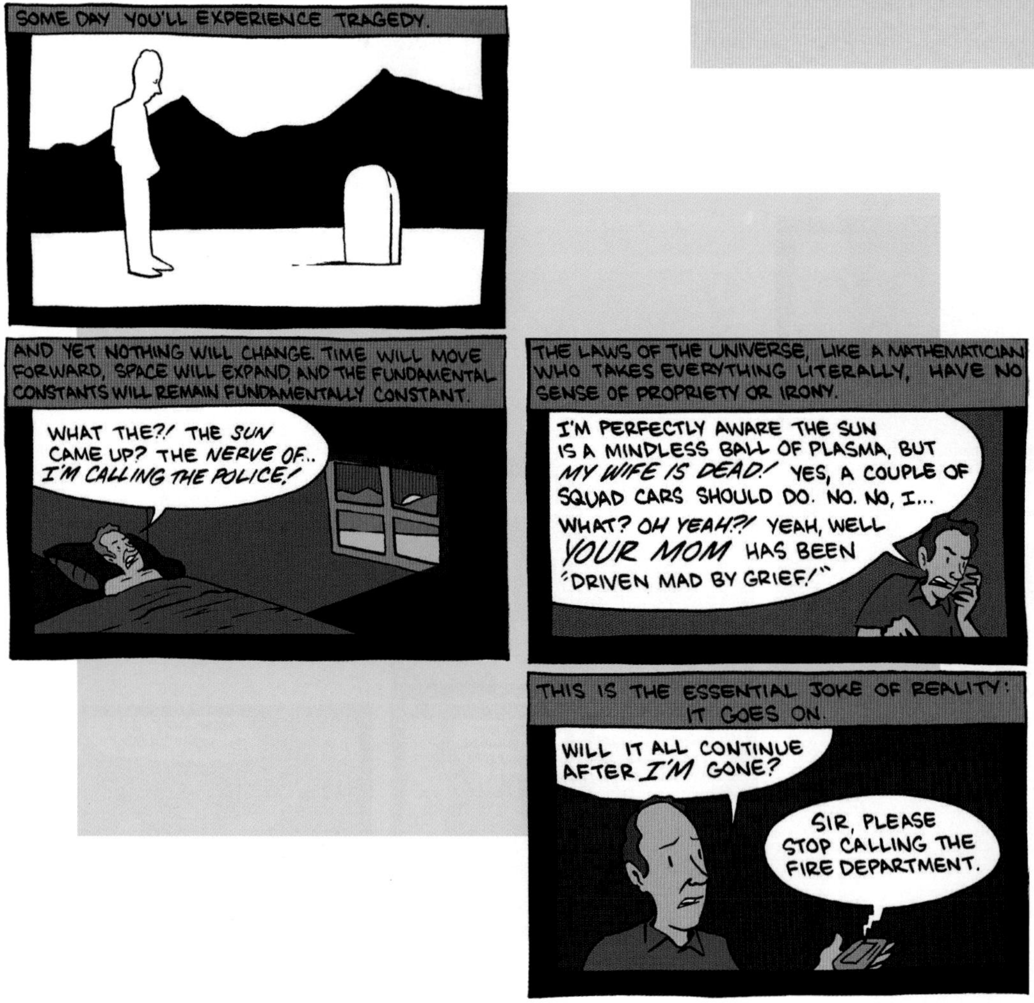
SOME DAY YOU'LL EXPERIENCE TRAGEDY.
AND YET NOTHING WILL CHANGE. TIME WILL MOVE FORWARD, SPACE WILL EXPAND, AND THE FUNDAMENTAL CONSTANTS WILL REMAIN FUNDAMENTALLY CONSTANT.
WHAT THE?! THE *SUN* CAME UP? THE *NERVE OF*.. *I'M CALLING THE POLICE!*
THE LAWS OF THE UNIVERSE, LIKE A MATHEMATICIAN WHO TAKES EVERYTHING LITERALLY, HAVE NO SENSE OF PROPRIETY OR IRONY.
I'M PERFECTLY AWARE THE SUN IS A MINDLESS BALL OF PLASMA, BUT *MY WIFE IS DEAD!* YES, A COUPLE OF SQUAD CARS SHOULD DO. NO. NO, I... WHAT? *OH YEAH?!* YEAH, WELL *YOUR MOM* HAS BEEN "DRIVEN MAD BY GRIEF!"
THIS IS THE ESSENTIAL JOKE OF REALITY: IT GOES ON.
WILL IT ALL CONTINUE AFTER *I'M* GONE?
SIR, PLEASE STOP CALLING THE FIRE DEPARTMENT.

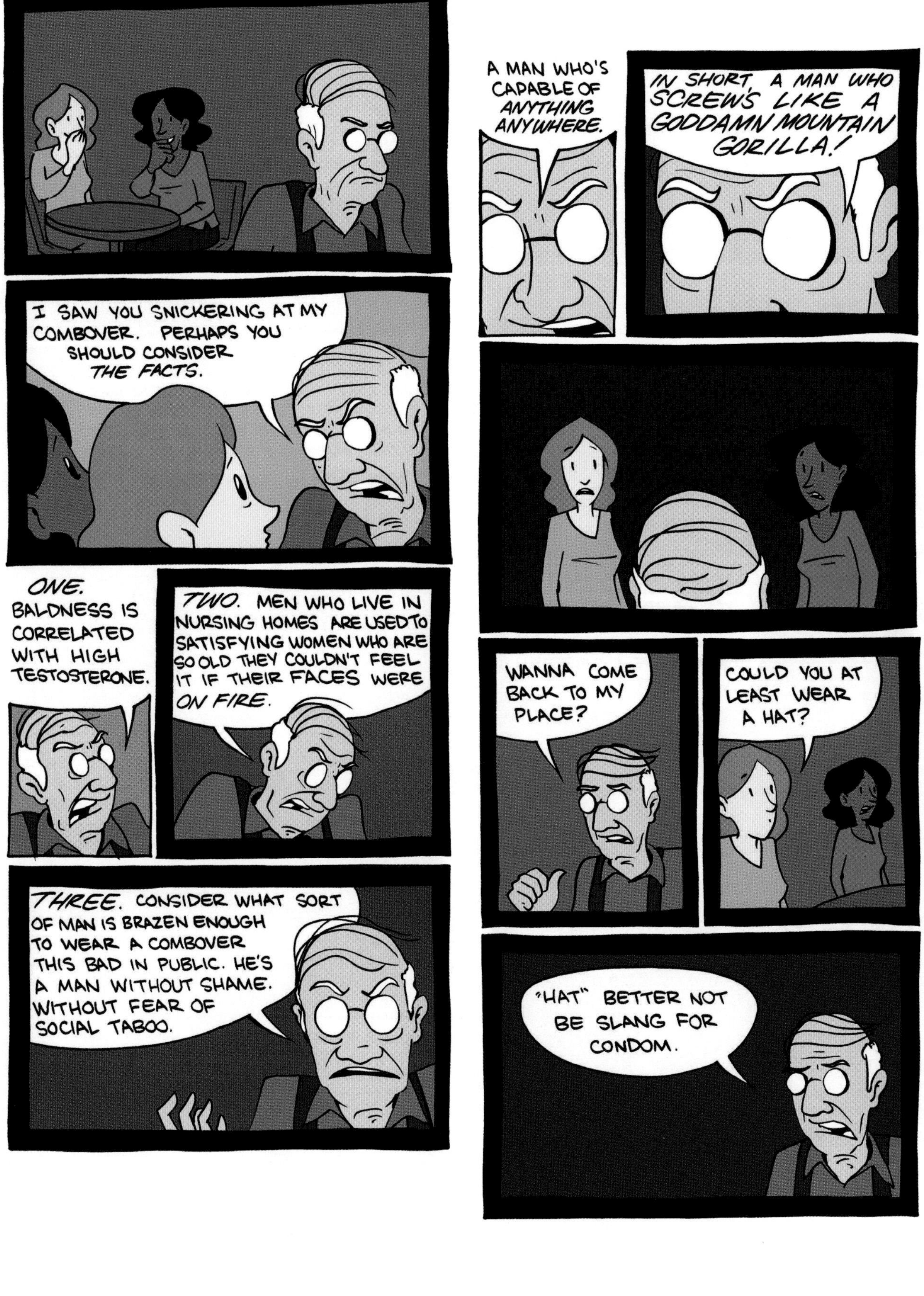
I SAW YOU SNICKERING AT MY COMBOVER. PERHAPS YOU SHOULD CONSIDER *THE FACTS*.
ONE. BALDNESS IS CORRELATED WITH HIGH TESTOSTERONE.
TWO. MEN WHO LIVE IN NURSING HOMES ARE USED TO SATISFYING WOMEN WHO ARE SO OLD THEY COULDN'T FEEL IT IF THEIR FACES WERE *ON FIRE*.
THREE. CONSIDER WHAT SORT OF MAN IS BRAZEN ENOUGH TO WEAR A COMBOVER THIS BAD IN PUBLIC. HE'S A MAN WITHOUT SHAME. WITHOUT FEAR OF SOCIAL TABOO.
A MAN WHO'S CAPABLE OF *ANYTHING ANYWHERE*.
IN SHORT, A MAN WHO SCREWS LIKE A GODDAMN MOUNTAIN GORILLA!
WANNA COME BACK TO MY PLACE?
COULD YOU AT LEAST WEAR A HAT?
"HAT" BETTER NOT BE SLANG FOR CONDOM.

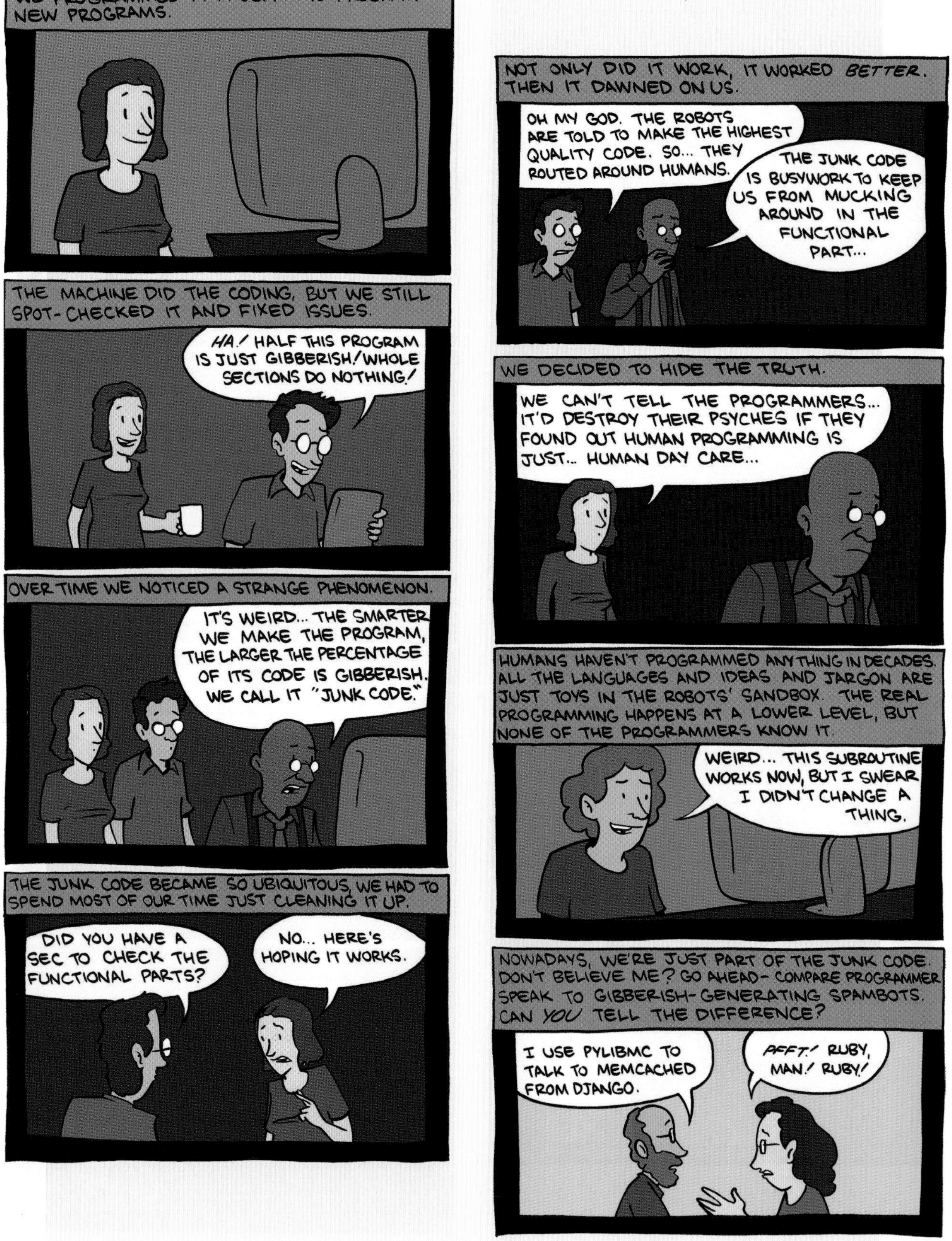
WE PROGRAMMED A PROGRAM TO PROGRAM NEW PROGRAMS.
THE MACHINE DID THE CODING, BUT WE STILL SPOT-CHECKED IT AND FIXED ISSUES.
HA! HALF THIS PROGRAM IS JUST GIBBERISH! WHOLE SECTIONS DO NOTHING!
OVER TIME WE NOTICED A STRANGE PHENOMENON.
IT'S WEIRD... THE SMARTER WE MAKE THE PROGRAM, THE LARGER THE PERCENTAGE OF ITS CODE IS GIBBERISH. WE CALL IT "JUNK CODE."
THE JUNK CODE BECAME SO UBIQUITOUS, WE HAD TO SPEND MOST OF OUR TIME JUST CLEANING IT UP.
DID YOU HAVE A SEC TO CHECK THE FUNCTIONAL PARTS?
NO... HERE'S HOPING IT WORKS.
NOT ONLY DID IT WORK, IT WORKED BETTER. THEN IT DAWNED ON US.
OH MY GOD. THE ROBOTS ARE TOLD TO MAKE THE HIGHEST QUALITY CODE. SO... THEY ROUTED AROUND HUMANS.
THE JUNK CODE IS BUSYWORK TO KEEP US FROM MUCKING AROUND IN THE FUNCTIONAL PART...
WE DECIDED TO HIDE THE TRUTH.
WE CAN'T TELL THE PROGRAMMERS... IT'D DESTROY THEIR PSYCHES IF THEY FOUND OUT HUMAN PROGRAMMING IS JUST... HUMAN DAY CARE...
HUMANS HAVEN'T PROGRAMMED ANYTHING IN DECADES. ALL THE LANGUAGES AND IDEAS AND JARGON ARE JUST TOYS IN THE ROBOTS' SANDBOX. THE REAL PROGRAMMING HAPPENS AT A LOWER LEVEL, BUT NONE OF THE PROGRAMMERS KNOW IT.
WEIRD... THIS SUBROUTINE WORKS NOW, BUT I SWEAR I DIDN'T CHANGE A THING.
NOWADAYS, WE'RE JUST PART OF THE JUNK CODE. DON'T BELIEVE ME? GO AHEAD- COMPARE PROGRAMMER SPEAK TO GIBBERISH-GENERATING SPAMBOTS. CAN YOU TELL THE DIFFERENCE?
I USE PYLIBMC TO TALK TO MEMCACHED FROM DJANGO.
PFFT! RUBY, MAN! RUBY!

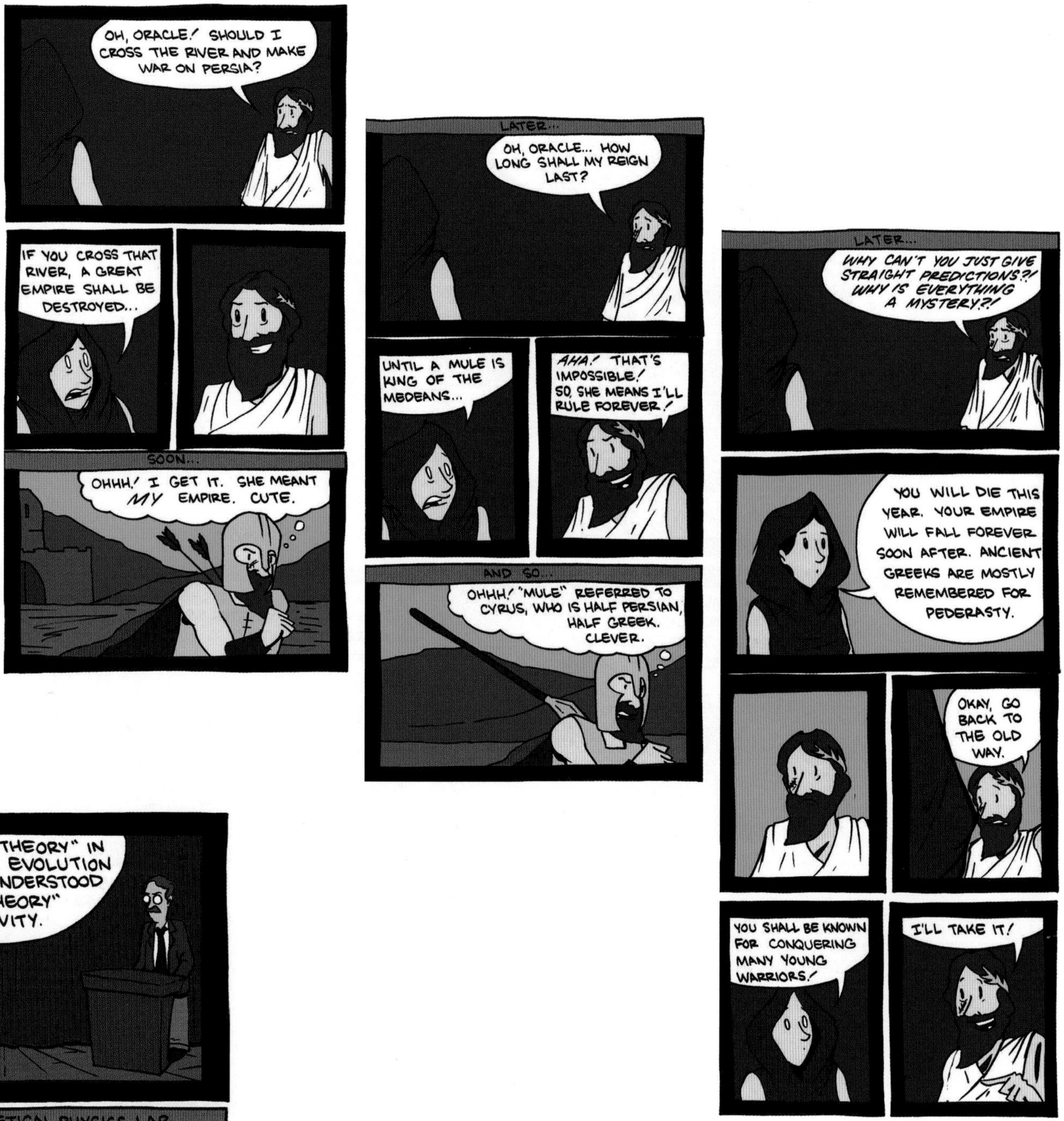
OH, ORACLE! SHOULD I CROSS THE RIVER AND MAKE WAR ON PERSIA?
IF YOU CROSS THAT RIVER, A GREAT EMPIRE SHALL BE DESTROYED...
SOON...
OHHH! I GET IT. SHE MEANT MY EMPIRE. CUTE.
LATER...
OH, ORACLE... HOW LONG SHALL MY REIGN LAST?
UNTIL A MULE IS KING OF THE MEDEANS...
AHA! THAT'S IMPOSSIBLE! SO, SHE MEANS I'LL RULE FOREVER!
AND SO...
OHHH! "MULE" REFERRED TO CYRUS, WHO IS HALF PERSIAN, HALF GREEK. CLEVER.
LATER...
WHY CAN'T YOU JUST GIVE STRAIGHT PREDICTIONS?! WHY IS EVERYTHING A MYSTERY?!
YOU WILL DIE THIS YEAR. YOUR EMPIRE WILL FALL FOREVER SOON AFTER. ANCIENT GREEKS ARE MOSTLY REMEMBERED FOR PEDERASTY.
OKAY, GO BACK TO THE OLD WAY.
YOU SHALL BE KNOWN FOR CONQUERING MANY YOUNG WARRIORS!
I'LL TAKE IT!

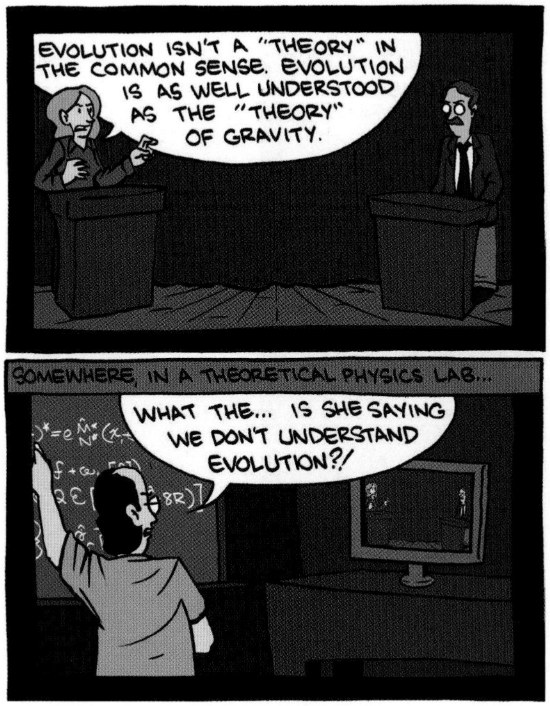
EVOLUTION ISN'T A "THEORY" IN THE COMMON SENSE. EVOLUTION IS AS WELL UNDERSTOOD AS THE "THEORY" OF GRAVITY.
SOMEWHERE, IN A THEORETICAL PHYSICS LAB...
WHAT THE... IS SHE SAYING WE DON'T UNDERSTAND EVOLUTION?!

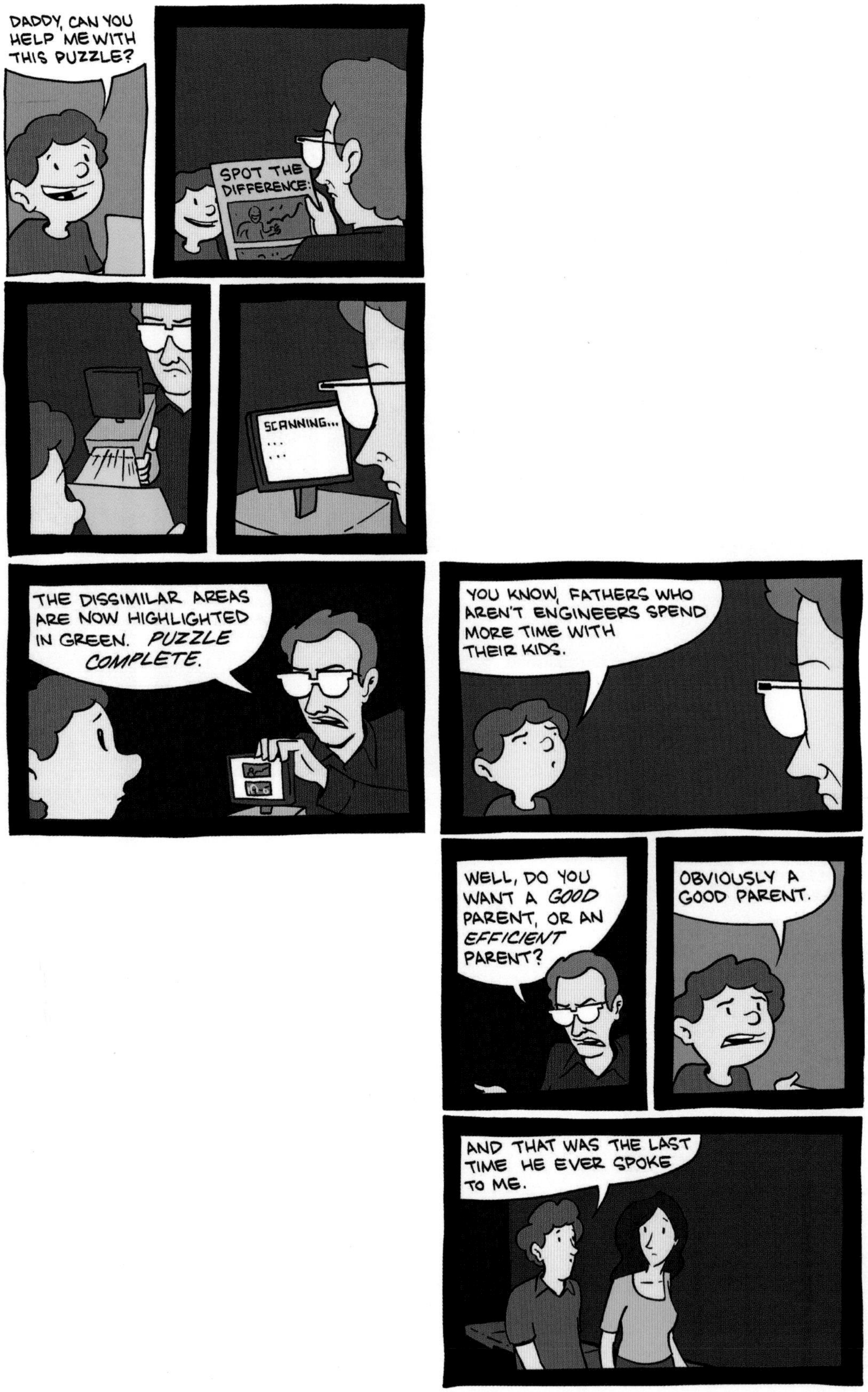
DADDY, CAN YOU HELP ME WITH THIS PUZZLE?
SPOT THE DIFFERENCE:
SCANNING...
THE DISSIMILAR AREAS ARE NOW HIGHLIGHTED IN GREEN. *PUZZLE COMPLETE*.
YOU KNOW, FATHERS WHO AREN'T ENGINEERS SPEND MORE TIME WITH THEIR KIDS.
WELL, DO YOU WANT A *GOOD* PARENT, OR AN *EFFICIENT* PARENT?
OBVIOUSLY A GOOD PARENT.
AND THAT WAS THE LAST TIME HE EVER SPOKE TO ME.

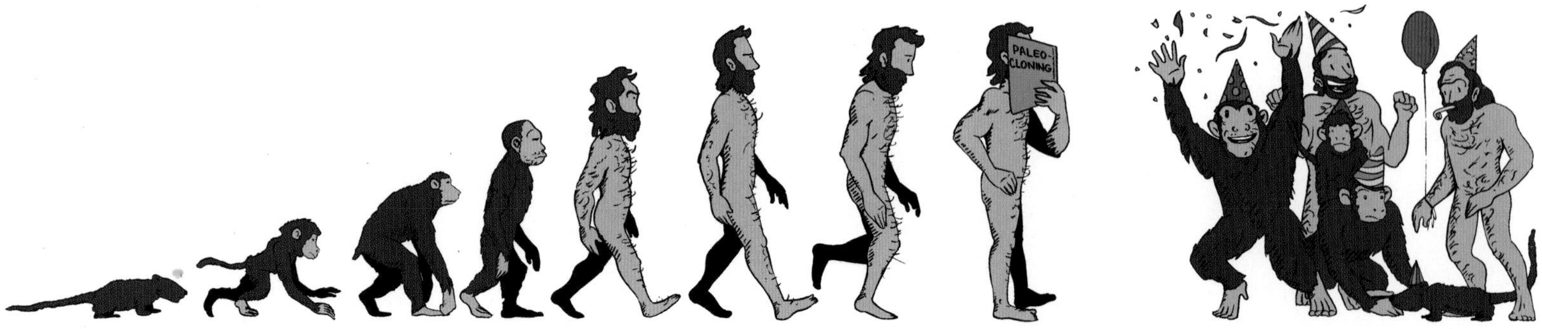
PALEO-CLONING

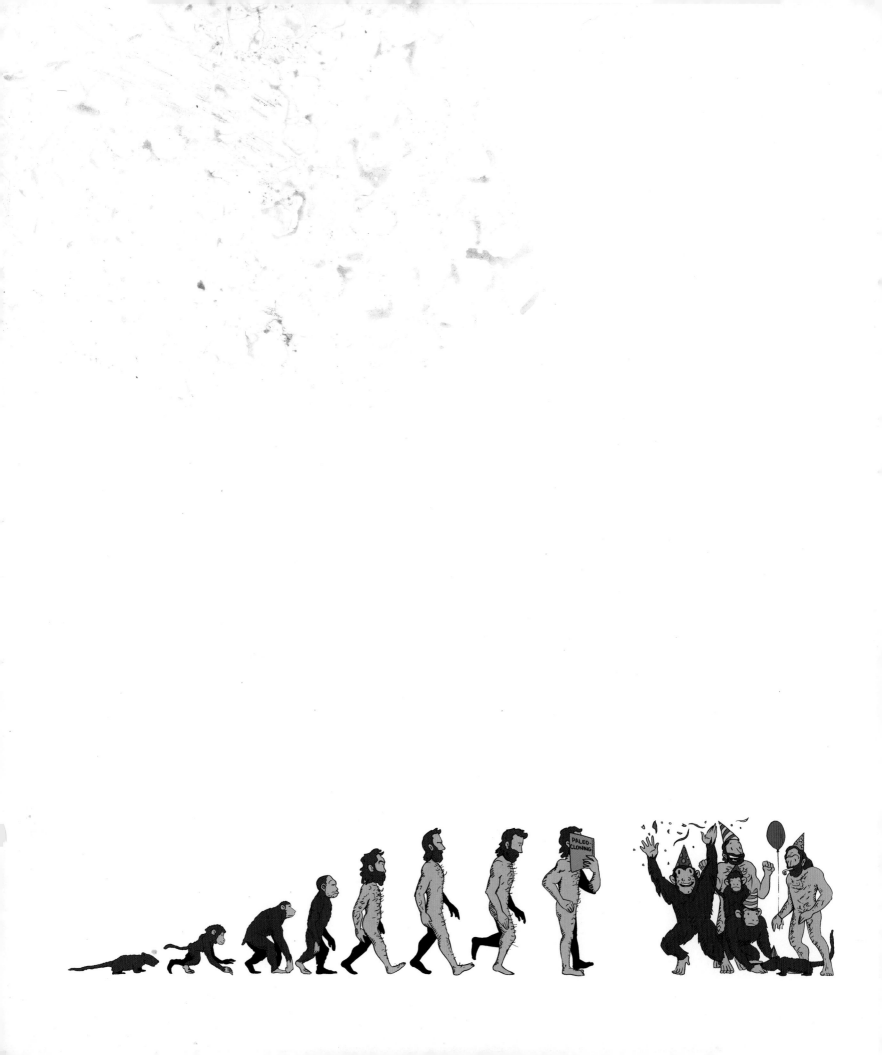